# Capitalism, Democracy, and Morality

## Scott R. Stripling, Ph.D.

Director
The National Center for America's Founding Documents
Boston University

*Copley Publishing Group*
Acton, Massachusetts 01720

ISBN 0-87411-684-8

10 9 8 7 6 5 4 3 2 1


Library of Congress Cataloging-in-Publication Data

Stripling, Scott Randall.
    Capitalism, democracy, and morality / Scott R. Stripling.
        p.        cm.
    Includes bibliographical references and index.
    ISBN 0-87411-684-8 : $24.95
    1. Democracy—Moral and ethical aspects.  2. Capitalism—Moral and ethical
aspects.  3. Democracy—United States.  4. Capitalism—United States.  I. Title
JC423.S868  1994
320.473—dc20                                                94-21847
                                                                CIP

# Contents

# *Preface*

This book is based upon a course I designed and taught to undergraduate students in the School of Management at Boston University in the Spring of 1990. The course was entitled "The Foundations of Capitalism and Democracy." Its syllabus comprised readings from the works of the great theoreticians of modern representative democracy and free enterprise: John Locke, Adam Smith, Alexis deTocqueville, and Publius (the pseudonym used by Jay, Hamilton, and Madison—the authors of *The Federalist*). The readings for this course departed considerably from those one usually finds in the curriculum of a business school; and I am grateful to the administration of Boston University, particularly to Mr. Jon Westling, Provost and Executive Vice President, for having confidence in me, and for giving me the opportunity to teach it.

I decided to offer the course especially to business students because of my conviction, based upon my professional experience in both education and commercial banking, that a genuinely liberal education is both useful and good for students who have chosen a business career. The good uses to which a liberal education may be put in business are manifold; and the benefits that accrue to students thus prepared become clear once one understands the true nature of both work and leisure.

As for the utility of a liberal education to a career in business, there are the obvious benefits of being able to speak, write, and calculate well. Indeed, these are indispensable to success in business. There is more, however. One rarely succeeds in business without a sound understanding of human nature. This understanding may be obtained through one's own experience, to be sure; but art is long and life is short. One therefore needs good teachers. The best teachers are those who were not obliged to learn from other teachers. Rather, because of their genius and intellectual daring, they learned from the "great book of the world" itself. A genuinely liberal education will consist principally in studying the books written by such teachers.

Despite Marx's view to the contrary, the true measure of work is not the mere expenditure of labor power. That is, one does not understand work if one attempts to understand it solely or primarily in terms of quantity. Rather, the true measure and nature of work are understood in the light of, or are identical with, the purpose or end to which work is put. What is work for? When one has truly answered that question, one has understood work.

The work in question here is, of course, not just any work, but human work. What is human work for? What work is proper to a human being, and what improper? Aristotle raises and answers this question in the *Nicomachean Ethics*. His answer is characteristically sensible and profound at the same time. Aristotle says that all human action is for the sake of some apparent good; and the final good, the good at which all human action aims, the good desired for its own sake and not for the sake of anything else, is happiness. One indication of the self-sufficiency of happiness as a human good is that it makes no sense to ask someone why he wants to be happy.

Having arrived at this conclusion, we do not, of course, necessarily know what happiness is; but we do know that it is something sought for itself and not for anything else. There is a great question in Aristotle, though, as there is in the teachings of the ancient philosophers generally, whether any human *action*, however noble, can ever be for its own sake and not for the sake of anything else. That virtue is its own reward is an ancient and noble sentiment; but Aristotle teaches that, finally, the life of human action is not the highest, most self-sufficient life, the life that fulfills our desire for that good which is sought for itself alone and not for the sake of anything else. Aristotle teaches that the highest and most satisfying human life is the life of philosophic contemplation, or what he calls the "theoretical life."

By "theoretical," Aristotle does not mean what we mean today when we use that term. We often use the words "theoretical" and "speculative" to mean "hypothetical." When we describe a statement as theoretical or speculative, we mean that it goes beyond the plain evidence of our senses, into the domain of conjecture. By contrast, Aristotle uses "theoretical" to mean "having to do with seeing." "Theoretical" is related to the Greek verb "theorein," which means "to see," just as "speculative" is related to the Latin verb "speculare." From these two words we get "theater" and "spectacle," whose relation to seeing is immediately evident. Thus, in Aristotle's thought, the most completely satisfying human life is the theoretical life, the life devoted to seeing.

The kind of seeing Aristotle means is "seeing with the mind's eye," intellectual seeing, the sort of seeing we all experience when we say, "Oh, I see what you mean;" the kind of seeing that brings such pleasure when, after struggling to understand a difficult problem, we suddenly "get it." The life devoted to study, contemplation, learning, and conversation, is the life motivated by the desire to see with the mind's eye the way things really are, to see them only for the sake of seeing them and for no other reason.

In denying that the life of human action, and in particular the life devoted to morality and politics, is the highest or most satisfying human life, Aristotle is not denigrating morality. He is not saying that the life devoted to morality is futile or foolish. He is merely saying that there is something higher for human beings. To be sure, only a few rare human beings ever attain to the theoretical life; but we who are not among the necessarily small number of rare human beings know from our own experience that in life the quest is often more invigorating and satisfying than the finding. The completion of a great project, once the novelty is gone, may leave us feeling, in Hamlet's words, "stale, flat, and unprofitable."

The Bible, however much it may disagree with Aristotle's teaching in other respects, agrees with him in this, namely, that the life of moral and political action is not the highest kind of human life. To see this, we have only to recall the great words of the prophet Isaiah:

In the year that king Uzziah died I saw also the Lord sitting upon a throne, high and lifted up, and his train filled the temple. Above it stood the seraphim: each one had six wings; with two he covered his face; and with two he covered his feet, and with two he flew. And one cried unto another, and said, Holy, holy, holy, is the Lord of hosts: the whole earth is full of his glory . . . Then I said, Woe is me! for I am undone; because I am a man of unclean lips, and I dwell in the midst of a people of unclean lips: for mine eyes have seen the King, the Lord of hosts.

There is, to be sure, a moral teaching to be found in the Bible; but we are told by Scripture that there is more rejoicing in heaven over the repentance of one sinner than over the righteous acts of many. Or, as the two great commandments found in both the Old and New Testaments teach, we are first to love the Lord our God with all our heart, mind, and strength, and then to love our neighbor as ourselves.

But let us get back to business. I frequently observed during my career as a commercial banker that those who had succeeded in business often did so, not because they had decided to make a lot of money, but because they had found a way of making a lot of money doing something they loved to do, something they might have chosen to do with their free time even if it did not get them a living, much less great wealth.

The important word here is "free." As its name indicates, liberal education is education in the proper uses of human liberty or leisure. Thus understood, a liberal education can equip one to succeed in business by helping to place business in its proper human perspective. Business exists for the sake of giving us the freedom to do what we love most; and liberal education, by which I understand primarily the study of the best books, educates and refines our sense of what is genuinely lovable for human beings. Liberal education raises us above the concern with the necessities of life, and trains us to love what is truly lovable.

Hence, the course and this book. Indeed, one motive for writing this book was to provide an introduction to the study of those great books that laid the foundations of liberal democracy and free enterprise, an introduction that could itself be used in a business school curriculum. There is, of course, no substitute for reading the books themselves; but perhaps someone in a business school somewhere will read this book and see that what I propose here is both possible and desirable.

Finally, I hope that others who read this book will at least be persuaded to undertake the task of discovering and thinking through for themselves the understanding of human nature and moral vision that animated the thought of those philosophers and statesmen to whom we look as the founders of America.

I here take the opportunity of thanking those who helped and encouraged me during the writing of this book, particularly my publisher, Mr. Frank Ellsworth; Dr. Edwin J. Delattre, Dean of the School of Education at Boston University; and most especially my wife, Victoria.

# Introduction

This book was written to set forth and defend two propositions concerning the American system of liberal democracy and capitalism: 1) The American system is a *fundamentally* decent system; 2) The American system is not heaven on earth. A healthy appreciation of liberal democracy and capitalism requires an informed understanding of both propositions. Without such an understanding, one exposes oneself to two related risks: unrealistic hopes and cynical despair. One may come either to expect too much of America's potential, or to abandon hope of improving its prospects.

It is necessary to say more about both propositions, and why they must be defended. By "fundamentally decent," we mean "morally decent in principle or intention." Thus, one purpose of this book is to set forth and defend the moral decency of the fundamental principles of liberal democracy and capitalism.

Our system of democratic capitalism needs to be defended because it is under attack, and deserves to be defended because it is good. The attack upon democratic capitalism in the United States is carried out primarily by the radical Left, and is directed against capitalism's alleged immorality.[1] It continues unabated, despite the evident triumph throughout the world of the principles of democratic capitalism. This attack is unrelenting, and its effects are ubiquitous. Our news media regularly distort or overstate bad economic news, while failing to note or accurately report the good; many of our educational institutions teach their students that American capitalism and democracy are oppressive, if not simply evil, while leaving them ignorant of even the rudiments of our constitutional form of government; our arts and popular culture routinely portray American business people in a way which is hostile to the point of pure distortion; and the United States Congress imposes regulations, taxes, and legal liabilities on business and

---

[1] It must be added that two of the most powerful modern critics of liberal democracy, Nietzsche and Heidegger, attack it from the Right, not the Left. As Allan Bloom noted, in *The Closing of the American Mind*, the contemporary assault on liberal democracy is a curious mixture of the teachings of these two thinkers and Karl Marx. The contemporary critics of liberal democracy and capitalism occasionally seem oblivious to this fact.

financial institutions, which are ostensibly meant to correct certain injustices in our economic system, but which often succeed only in blunting the competitiveness of American businesses, or in jeopardizing their viability, thus harming the general economy.

The contemporary critique of American capitalism and democracy is essentially a *moral* critique. It is not the efficacy of our principles that is under assault, but their morality. Unfortunately, for various reasons many American business schools fail to teach their students the fundamental principles and moral vision of liberal democracy and capitalism. Therefore, business people themselves are ill prepared to defend them against the charges of their critics.

For example, accounting students will be familiar with the "arm's-length transaction" criterion, which is used to determine whether fair consideration has been given in exchange for assets purchased. Perhaps they will also have heard of the principle of "enlightened self-interest," upon which this criterion is based. It is highly unlikely, however, that those students will have studied the great debate between ancient and modern political thinkers, whose outcome was to distinguish enlightened self-interest from mere greed, and to justify the liberation of acquisitiveness, the engine which drives economic expansion. Business students are unlikely to know firsthand the great arguments of Adam Smith, which demonstrate how free enterprise enables the public welfare to be served, not *in spite of,* but *because of* enlightened self-interest.

Adam Smith to the contrary notwithstanding, many critics of capitalism assert that it is a system of economy fundamentally intended merely to legitimate or encourage greed and concentrate political power in the hands of the wealthy few. The world-wide collapse of socialism, and the subsequent spread of capitalism and democracy, have not dissuaded these critics. For them, the triumph of capitalism is a great moral catastrophe. Those whose interests would otherwise move them to defend democratic capitalism against its critics, cannot do so credibly, unless they know, for example, that John Locke and Adam Smith stated the case for combining democracy with free enterprise at least as powerfully as Marx attacked it; or that Smith himself noted certain undesirable effects of capitalism, and anticipated most of Marx's most powerful criticisms. Indeed, Smith may very well have been a more penetrating critic of capitalism than Marx. Thus, whether one intends to defend or criticize, to reform or destroy free market economies, one will increase one's chances of success if one has first understood the best arguments that have been made in their defense.

Certainly, the confidence of American business in its own goodness could be enhanced by an informed appreciation of the intellectual traditions of free markets and popular government. To this it will be replied that business schools are practical places. Their primary job is to teach their students the practice of business, or to teach the principles of business only as they relate immediately to business practice. Let this be granted. There is an eminently practical reason to teach business students the theoretical and moral principles of capitalism and democracy. People who succeed in business—really succeed—usually do so in part because they have a deep understanding of human nature. The authors of the books which lay the intellectual foundations of the American system, and whose teaching is presented in what follows, possessed such an understanding to an unusually high degree.

This book, accordingly, considers both the legal and constitutional theory which guided the Founders in framing the American system, as well as the more fundamental and problematic question concerning human nature and its proper relation to political life.

We do not aim to proselytize for the American system of democratic capitalism. Rather, we attempt to explain, and, where it is right to do so, defend or criticize democratic capitalism, or the American combination of representative democracy and capitalism. We thus implicitly reject two prevailing contemporary views, namely, that economics and political science are separate, autonomous disciplines; and, that economics and political science are "morally neutral," or "value-free," disciplines. Capitalism and liberal democracy do not go together accidentally; rather, they complement one another's vision of a good society. Therefore, to explain the theoretical foundations *and* moral vision of capitalism and liberal democracy, is to see how the two are connected.

The kind of explanation meant here is primarily theoretical, or philosophical, without intending to deny that theory may have important implications for practice. What is intended is an explanation that will answer two questions: 1) What is the American system of economy and politics; that is, What are the principles on which this system rests?; and 2) What is the moral vision of this system; or, What kind of human being does it intend to produce?

These questions are raised and discussed in the light of a reading, intended to be both sympathetic *and* critical, of the primary texts and documents of America's intellectual foundations, namely, the books written by the great teachers of liberal democracy and capitalism: John Locke, Alexis de Tocqueville, and Adam Smith. The discussion also takes its bearings from the *Federalist Papers*, a work which may be regarded as *the* authoritative guide to the U.S. Constitution, and from the speeches of our most profound student of the Declaration of Independence, Abraham Lincoln.

This book is not a manual or handbook for how to fix what is wrong with our country. It may, however, be regarded as contributing to that worthy project in the following way. We cannot be properly motivated to fix what is wrong with our country unless we believe it to be worth fixing. We cannot know how to fix our country, unless we know what its original, unbroken condition is; and we cannot acquire this knowledge without first understanding the principles upon which our country is founded. The knowledge we seek is primarily moral. It is an *understanding*, not an uncritical, chauvinistic acceptance, of the propositions with which this introduction began: despite its defects, the American system of democratic capitalism is *fundamentally* decent, and worthy of the allegiance of all reasonable human beings of good will.

# CHAPTER ONE

## *Reclaiming Our Foundations*

### I

The principles of capitalism and liberal democracy complement one another. Together, they provide the theoretical justification for the American experiment in self-government, what Publius,[1] the pseudonymous author of *The Federalist*, called a "large commercial republic." According to classical republican theory, this phrase is an oxymoron: republics can be neither large nor commercial. Classical republican virtue required republics to be small, agrarian, and devoted to the inculcation of virtue in their citizens. The large commercial republic, by contrast, although not indifferent to the virtue of its citizens, would not intrude in that sphere of privacy, namely society, wherein moral education was to be accomplished. According to Publius, the discovery of the principles that make possible a large commercial republic, and their embodiment in the Declaration of Independence and the United States Constitution, are the great achievements of modern political thought.

Although John Locke is justly regarded as *the* great theoretician of the American Revolution, Adam Smith, whose *The Wealth of Nations* was itself first published in 1776, must also be seen in this light. In this great work, Smith elaborated the principles of an economy that would happily correspond to what *The Federalist* intended by the phrase "large commercial republic." In particular, Smith may be said to have provided America with the economic system best suited to the creation of a large, affluent middle class, whose stabilizing influence would counteract the well-known vulnerability of democratic governments to faction and demagoguery.

---

[1] "Publius" was the name chosen by John Jay, Alexander Hamilton, and James Madison, the authors of *The Federalist*, to be their common pseudonym. We discuss the reasons for this choice in the Appendix to Chapter II.

1

Moreover, Smith showed how to encourage, albeit in economic terms, what Thomas Jefferson called a "natural aristocracy,"[2] by elaborating a system wherein the naturally gifted and ambitious could flourish both economically and politically. While it might be true that in such a system there would be permanent economic classes of people, given the equality of opportunity for material improvement available to all, there would be no permanent members of those classes. That is, one born talented but poor need not despair of the possibility of escaping his poverty; nor could one fortunately born to wealth and influence complacently regard his good fortune as his entitlement, secured in perpetuity to himself and his offspring. A society that cultivated a natural aristocracy would, thought Jefferson, go farther toward encouraging achievement, while discouraging resentment or envy over the good fortunes of others, than could those societies where rank was based upon wealth and good birth.

Finally, although in the main Smith accepted Locke's teaching on human nature, he modified it in one crucial respect. Locke appeared to teach that the primacy of self-interest in human nature implies that any duty to promote the general welfare must always result from a calculation of reason based upon self-interest. Duty would always be subordinated to self-interest. Reason itself, according to Locke, does not supply or discern the good for man as man. The good for man as such is supplied by his passionate attachment to his own preservation, which is itself rooted in human nature. Accordingly, Locke taught that duty would always be considerably less effectual as a motive for action than would self-interest. Smith, however, believed he had discerned in human nature a second principle, which he called "sympathy," by which he meant our natural fellow-feeling with the suffering and joy of other human beings. Smith taught that this principle, because it is a passion, influences our actions more immediately and surely than any duty or precept of reason, but nonetheless prompts us to act out of concern for the well-being of others. We are, says Smith, naturally

---

[2] In his correspondence with John Adams, Jefferson distinguished natural aristocracy, whose grounds are "virtue and talents," from artificial aristocracy, "founded on wealth or birth," without regard for virtue or talents. Jefferson believed that "that form of government is the best which provides most effectually for a pure selection of these natural *aristoi* in to the offices of government." See *The People Shall Judge* (Chicago: University of Chicago Press, 1949), 1: 228ff.

interested in the fortune of others, "though [we derive] nothing from it but the pleasure of seeing it."[3]

Therefore, Smith clearly intended that the liberation of the desire for material gain advocated by the system of economy set forth in *The Wealth of Nations*, be understood in the context of a political system which encouraged, rather than coerced, our natural compassion for others, but which did not demand of human nature what is impossible to it, namely, the complete overcoming of self-interest. There is, Smith believed, a legitimate difference between encouraging self-interest through healthy economic competition, and encouraging cheating. Others will indulge, and even approve, him who competes as hard as he can in "the race for wealth, honours, and preferment . . ." They will not, however, approve any violation of the rules of fair play. A man may place his own interests ahead of the interests of others to the degree necessary to spur him to compete against them; but his preference for his own self-interest cannot justify ignoring those laws that define and protect the common good. The liberation of self-interest on the grounds of promoting the general welfare, emphatically presupposes a level playing field, while it just as emphatically rejects any attempt to eliminate inequalities of ability, or to reward unequal effort equally. Thus, Smith taught that, under a system of relatively unintrusive government, the two fundamental passions of self-interest and sympathy may complement one another, with salutary economic effect.

The foregoing account contrasts with the opinion now popular with some Americans according to which true democracy, being thoroughly egalitarian, cannot permit the unequal distribution of wealth. Equality of opportunity, they argue, is not a sufficient condition for a just society. The unequal distribution of wealth, power, and influence is also unjust, and needs to be rectified by government policy. Thus, these critics will interpret or criticize the Declaration of Independence and Constitution in the light of this conviction, finding fault with those elements which, in their view, merely reflect the unacknowledged class interests of the anti-democratic group: the combination of democracy and capitalism that characterizes the American system produces disparities of wealth, which are thought to be unjust because they allegedly contravene the egalitarian principles of democracy. Capitalism contradicts democracy. In a democratic society, disparities of wealth must be regarded as unjust. A truly just democratic system will therefore be obliged to re-distribute wealth more equitably. Its ruling principle will

[3] Adam Smith, *The Theory of Moral Sentiments,* ed. Raphael and MacFie (New York: Oxford University Press, 1976), 9.

resemble the famous saying of Marx: "from each according to his ability to each according to his need."

According to the Marxist view, *true* democracy cannot consist with capitalism. In a capitalistic state, so Marx believed, what may appear to be democratic institutions and laws, merely reflect the interests of the ruling class, the capitalists. True democracy, as Marx understood it, will be established only in the post-revolutionary world from which all class conflicts will have disappeared or will have been made to disappear.

The thesis argued here rejects this view. In particular, and contrary to the Marxist teaching, we argue that capitalism is not fundamentally anti-democratic, and that the unequal distribution of wealth is not inherently unjust; that democracy, or at least the American version of democracy, was not intended to be radically egalitarian; and, that the existence of classes defined by interests which mutually conflict need not be taken as a sign of an "internal contradiction," which must be overcome, either by the dialectic of history, or, if history should prove dilatory, by direct revolutionary action.

The American Founders, agreeing with Aristotle, rejected the opinion that equality in some respects implies equality in all respects. They accepted the classical view, according to which justice means treating equals equally, the corollary to which is that it is unjust both to treat unequals as though they were equals, and to treat equals as though they were unequal. Thus, the classic view would hold that radical egalitarianism is radically unjust, precisely because it rejects the principle that merit and reward should be proportioned to one another. Furthermore, the Founders accepted the proposition that all human beings, however unequal in respect of natural gifts or accident of birth, are naturally equal in respect of certain unalienable rights, with which they have been endowed by their Creator, the God who governs the natural order. It is this sense of equality which they regarded as having political consequences, and for the securing of which governments are legitimately instituted.

The Founders generally held that efforts to achieve equality of *condition* cannot succeed, but will lead to disaster. Such efforts do immeasurably more harm than those inequalities that inevitably result from securing equal opportunity to unequally gifted human beings. In the justly famous *Federalist* #10, Publius demonstrates that the attempt to ensure equality of condition tends to destroy the very freedom necessary to the enjoyment of equality of opportunity.

4

A corollary to this proposition is the Founders' view that disparities of wealth are not *per se* unjust. This does not mean that they lacked compassion for the plight of the poor, or that they believed society has no obligation to help the poor. Rather, the Founders believed that when each man has the same opportunity for improving his lot as every other man, some will inevitably be more successful than others, because of superior natural ability or effort. Not all differences of success result from invidious discrimination or other form of injustice; and, not to allow superior natural ability to succeed, or not to reward superior effort, in the name of "equality," is unjust, particularly if justice means the equal treatment of equals, or, to state the principle more generally, if justice means that reward should be proportionate to merit. The opportunity to succeed cannot be divorced from the risk of failure. This principle results directly from the proposition, held by the signers of the Declaration of Independence to be self-evidently true, that each human being is naturally endowed with the right only to the *pursuit*, and not to the attainment of happiness.

## II

The Marxist critique of capitalism has been particularly successful in defining the terms and principles of the contemporary debate over American liberal democracy. Many defenders *and* critics of America, wittingly or not, have accepted certain premises and terms from Marxism, which are not themselves "scientific," in the sense of being disinterested; rather, those terms and premises derive from a critique of democratic capitalism which is motivated by a revolutionary animus against democratic capitalism.[4]

This fact alone compels us to return to the intellectual sources of American democracy and capitalism, and to consider them for ourselves, apart from the revolutionary animus that drives the Marxist critique. Revolutionary animus is often indistinguishable from righteous indignation, and righteous indignation has been known to cloud judgment. In a word, one cannot know whether the Marxist critique of democratic capitalism is fair unless one has first tried to understand democratic capitalism on its own terms.

---

[4] An example of this is the continuing debate over "fairness" regarding taxation and the distribution of wealth in America. One seldom hears it said in this debate that, within certain limits, there is nothing inherently unfair about unequal distribution of wealth, and that efforts by the government to redistribute wealth are unjust or destructive; yet precisely this is the view of men like James Madison and Adam Smith.

5

Having made the effort necessary to achieve this understanding, one finds that democratic capitalism emphatically disagrees with Marxism over the issue of human nature, or of nature, generally. Accordingly, what at first may have appeared as a critique of capitalism by Marx, comes to be seen as a profound disagreement between two worthy antagonists. There is no *prima facie* reason for democratic capitalism simply to concede the moral high ground to Marxism from the very start.

Marx confidently predicted the collapse of capitalism and liberal democracy, and the inauguration of the classless society, partly because he believed that human nature is plastic, or indefinitely malleable. He denied the existence of a permanent human nature, common to all human beings everywhere and always. The American Founders, on the other hand, generally believed that there *is* something permanent in human beings, which directs and limits what is possible for political life, and which sets the given conditions for one's reflection upon political life and its purposes.

Our Declaration of Independence and Constitution express this permanent element in the great principles upon which the American form of republican government is founded: the natural equality of all human beings with respect to the unalienable rights of life, liberty, and the pursuit of happiness; the institution of government for the purpose of securing these rights; and the consent of the governed as the only source of the just powers of government.

These principles are themselves the consequence of a certain conception of human nature. So surely do they follow from this conception that the Declaration calls them "self-evident truths"; that is, once one has understood the essence of human nature, one immediately sees the truth of propositions such as "All men are created equal." The principles of the natural equality of rights and unalienable liberty, properly understood, are rooted in human nature and determine the possibilities for political life.

Moreover, these principles decisively connect the American form of democracy to capitalism. The mutually congenial character of liberal democracy and capitalism is rooted in their shared conception of human nature. The Founders well knew that the unalienable right to the pursuit of happiness essentially entails the right to acquire and own property. One's property and one's right to acquire property are a part, or an extension of one's identity as both a natural and a civil person; but property rights are insecure outside civil society. Therefore, the security of one's civil person is not complete unless one's property rights are secure.

The Founders also knew that, by protecting the right to own and acquire property, the Constitution guaranteed that an unequal distribution of property would result, given the unequal distribution of talents and ambition among mankind; but they did not believe that the unequal distribution of property is necessarily unjust. All other things being equal, the unequal distribution of property may only be the result of differing degrees of effort or talent. All other things *not* being equal, one can admit that there is injustice in the world, without being forced to believe that injustice can be entirely eliminated from the world, or that we have a duty to eliminate all injustice.[5] It is not the case that those who fail and those who succeed always deserve what they get.

The Founders knew this as well as anyone; but they believed that, because of certain ineradicable weaknesses in human nature, any system of government that attempts to redistribute property according to some conception of "fairness," inevitably tends toward tyranny. Someone must decide what the standard of fairness will be which determines that redistribution; and those who decide, being human, will be as likely as anyone else to be motivated more by self-interest than by concern for the common good. As James Madison wrote in

---

[5] To this it will immediately be responded that, of course, all other things are *not* equal. Because of various inequities in our society, some people have more property than others, not because they worked harder or were more talented, but because they were lucky, or were born to wealth and privilege, or because they happen to have been born with the right skin color, or because they cheated, and so on. It is obviously true that disparities of wealth do not always reflect different degrees of ability and effort; and the Founders knew this at least as well as we do. It was precisely for this reason that they insisted so strongly on the natural and unalienable character of the right to own and acquire property. One cannot reasonably expect to eliminate from society all the inequities which result from chance, good fortune, or occasional injustice; but one can reasonably expect to aspire to a society which protects the right of everyone to exert himself on behalf of improving his material well-being. In such a society, argued Jefferson in his correspondence with John Adams, natural ability will be allowed to flourish. Those inequities which inevitably result in aristocracies based on wealth and birth, will be less likely to occur in a society where talented and hard-working people, of whatever station, are allowed and encouraged to succeed. In particular, if disparities of wealth result from certain invidious kinds of discrimination, racial or otherwise, this is not a reason to re-distribute wealth; rather, it is a reason to redouble one's efforts to protect the rights of all citizens to own and acquire property.

*The Federalist*, #51, "In framing a government which is to be administered by men over men, the great difficulty lies in this: you must first enable the government to control the governed; and in the next place, oblige it to control itself."

Therefore, the Founders, in agreement with Adam Smith, concluded that it is generally better to allow the creation and distribution of wealth to proceed in accordance with a more impartial system, a system which, to be sure, has its defects, but which nevertheless has the virtue of being no respecter of persons. This system, which we have been taught to call "capitalism," is better described as a system of free markets and free enterprise. This system best accommodates the inevitable human tendency to acquire property, and allows the naturally gifted and ambitious ample scope for their talents. Smith was convinced that the successful efforts of gifted and enterprising individuals in a free economy will usually benefit others more assuredly than will a reliance upon philanthropy or charity; and, because it is not compulsory, the natural sympathy of human beings for their fellows will incline them toward philanthropy and charity.

Thus understood, capitalism is the natural economic complement to the principles announced by the Declaration. Accordingly, in what follows, we employ the term "democratic capitalism" to refer to the combination of government and economy which characterizes the American system.

### III

What is offered here is not an apology for any destructive excesses of the American system of democratic capitalism, or for any deviation from the rectitude of its principles. No attempt is made to defend the misbehavior of greedy individuals or corrupt institutions; however, we shall not moralize over the occasionally unscrupulous actions of those people called "capitalists." Nor do we simply blame the moral shortcomings of individuals upon the capitalist system. It is possible simultaneously to be both a capitalist and morally decent. We reject the opinion that would make the ultimate subject of moral responsibility anything other than individual, freely acting, human beings.[6]

---

6 Accordingly, we do not excuse the pathological or criminal behavior of certain people on the grounds that they are the victims of an American society which has become (if it was not always) racist, sexist, and greedy. It is obviously true that the moral character of a human being is determined in part by conditions over which he has no control, and for which he should not be blamed. Nevertheless, one ought to beware of according too much to these

We have said that the attack upon democratic capitalism is carried out principally by the intellectual Left, and is directed against the alleged immorality of both its practice and principles. According to the Left, the American system is not in fact democratic, but "elitist." It is dedicated, not to the true principles of America's founding, which, the critics assert, are radically egalitarian; rather, democratic capitalism tends to perpetuate certain invidious class distinctions.

As a result of this critique, some intelligent people, including business people, appear to be embarrassed by capitalism. This interesting phenomenon is particularly evident on the campuses of many of our most prestigious universities, where embarrassment over capitalism frequently transforms itself into outright hostility. This phenomenon also displays an element of imprudence, not to mention ingratitude. It ought to be obvious to anyone that the very existence of our colleges and universities, not to mention their ability to give financial assistance to poor but talented students, depends decisively upon the successful management of funds invested by their endowments. No endowment could succeed as well, for example, in the economy of Communist China, or Cuba. The ability of any educational institution to offer scholarships, and thus make good the promise of equal educational opportunity for all, depends decisively, in this and many other ways, on a system of free markets and investment.

However obvious this may be, many in America evidently doubt the moral goodness of this country's system of government and

---

external conditions. If my character and actions are simply and completely determined by my rage and frustration at conditions which I did not cause, then it is certainly true that I cannot be blamed for my actions, however brutal or lawless, because I cannot be held responsible for them; but, for the same reason, neither can I be praised for having overcome them. I must be helped to overcome the pathologies of the ghetto, and thus require helpers, for example, in the form of government subsidies and bureaucracies. By the same logic, one ought to be prepared to excuse the alleged rapacious and greedy behavior of capitalists on the same grounds: they are as much victims of the capitalist system as are the most impoverished and downtrodden ghetto dwellers. It matters not that the capitalists have power and the ghetto dwellers are powerless. Being a victim of the system, one's abuse of one's power and privilege is as beyond one's control as are rioting and looting for the ghetto dwellers, actions which themselves require power in some sense of that term. The critics of free enterprise may, of course, reply that this is precisely *why* government regulation of markets is necessary. Such a reply would at least have the virtue of sharpening the debate over the relation of individual responsibility to society.

economy. This does not necessarily mean that they would abolish it if they could, in order to replace it with a more humane, compassionate system; but they cannot give capitalism their wholehearted, or perhaps even half-hearted, support. They will not rise to its defense. They will look beyond capitalism, in an effort to find some means to mitigate its alleged harshness, means that may not always be consistent with the ends of capitalism.

In failing to see that capitalism has its own built-in means for correcting itself, however, many people of otherwise good intentions sometimes do more harm than good. It is true that Adam Smith himself insisted that capitalism has certain unavoidable ill effects which need to be remedied by government regulation. In Smith's case, however, regulation was not motivated by hostility to capitalism, but by a conception of human nature, coupled with a clear understanding of the shortcomings of capitalism relative to the deepest needs of human nature.

There is certainly no harm in agreeing with the critics of capitalism that capitalism has its defects. Indeed, the fact that we ourselves often refer to our system of free enterprise and private ownership of capital as "capitalism," is due largely to the influence of Marx, whose teaching is *primarily* a critique of capitalism; and the Left's critique derives principally from Marx's teaching. By admitting that capitalism is not heaven on earth, the supporters of capitalism may agree with Marx's critique at least to the extent that it regards capitalism as being deficient in certain respects. We can be broad-minded enough to learn from our critics, particularly one as intelligent and learned as Marx.

Yet, in order to learn from Marx's critique, we need not share the passion that animates it. It appears to be a fact of human nature that those most acutely sensitive to the world's injustice are frequently the most deficient in precisely the good judgment and prudence necessary to guide or restrain their passion for justice. To benefit from Marx's critique in a manner worthy of reasonable people, we must liberate ourselves, at least temporarily, from the power of Marx's rhetoric to arouse our moral indignation. We must resist the temptation to succumb to the pleasures of moral indignation.

We may admit that capitalism is defective in certain respects, without thereby being obliged to assist in or wish for its destruction. Perhaps its good qualities outweigh or balance its defects. Our reserve here is due to one simple consideration: it is unreasonable to destroy capitalism without first assuring ourselves that there is a better system to take its place, and that such a system is practicable here and now.

This assurance presupposes, however, that we have understood capitalism on its own terms. We cannot know whether something is good or bad without first knowing what it is.

It is important to state this, even at the risk of belaboring the obvious, for the simple reason that we must avoid throwing the baby out with the bath. It seems to be the peculiar fate of humankind always to want more than it has, while being compelled to live with less. Thus beset by its own peculiar combination of desire and necessity, human nature is always in danger of falling into moral extremism. The intensity of human longing for what it lacks is mocked by the compulsion to accept the shortcomings of human life as it is lived here and now. Human nature thus tends to overlook the good it has, and overestimate the good it lacks: we criticize too harshly and hope too fervently.

Accordingly, in what follows, it is necessary to avoid the extremes of praise or blame which inevitably accompany blindness to morally relevant distinctions and facts. Our system of democratic capitalism is not perfect; but neither ought it be consigned to the realm of those things which are beneath contempt. Our task, therefore, is to see our system as it is, without wrath or zeal.

## IV

Our failure to see democratic capitalism as it is, and our consequent inability to judge its true worth, are due to our having forgotten the meaning of the principles upon which our nation was founded. This forgetting is at once the cause of our diffidence regarding the moral goodness of our system, and of our vulnerability to the attacks of radical critics. In order to judge the moral worth of our principles for ourselves, we must overcome certain contemporary biases against the possibility of understanding those principles as they were originally intended. We must try to recover the conception of human nature upon which they were originally based.

This effort is made more difficult because, as we said above, the prevailing contemporary understanding of the founding principles of American civil society—rights, justice, the common good—has been decisively shaped by the very teaching most inimical to the principles of the Declaration and Constitution. This teaching obscures those principles, and prevents our seeing them as they are. We are therefore kept from acquiring a true understanding of liberal democracy, both of its problems and its resources for solving them. We come to have expectations of liberal democracy which it cannot possibly fulfill; and, we blame it for failing to keep promises it never made.

The following example illustrates how the contemporary critique of democratic capitalism obscures the true nature of both its defects and resources for remedying them. From the beginning, the Founders of this country knew that *the* great difficulty for a political society such as ours is somehow to reconcile individual rights with public-spiritedness, where public-spiritedness is understood to mean dedication to the *common* welfare.

The common welfare, or the common good, is some good which can be shared in equally by all citizens. Obviously, not all goods can be common. Some goods are scarce, or are otherwise depleted by being shared in; but a common good, such as justice, cannot be depleted. Moreover, the common good is not merely the aggregate of individual goods; neither is it equivalent to the sum of the interests of allegedly disenfranchised groups, nor to the sum of all special interests. Rather, the common good is a good which is not a *sum* at all, but an integral whole. By transcending individual differences and interest, the common good unites all members of a community, precisely by being common. The common good is that which transforms a collection of individual human beings into a community.

How, then, is it possible to inculcate a people with dedication to the common good in a political society based upon the principle that individual rights are primary? Is this not manifestly impossible in a political society such as ours? This is the meaning of Publius' assertion in *The Federalist*, that "[r]epublican government presupposes the existence of these qualities [that is, the qualities dedicated to promoting the common good of society] *in a higher degree than any other form.*" [emphasis added]

In our time, the original conception of public-spiritedness, which itself presupposed a view of the common good of society, has been replaced by a new civic virtue, called "compassion." The new compassion is a revised version of the old compassion, now transformed to accommodate a particular political agenda. It no longer means the benevolent or humane sympathy for the suffering of other human beings simply as such. The new compassion is selective and divisive; but, the rhetoric of the new compassion dissembles its true intention, by using words like "inclusive" and "caring." Whereas the old-fashioned sort of public-spiritedness extended to citizens only as citizens, the new compassion extends, not to all the citizens of a society, but to its victims.

The division in society required by this understanding of compassion, between the victims and the non-victims, is thought to impose an obligation on the non-victims to help the victims. Indeed, the new compassion holds the non-victims partly responsible for the plight of the victims. The new compassion is therefore a source of civic duty. Dedication to the public good thus means serving, not the unfortunate, whatever their station in life, nor one's fellow citizens, but the alleged victims of certain invidious practices of society. Public dedication based upon the new compassion is therefore an attempt to make propitiation for one's complicity, however tenuous, in society's assault upon the victims.

However noble may be the intent of those who advocate compassion in the sense discussed here, the result of public policies animated by this alleged virtue is almost always to divide rather than unite. The non-victims come to resent being obliged to atone for the sins of their fathers, or for the sins of some impersonal entity called "society." The victims, and their advocates, come to resent any suggestion that their own occasionally pathological behavior might be partially responsible for their deprived condition, or that they have the means for rising above that condition, and thus must be held responsible for failing to make the effort necessary to improve their lives. Much of the peevish and hostile tone of contemporary public debate over domestic policy results from substituting "compassion" for public-spiritedness.

The replacement of public-spiritedness by compassion makes it impossible for us to understand the intransigence of the difficulty referred to by Publius, namely, the difficulty of inculcating a concern for the general welfare in a political society founded upon the primacy of individual rights. Contemporary compassion *cannot* be the public virtue required by liberal democracy, precisely because it depends upon a vision, not of society taken as a whole, but of society divided between the complacent and the aggrieved. The old compassion, or *charitas*, was directed to the suffering and exposed condition of individual human beings as such: we are all human, and we all suffer. The fundamental premise of the new compassion is the irreducible division of mankind into mutually antagonistic groups, confronting one another as oppressor and oppressed. Compassion is reserved for the powerless of the world; and the only remedy for powerlessness is the redistribution of power. The redistribution of power, which is the goal of the new compassion, is undertaken, however, without regard to the question of the good use of that power, or the good of society; but, this question was *the* question for the most thoughtful proponents of a liberal democracy based on the natural rights of individual human beings. Thus, the contemporary version of compassion is the antithesis of the kind of virtue required by genuinely republican government.[7]

## V

We have said that liberal democracy and Marxism disagree fundamentally over whether there exist natural principles or standards, which govern or decisively affect or limit political life. According to the Declaration of Independence and the Constitution, man both has a nature, and is a part of a larger and comprehensive natural whole, both of which are subject to "the laws of nature and nature's God." The American system explicitly and most emphatically bases itself upon a certain understanding of human nature, and of the place of human nature in the comprehensive natural order. If one ignores this, one fails even to begin to understand the momentous achievements of our national founding, and will be unequipped to criticize these achievements intelligently. Insofar as contemporary criticisms of liberal democracy and capitalism discount this appeal to nature, they beg the question that was, from the perspective of the Founders, the most important question: What is human nature, and what are the implications of human nature for the shape and purpose of civil society?

Our authoritative answer to this question is supplied by Publius in *The Federalist*. Reflecting upon human nature and the history of political societies, Publius teaches us to moderate our hopes and expectations of political life. Politics is not everything there is to life. Politics alone cannot solve all the problems of human life. The political, or public sphere must be kept separate from the private. Admittedly the two spheres intersect in the plane where one's exercise of one's rights may conflict with the exercise by others of their rights; but, beyond this, government and politics are constitutionally incapable of directing certain dimensions of the private lives of citizens.

For example, government is thought not to be the primary vehicle for directly influencing or shaping the moral character of a people. This emphatically does not mean that the Founders thought that government is amoral, or that it may be indifferent to morality. Rather, they believed that any government, remaining within its legitimately circumscribed sphere of influence, may seek to influence the moral character of its citizens, albeit only indirectly, in accordance with those

---

[7] It should be obvious that the sense in which we have criticized "compassion" does not at all correspond to the unpoliticized sense of the term, which enjoins us to sympathize with the suffering of our fellow human beings, regardless of station or victim status.

14

qualities necessary to republican government; but, the private sphere may not legitimately be deprived of its primary responsibility for the moral education of the people.

Accordingly, even in the best civil society, there will be moral irregularities; but their tendency to cause mischief can be mitigated by public and private education, as well as by the moral and religious instruction of the young by their parents, the moral exhortations of religious leaders, and, by participation in public life, in the civic life of a free, self-governing people.

There are, indeed, certain habits of mind and character required of the people by republican government, and government may legitimately seek to encourage those qualities. The prudent statesman, however, will be guided by the principle that human beings love themselves at least as much as, if not more than, they love truth and justice. They tend to form factions, or what are now called "special-interest groups." These groups are animated, not by civic zeal, but by their desire to promote their own particular interest, even at the expense of the public welfare. To decrease the tendency of democracies to be ruled by any one faction, one must supplement the effort to inculcate public virtue, by relying upon the following principle: you decrease the likelihood that any one faction will prevail over the public interest by permitting the number of factions to increase. The greater their number, the less likely that any one special interest will predominate.

The necessity to accommodate democracy's tendency to be ruled by factions, a tendency rooted in human nature, is one reason Publius teaches the wisdom of moderating one's expectations from politics. His teaching is not new; rather, it is a teaching with which most Western political thinkers agree.[8] Almost every political thinker of the first rank, from Plato and Aristotle, to John Locke, Alexis de Tocqueville, and Adam Smith, however they may have disagreed in other respects, taught the wisdom of limiting one's expectations of the human good that may be achieved by politics. The principal reason for the virtual unanimity of these thinkers is their shared belief in the existence of human nature's permanent possibilities, for both good and evil. The great political thinkers occasionally disagree sharply over what human nature is; but, they do agree that it exists, and that it both directs and limits what is politically possible.

Certain prevailing contemporary opinions make it necessary to state that believing in the existence of human nature is not inconsequential.

---

[8] There are, of course, some exceptions to this consensus, Karl Marx being the most obvious.

Indeed, in our century, what has fundamentally separated the free nations from the totalitarian nations is the belief in two things: God and human nature. Twentieth-century totalitarianism in both its forms, German National Socialism and Communism, has been both militantly atheistic and opposed to the belief in an unchanging human nature. The inevitable result of these two opinions was the exaltation of the human will. Both the Nazis and the Communists maintained that there is no permanent nature in man to limit his possibilities. Man is limited neither by nature or God. Man is radically free. Radical freedom is freedom *from*, unfettered by freedom *for*: freedom is for whatever you will it to be.

That man is radically free means that man makes himself to be what he is. Man is what he is at any given time as the result of a process called "history," which is itself the product of free human action. Man at any given time has certain characteristics, which are determined by the prevailing historical conditions; but these conditions are themselves the products of prior human activity. The only limit set to freedom is set by freedom itself. As Leo Strauss has written, "The so-called discovery of history consists in the realization, or in the alleged realization, that man's freedom is radically limited by his earlier use of his freedom, and not by his nature or by the whole order of nature or creation."[9]

It may be added, without much exaggeration, that the future of the United States, and of the West generally, is threatened more than anything else by the possibility that some form of the teaching which denies the existence of both God and human nature will prevail. In particular, one must take seriously the possibility that this teaching will prevail in the United States, or that it will prevail (if it has not already) among the intellectual and cultural elites in the United States.

To state the case specifically: if one believes there is such a thing as human nature, something permanent and definitive in all human beings, such that human beings are equipped with both capacities and weaknesses, then one will not expect the perfectly just and equitable society ever to be achieved, or evil to be entirely eliminated, or good always and everywhere to triumph. One will not expect to see poverty and suffering vanish, or war to cease, or the comity of nations ultimately prevail. One will agree with the framers of the Constitution that

---

9 Leo Strauss, "Progress or Return? The Contemporary Crisis in Western Civilization," in *Modern Judaism I* (Baltimore: The Johns Hopkins University Press, 1981), 32-33.

reasonable human beings will expect, even in the best case, only "a *more perfect union*."

The very language of the Constitution thus recalls the lesson of political moderation; and, the structure of the system set forth by our Constitution, "partly federal, partly national,"[10] itself indicates the belief that perfect political unity is neither possible nor desirable. We are a nation of states. As such, we reflect a political compromise, perhaps one of the most remarkable in history, whereby the integrity, autonomy, and interests of each state, are made to consist with a unifying national interest, under the rule of national law. To grasp the enormous difficulty of this achievement, one need only reflect upon the fates of similar attempts, in the European Community, Yugoslavia, and the former Soviet Union.

*The Federalist* reinforces the teaching that perfect political union is not to be expected. Human nature being a combination of self-love and reason, each person is more likely to be attached to his own opinions because they are his, than because they are true. Accordingly, as we noted above, the Founders believed political factions to be inevitable. One might, of course, try to achieve political unity simply by eliminating factions altogether. To get rid of factions, however, you must first eliminate freedom; but, to be a free individual human being means, in part, to be separate from other human beings, with the liberty, among other things, to associate with those with whom one shares important interests. Therefore, to say that perfect union is impossible is the negative way of expressing the fact that human beings are by nature free.

The great divide between modern liberal democracy and modern totalitarianism is, therefore, not primarily the presence or absence of an expressed devotion to justice, or to "human rights" as such. What separates the two forms of government is dedication to the principle that all human beings are *by nature* equally endowed with rights, among which is the right to liberty, a right that inevitably entails the occasional abuse of liberty in behalf of selfish interests.

Liberal democracy may be said to differ from totalitarianism in that it saw human nature for what it is, and did not blink. Modern liberal democracy simultaneously tries to accommodate the permanently unsociable element in human nature, while mitigating its unsociable effects; but, liberal democracy, unlike totalitarianism, also insists upon the irreducible uniqueness and liberty of each human being.

---

[10] See Harry Jaffa, "Partly Federal, Partly National," in *The Conditions of Freedom* (Baltimore: The Johns Hopkins University Press, 1975).

The impossibility of perfect political union implies the impossibility of perfect political justice, in the sense of the complete overcoming of private interest in favor of the common good. This is not, however, a counsel of despair. To deny the possibility of perfect justice is not to deny the possibility of justice. We may have a duty to obtain and promote justice, even if, or especially if perfect justice is impossible. Indeed, it is rather the expectation that perfect justice will be achieved that leads inevitably to fanaticism and despair, even to the denial of the very possibility of duty itself. On this point, the great tradition of Western political thought reaches virtual unanimity: justice is necessary and perfect justice is impossible.

# CHAPTER TWO

## *What Is Liberal Democracy?*

### I

On January 27, 1838, Abraham Lincoln delivered his "Address Before the Young Men's Lyceum of Springfield, Illinois." In it, he said:

> We find ourselves in the peaceful possession, of the fairest portion of the earth, as regards extent of territory, fertility of soil, and salubrity of climate. We find ourselves under the government of a system of political institutions, conducing more essentially to the ends of civil and religious liberty, than any of which the history of former times tells us. We, when mounting the stage of existence, found ourselves the legal inheritors of these fundamental blessings. We toiled not in the acquirement or establishment of them—they are a legacy bequeathed us, by a *once* hardy, brave, and patriotic, but *now* lamented and departed race of ancestors. Their's was the task (and nobly they performed it) to possess themselves, and through themselves, us, of this goodly land; and to uprear upon its hills and its valleys, a political edifice of liberty and equal rights; 'tis ours only to transmit these, the former, unprofaned by the foot of an invader; the latter, undecayed by the lapse of time and untorn by usurpation, to the latest generation that fate shall permit the world to know. This task gratitude to our fathers, justice to ourselves, duty to posterity, and love of our species in general, imperatively require us faithfully to perform.[1]

Lincoln then went on to ask whether and from what source the people of the United States might apprehend the greatest danger in transmitting to their posterity the inherited blessings of a free land, liberty, and equal rights for all citizens: "At what point then is the approach of danger to be expected? I answer, if it ever reach us, it must spring up amongst us. It cannot come from abroad. *If destruction be our lot, we must ourselves be its author and finisher. As a nation of freemen, we must live through all time, or die by suicide.*"[2] [emphasis added]

---

[1] Roy P. Basler, ed., *Abraham Lincoln: His Speeches and Writings* (New York: World Publishing Co., 1946), 76ff.

[2] Ibid., 76.

Lincoln's description of the conditions of his time applies with equal force to our own. Our legacy is the same as, if not greater than that of past generations of Americans. We enjoy the fundamental blessings of liberty and equal rights to an even greater extent than did the members of Lincoln's audience. Standing between us and them are certain momentous achievements in behalf of liberty and equality: the Civil War, the Emancipation Proclamation, the Amendments abolishing slavery and prohibiting the denial of voting rights on the grounds of race or sex, *Brown v. Board of Education*, and the civil rights legislation of the Great Society.

Yet, despite these great achievements, many Americans doubt whether we have genuinely progressed in our efforts to live up to the principles of our Declaration and Constitution. Indeed, some even doubt the decency of those very principles themselves. America's critics, ever vigilant, are continually discovering new forms of discrimination and inequality, even in those areas of American life where the greatest progress seemed to have been made. An impartial observer might indeed be baffled by the relentless and unforgiving quality of America's self-criticism, a quality which is evident daily in our news media, popular culture, and educational institutions.

It seems that nothing we do to promote equal opportunity and racial harmony, or to eliminate sexual discrimination is ever good enough. The words of Alexis de Tocqueville would appear to have been confirmed:

It is possible to conceive of men arrived at a degree of freedom that should completely content them; they would then enjoy their independence without anxiety and without impatience. *But men will never establish any equality with which they can be contented.* Whatever efforts a people may make, *they will never succeed in reducing all the conditions of a society to a perfect level;* and even if they unhappily attained that absolute and complete equality of position, *the inequality of minds would still remain, which, coming directly from the hand of God, will forever escape the laws of man.* However democratic, then, the social state and the political constitution of a people may be, it is certain that every member of the community will always find out several points about him which overlook his own position; and we may foresee that his looks will be doggedly fixed in that direction. When inequality of conditions is the common law of society, the most marked inequalities do not strike the eye; when everything is nearly on the same level, the slightest are marked enough to hurt it. *Hence the desire of equality always becomes more insatiable in proportion as equality is more complete.* [emphases added][3]

Equality, however, is not the sole principle upon which our republic was founded, as Tocqueville himself knew quite well. Our other great founding principle is liberty. In a chapter in *Democracy In America* entitled "Why Democratic Nations Show a More Ardent And Enduring Love Of Equality Than Of Liberty," Tocqueville writes:

> The first and most intense passion that is produced by equality of condition is, I need hardly say, the love of that equality . . . Everybody has remarked that in our time . . . this passion for equality is every day gaining ground in the human heart. It has been said a hundred times that our contemporaries are far more ardently and tenaciously attached to equality than to freedom. It is possible to imagine an extreme point at which freedom and equality would meet and blend. Let us suppose that all the people take a part in the government, and that each one of them has an equal right to take a part in it. As no one is different from his fellows, none can exercise a tyrannical power; men will be perfectly free because they are entirely equal; and they will all be perfectly equal because they are entirely free. *To this ideal state democratic nations tend. This is the only complete form that equality can assume upon earth; but there are a thousand others which, without being equally perfect, are not less cherished by those nations.* [emphasis added]

However imperfectly we may realize it in practice, the ideal state Tocqueville describes, wherein freedom and equality "blend," is precisely what is intended by the Declaration of Independence: each human being is the equal of every other in being naturally and unalienably endowed with the right to liberty. In any legitimately instituted government, therefore, each citizen is the equal of every other in his right to participate in that government. This is the Declaration's way of saying what Tocqueville means by the phrase "men will be perfectly free because they are entirely equal; and they will all be perfectly equal because they are entirely free."

A moment's reflection, however, shows why these two principles, equality and liberty, are difficult to combine in practice. This reflection is strengthened by a review of the history of nations, including our own. The example of the Soviet Union shows that equality of conditions, albeit equality in misery but not freedom, may exist among the citizens ruled by a totalitarian regime; and, the history of America provides

---

[3] Alexis de Tocqueville, *Democracy In America*, vol. 2, ed. Henry Reeve (New York: Alfred A. Knopf, 1976).

examples of the abuse of liberty at the expense of the equality of others.[4]

Tocqueville himself makes some similar remarks about the relation of equality to liberty. In practice, equality of condition "may be established in civil society without prevailing in the political world." That is, it is possible for there to be a political society in which all citizens have the equal right "of living in the same manner and seeking wealth by the same means," without there simultaneously existing the right of all to participate equally in governing. Monarchy is an example of such a society. Tocqueville adds that one may easily imagine other combinations "by which very great equality would be united to institutions more or less free or even to institutions wholly without freedom."

Tocqueville continues by stating that equality, pushed "to its furthest extent, may be confounded with freedom," precisely because "men cannot become absolutely equal unless they are entirely free." Tocqueville, however, appears to agree with ancient writers like Plato and Aristotle, that it is equality, and not freedom, that is the characteristic mark of democracy. Moreover, because of the human tendency to confuse liberty with equality, it is especially important to understand how they differ, and why it is that human beings tend to prefer equality to freedom.

The preference for equality over freedom is due in part to the natural human tendency to want to esteem oneself as highly as one does others, and in part to the fact that political liberty is more easily lost than is equality. Accordingly, "not only do men cling to equality because it is dear to them; they also adhere to it because they think it will last forever." Moreover, anyone may easily see for himself what evils flow from the excesses of political freedom. Where freedom is excessive or unrestrained, "the tranquillity, the property, [and] the lives" of individual human beings are jeopardized. The evils that extreme freedom brings "are immediate; they are apparent to all, and all are more or less affected by them."

It is much more difficult to discern the evils that are caused by extreme equality: they are "slowly disclosed; they creep gradually into the social frame; they are seen only at intervals; and at the moment at which they become most violent, habit already causes them to be no longer felt." Conversely, whereas the advantages and pleasures associated with freedom are discerned only over time, the benefits and

---

4 The reader ought not conclude from the juxtaposition of these two examples that we intend anything like the "moral equivalence" of the United States and the former Soviet Union.

charms of equality are immediately and everywhere manifest. Tocqueville writes that equality "every day confers a number of small enjoyments on every man." Moreover, the "charms of equality are every instant felt and are within the reach of all; the noblest hearts are not insensible to them, and the most vulgar souls exult in them." Everyone may, without exerting himself, immediately enjoy the pleasures of equality; but, the pleasures of liberty are never obtained without sacrifice.

Tocqueville concludes this chapter by observing:

> I think that democratic communities have a natural taste for freedom; left to themselves, they will seek it, cherish it, and view any privation of it with regret. *But for equality their passion is ardent, insatiable, incessant, invincible; they call for equality in freedom; and if they cannot obtain that, they still call for equality in slavery.* They will endure poverty, servitude, barbarism, but they will not endure aristocracy. [emphasis added]

The fact that our republic is founded upon the twin principles of equality and liberty is reflected by the term "*liberal* democracy." Our republic is a democracy, to be sure, but it is a liberal democracy, as well. Not all democracies are liberal democracies. Democracy means "rule of the people," where each person is the equal of every other person in regard to ruling and being ruled. Liberal democracy, however, is dedicated to the preservation of individual liberty: within certain limits, each citizen in a liberal democracy may live as he pleases. Some of the cities of ancient Greece, for example, were non-liberal democracies. Religion, which we regard as a private matter of personal liberty, was a public matter in the Greek cities: one's religion was the religion of one's city.

Our democracy, then, is emphatically based upon both liberty and equality; but, as our current situation and the quotes from Tocqueville illustrate, we get into difficulty when we abandon one of these principles for the sake of the other. Given the unequal distribution of talent and ability, good birth, and fortune, unrestrained liberty leads inevitably to political inequality; but, the passion for equality, unchecked by tolerance both for natural distinctions among human beings, as well as for the rewards which are rightly due those who exert themselves to succeed, leads to a fanatical intolerance of *all* inequalities, however benign or insignificant they may otherwise be.[5]

---

[5] This seems to be our plight, namely, radical egalitarianism. In current political parlance, liberalism and radical egalitarianism tend to be identified with

Accordingly, our present unhappiness with America is partly due to our having forgotten the original intent of our founding principles. In that case, the required therapy would involve recalling those principles to mind, and rehabilitating our appreciation for their worthiness to serve as the ideals of a free and decent people. Having thus been restored to health, we could then be confident that, even though we occasionally fail to live up to them, our principles are nevertheless still worthy of our allegiance. Our principles are not at fault, even though we sometimes fail to act according to them. We could say with Lincoln that our Declaration of Independence and Constitution declared human rights so that enforcement might follow as soon as circumstances allowed.

Unfortunately, our problems appear to be deeper than this. It would indeed be a good thing if we were to return occasionally to the Declaration of Independence and the Constitution, to remind ourselves of the nobility of our principles; but, these great documents themselves, and the principles upon which they stand, have become problematic. Many contemporary Americans regard them with diffidence, if not outright hostility. We give them only tentative approval. We have been taught to do this by a version of our founding which is now ubiquitous in American life. According to this view, our founding is fundamentally flawed. It deliberately, if not cynically, compromised the principles of natural equality and liberty, by an accommodation to the institution of slavery, in order to establish the Union. The very morality of our founding documents must therefore be questioned.

The charges are familiar and relentless. We are told that our nation was founded by a group of elitists, slave-owners, racist white males, and misogynists, intent on perpetuating their own hegemony, while dissimulating their true intent behind the rhetoric of human equality, liberty, and the principle of the consent of the governed. To be sure, the arguments offered to support this view are often weak, and rely upon tendentious scholarship.[6] Nevertheless, faulty reasoning to the contrary notwithstanding, many Americans have been convinced by this logic, and have accepted the conclusion that our founders intended only to preserve their "white skin privilege," and merely glorified it with grand talk about the equality of all human beings.

It is particularly ironic, in the light of recent history, that many Americans now doubt the wisdom and goodness of our institutions,

one another; however, modern liberalism in its original conception is not radically egalitarian.

6 We consider some of these in Chapter Five, "Critiques."

and thus question whether indeed we are obliged to perpetuate them, or to help other countries in their efforts to establish democratic governments and free-market economies. The recent collapse of most of the socialist nations in the world, along with their efforts to replace socialism with democracy and free enterprise, would seem to have vindicated the superiority of our principles to the principles of socialism, the only serious twentieth-century rival to democratic capitalism. The great events of our time, in particular the peaceful collapse of the regime that most intransigently opposed our system of democracy and free markets, would seem to be cause for great joy and hope. The most murderous regime in the history of mankind simply ceased to exist.

From the end of World War II, the free nations of the earth were separated from the unfree by what Winston Churchill had called "The Iron Curtain." The non-communist West and the communist East divided the world between them. The resolution of their implacable enmity appeared to be impossible without war, perhaps the last war, the war that would eliminate the possibility of future wars by eliminating all combatants; and then, the Soviet Union simply disappeared, its principles rejected by those who knew best what life under communism really is.

Thus, like the Americans Lincoln addressed in 1838, we now have no foreign invader to fear; and surely we live at a time when civil and religious liberty abound to an even greater degree than in Lincoln's time. We are not compelled, as are the countries of Eastern Europe and the former Soviet Union, to build a political system and an economy from scratch. These countries must overcome the spiritual and economic damage caused by decades of totalitarian rule and an economy controlled by a relatively small number of state bureaucrats. The life of luxurious material well-being reserved for a few party members was far removed from the life of the ordinary Soviet citizen, which was characterized by a degree of squalor and economic destitution that makes our own official poverty level appear sumptuous by comparison.

Perhaps, in Czechoslovakia or Ukraine, or somewhere unanticipated, there will re-appear that "once hardy, brave, and patriotic" race of ancestors, whose disappearance Lincoln lamented; surely such a race is as needful there as it once was here. We Americans, however, have only to transmit the legacy bequeathed us by our ancestors. We have good reason to believe, however, that we have failed to protect our legacy of liberty and equal rights from the decay of time, "untorn by usurpation."

Lincoln made another famous speech, his "House Divided" speech, in Springfield, Illinois, June 17, 1858. He began by saying "If we could first know where we are, and whither we are tending, we could better judge what to do and how to do it."[7] Lincoln was referring to a *crisis*, literally, a moment when a judgment must be made, concerning whether the nation would be ruled by the opponents or the advocates of slavery. That crisis, Lincoln said, was inevitable: the government could not "endure permanently half-slave and half-free." The house would not fall; but it would cease to be divided.

One might plausibly take Lincoln to mean that it was necessary to study the history of the United States, particularly the history of slavery, in order to see how to proceed. Lincoln was, however, thinking not merely of history. To know "where we are and whither we are tending" requires, not history, or not merely history, but a reflection upon the principles that motivate the human agents who make history. The crisis of the house divided was, therefore, essentially a moral crisis, a crisis of moral principles. Where we are and whither we are tending depend fundamentally upon principles: history depends upon principles.

This remains true of our contemporary situation. The world is no longer divided between democracy and communism. The world is no longer half-slave and half-free; or, to put it more prudently, the world is no longer divided between the free nations and those ruled by totalitarian regimes. It is, of course, always possible, if not likely, that new forms of tyranny will appear; but this possibility was not as compelling as was our danger, while communism was strong and relentless. We were obliged by our very peril to have confidence in our country and its principles. That enemy having destroyed itself, we now face the real crisis, the moment when we must judge whether our principles are worth defending. Aristotle said in his *Politics* that political societies come into existence for the sake of life and its preservation but remain in existence for the sake of the good life.[8] While our enemy flourished, we had primarily to defend ourselves from extinction. When he was defeated, we were obliged to confront the question of the goodness of our way of life, the reason for its continuing to exist. We, no less than Lincoln's audience in 1838, are obliged by "gratitude to our fathers, justice to ourselves, duty to posterity, and love of our species" to return to the reflection upon the principles of liberty and equal rights, the principles of liberal democracy.

---

[7] Basler, *Abraham Lincoln*, 372.
[8] Aristotle, *Politics*, 1280b30ff.

Our crisis is that liberal democracy, or the goodness of liberal democracy, has become problematic. However, it is misleading to state that liberal democracy has *become* problematic: being based upon certain principles which appear to stand in some tension with one another, liberal democracy is always or inherently problematic. Thus it is our permanent duty, as a free and reasonable people, to reflect upon the meaning of our nation's founding.

The crisis of liberal democracy is coeval with the beginnings of liberal democracy, because liberal democracy tries to hold together principles which have proved incompatible in the past, namely, liberty and equality. Moreover, being based on the primacy of individual rights, liberal democracy is constantly compelled, by its very principles, to confront the difficulty of inculcating in its citizens a sense of civic duty. The sense of civic duty, however, presupposes a sense of the common good, the good which, being shared by the members of a political society, makes it a *community*, and not merely an aggregate of human beings living in proximity to one another. In a society dedicated to protecting the individual right to the pursuit of happiness, however, the notion of the common good is inherently problematic.

Compounding this difficulty is the tendency in a democracy to identify the common good with the will of the majority. The common good, it seems plausible to say, is what the majority says it is. That this is emphatically not the case for the American republic was one of the guiding themes of the political career of Abraham Lincoln. As he argued in his great debates with Stephen Douglas, if you identify the two, then if the majority of the people want slavery, it follows that slavery must be regarded as conducing to the common good. Douglas was evidently willing to live with this conclusion; but Lincoln was not.[9] The common good of the American republic requires the protection of the civil rights of all citizens; but slavery denies the civil rights of some. If the civil rights of some citizens are insecure, then the civil rights of all are insecure. It is merely a matter of who has power.[10]

---

[9] I say that Douglas was "evidently willing," because, as Harry Jaffa has argued, in his excellent book, *Crisis of the House Divided*, there is good reason to believe that Douglas, like Lincoln, loathed slavery. Unlike Lincoln, however, Douglas was prepared to make certain concessions to slavery in the short run, because he believed it was on the way to extinction in the long run.

[10] Of course, there were those who tried to escape this conclusion by denying that slaves were citizens. This is one of the main points of the infamous Dred Scott case, about which we say more elsewhere. Chief Justice Taney, writing

The foregoing argument is, of course, merely negative; that is, it argues against slavery on the grounds that accepting slavery may lead to consequences which are otherwise repugnant. The strongest argument against slavery, and it too is an argument that Lincoln made, is that slavery contravenes the natural equality of each human being with every other. As Lincoln put it, the principle of natural equality means that, just as I would not own a slave, neither would I be a slave.

The problematic nature of liberal democracy is, therefore, a consequence of the primacy of the rights of the individual, and the difficulty in distinguishing the will of the majority from the common good. Therefore, one may say that our present crisis, like the earlier crisis of which Lincoln spoke in his "House Divided" speech, was inevitable. It is rooted in serious doubts concerning the very goodness of our principles, the efficacy of our system of government, and even our capacity for self-government. These doubts are not groundless; but neither are they necessarily overwhelming.

The difficulties that are inherent to liberal democracy do not necessarily coincide with those ills alleged by the radical Left to infect America. It is one thing to say that every reflective American ought to have certain reservations about liberal democracy because of certain tendencies endemic to it, but it is quite another simply to capitulate to a critique of America based on criteria which are themselves inconsistent with America's own founding principles.

Our doubts, therefore, are caused in part by our failure to transmit, from generation to generation, a clear comprehension of the principles on which our system of government and economy stands, but they are also partly due to the widespread success of the radical Left's critique of our principles. These two causes come together in the following way. The Left's critique has succeeded in large part because it has exploited our tendency to take the momentous achievements of America's past for granted. Accordingly we, like the Hebrew people after the giving of the Second Decalogue, do not meditate upon our principles day and night.

The national diffidence which the radical critique has produced prevents us from arming ourselves adequately to withstand its attacks upon liberal democracy, precisely because our diffidence extends to the things most needful, namely, the very documents and books that contain the original statement of our principles. To put the point simply:

---

for the majority, concluded that slaves are not citizens, on the grounds that, at the time the Declaration and Constitution were written, many white Americans did not regard them as citizens.

the radicals say, "Do not try to derive comfort or support from reading the Declaration, or the Constitution , or the *Federalist*. These are the writings of middle-aged, wealthy, corrupt, slave-owning white men, who are for this reason not to be trusted." By capitulating to, or even cooperating with the radicals, our public schools and other institutions of learning fail to teach their students the truth, both the bad *and* the good, about our national past, its principles and history. Many of those who control what is taught in our schools have accepted the radical critique of America's founding, and thus transmit the critique, but not the defense, to our children.

Every thoughtful and informed person is aware of the revisionism that now controls the way our children are taught the history of their country, by the schools, the news media, and popular culture. According to the revisionists, our Declaration of Independence and Constitution are corrupt, racist, hypocritical documents, expressing only the private interests of a certain class of elitists bent upon dominating the disenfranchised for their own personal gain.

So certain are the revisionists and their students of these alleged facts, that they are excused from making the effort to read, and understand on their own terms, the documents they condemn. One recalls teaching a class of adults in a continuing education course, the readings for which included the Declaration of Independence. A student objected to the following passage, on the grounds that it is racist: "He [i.e., King George] has excited domestic insurrections amongst us, and has endeavored to bring on the inhabitants of our frontiers, the merciless Indian savages, whose known rule of warfare is an undistinguished destruction of all ages, sexes, and conditions."

The student's argument consisted of reading the offending passage aloud, and concluding with a silence that signified a confidence that the self-evidence of Jefferson's racism made any further comment or argument superfluous. The major premise of the student's argument apparently was that it is racist to call Indians "savages," although the student was evidently unwilling to accord the same treatment to King George, of whom the Declaration asserts: "He is at this time transporting large armies of foreign mercenaries to complete the works of death, desolation, and tyranny, already begun with circumstances of cruelty and perfidy scarcely paralleled in the most barbarous ages, and totally unworthy the head of a civilized nation." Therefore, the major premise was that it is permissible for Jefferson to call King George barbaric when he behaves in a barbaric way; but it is impermissible for Jefferson to describe the behavior of certain Indians as barbaric.

The criterion according to which one may distinguish the permissible uses of "barbaric" from the impermissible uses is evidently supplied by the term "oppression": only oppressors, but never the oppressed, can behave barbarically. The Indians were oppressed by the American colonists. Therefore, they cannot be barbaric; and it is racist to call them barbaric. Q.E.D.

The student's presupposition concerned neither the facts of history nor of human nature. It was, rather, a moral postulate, which made possible the student's unshakable certainty of the moral superiority, never mind the truth, of that position to every dissenting view. It was a presupposition absorbed from the curious mixture of rigid absolutism and fanatical relativism that prevails today among America's intellectual elite. According to this view, all "values," that is, considerations of right and wrong, are "relative." That is, values depend, not upon what really is right or wrong, but upon what is held or posited to be right or wrong at a given time and place. On the other hand, according to this same view, Western civilization, and America in particular, really is immoral, on account of its racism, sexism, and the like. The opinion that racism, sexism, and other similar "isms," are immoral is not itself a "value"; rather, it is absolutely true. Thus, the position of the radical critic appears to be as follows: "All values are relative; but ours are absolutely true. Anyone who disagrees with us on the basis of their own values, is an absolutist, and therefore a fascist. We who disagree with them, on the basis of the absolute truth of our values, do so in the name of tolerance."

Perhaps this apparent contradiction is partially mitigated by the following consideration. The alleged source of Western civilization's racism and sexism is its belief in its own superiority to other civilizations, and, in general, in the belief in objective standards, expressed in the Declaration by what it calls "self-evident truths," according to which civilizations may be ranked as more or less civilized, that is, as better or worse, or more or less humane. Therefore, it is the belief in standards that is the source of invidious distinctions like "civilized" and "barbaric." If there really are no objective standards on which to base these distinctions, then, so this argument holds, they can be based only upon the latent or hidden racism or sexism of those who make such distinctions. That is, the belief in objective standards is itself merely an act of will, hidden from view, to be sure, but an act of will, nevertheless, the purpose of which is to conceal the true source of one's belief in "values." Thus, those who assert that all values are relative, while simultaneously maintaining that the immorality of racism is not relative, partially avoid contradicting themselves by their conviction that all values are ultimately products, or "projections," of the will.

Still, the contradiction is not altogether removed, because the radical critics do not admit that *their* values are merely projections of the will.[11] The radical critics of America's founding are sincere in their beliefs that racism and sexism are immoral, that this immorality is based upon rational and objective standards, and that America violates these standards. Yet, because they are convinced that our founding documents are corrupt, the radical critics are prevented from appealing to the principles of the Declaration and the Constitution—the natural equality of all human beings, the natural endowment of the rights of life, liberty, and the pursuit of happiness, and so forth—to vindicate their charge that America is immoral. Certain it is that if all human beings are equal in being naturally endowed with the rights of life, liberty, and the pursuit of happiness, then invidious distinctions based on race or sex are immoral. In that case, the radical critics would be doing this nation a great service by insisting that it live up to the principles that it professes.[12] The pathos of the radical critique, however, is that its own historical revisionism denies it the access to those very principles necessary to vindicate its moral critique of America.

However this may be, the radical critics remain convinced, for example, that when Thomas Jefferson wrote "all *men* are created equal," he did not mean all human beings; rather, he meant white, upper middle class, Anglo-Saxon males. To confirm this allegation, argue the critics, one has only to consider, for example, the concessions made to slavery by our Constitution. These concessions are held to prove the hypocrisy of our founding principal document. It is not, therefore, America's occasional failure to live up to its principles which

---

[11] This is not altogether true. Some of the more intellectually consistent adherents of the radical critique now recognize that their principles must, according to their own reasoning, be mere projections of the will. Accordingly, they no longer concern themselves with justice, but with power. For a good contemporary discussion of this phenomenon, see Thomas Pangle's *The Ennobling of Democracy*.

[12] This was indeed the principal source of the moral strength of the American civil rights movement in the beginning. The force of Martin Luther King's indictment of America was precisely in shaming it with the realization that it did not practice what it preached. The contemporary civil rights leadership, by contrast, appears to believe that America is *in principle* racist. If this charge is indeed true, one wonders what the remedy is, if there is any.

is the source of the injustices of our society. It is rather that our founding principles are themselves conceived in hypocrisy.

All other things being equal, it would therefore seem reasonable to return to the study of our intellectual foundations through a careful study of the Declaration and the Constitution, in order to see whether the radical critique is justified. That is, if we agree with the radicals that fundamental reforms are necessary, we must first see where we went wrong. Thus, the remedy for our condition is, in part, a clear comprehension of our founding principles, acquired through the open-minded study of our intellectual heritage. Our dilemma is that we feel ourselves unable to read the old books, the authoritative books, except in the light of the critique most hostile to the teaching of those very books; or except as we are predisposed by a certain contempt for the past and tradition, a contempt which we have been taught is appropriate to our sophisticated modernity, to look down on the past, or to smile condescendingly at its naivety. We must, at least temporarily, liberate ourselves from this dilemma.

Our effort to liberate ourselves is made difficult by the fact that contempt for the past is implied by a certain notion of progress which is itself implicit in the very meaning of modernity. Progress in general means that things go from worse to better, from an inferior to a superior condition: the current situation, the up-to-the-minute, the modern is, because of progress, superior to the past, the old, the outmoded. There is an obvious and unexceptionable sense of progress with which we are not here concerned, namely technological progress. No one can dispute that technology has progressed in human history. What is meant here is not technological progress, but intellectual progress, or progress in wisdom, moral understanding, or humanity.

Technological progress can only nominally be called progress, for the following reason. Technological progress may be described as the increase or refinement of the power or utility of tools. Increase or refinement of power or utility is not identical with increase of wisdom. Indeed, when foolishness is weak, it can do little harm; but, augment its strength, while leaving it in its benighted state, and you increase the likelihood and the extent of its doing great evil.

The history of the twentieth century alone amply demonstrates that wisdom or morality, do not necessarily advance together with technology. Indeed, their respective courses may run counter to one another.[13]

---

13 Consider, for example, Winston Churchill's reflections, in his *The Second World War*, on the implications for all future warfare of the technologies developed during the First World War. Thomas Jefferson, in a letter to John

However this may be, the point is that, as up-to-date moderns, we are vulnerable to being deceived by the opinion that we are justified in regarding the moral seriousness of those in the past, like Jefferson, with good-natured condescension. Therefore, when we read a sentence like "We hold these truths to be self-evident," we may admire the robust confidence of those who proclaimed it; but, because we are convinced that we have matured to the point where we no longer require consoling myths like the belief in self-evident truth, we cannot share that confidence.

There is a more radical version of the view that history is progressive, called historicism, which denies that there is even progress in history. Instead, there is only change. This view of history is, admittedly, more consistent than the naive moral relativism that it displaced. To speak of progress in the sense of going from a "worse" to a "better" condition is to make a value judgment; but, if there are no objective standards of good and bad, then, because progress means going from a worse to a better condition, it makes no sense to speak of progress. According to this more radical version of historicism, at various times and epochs, different opinions about good and bad prevail. These opinions are the products of certain conditions which obtain at that given time, and depend decisively on those conditions, for example, the material conditions of production, the spirit of the time, and so forth.

According to this view, the great thinkers of these epochs are as much the children of their times as are the common people, although they may have expressed the spirit of their times more powerfully or comprehensively than lesser minds. The consequence of either understanding of history, but particularly of historicism, is that we cannot seriously study the past, as though the teaching of the past, contained in old books, could guide us in the most urgent matters, matters of life and death, or good and bad. That is, it follows from either understanding of history that it makes no sense to study old books as though they contained *the* truth.

---

Adams, also discussed the effect upon what may be called the moral qualities, of technological advances in the making of weapons: "I agree with you that there is a natural aristocracy among men. The grounds of this are virtue and talents . . . But since the invention of gunpowder has armed the weak as well as the strong with missile death, bodily strength, like beauty, good humor, politeness, and other accomplishments, has become but an auxiliary ground of distinction." Quoted in *The People Shall Judge* (Chicago: University of Chicago Press, 1949), 1: 229-230.

It is true that those who believe that intellectual and moral history is progressive, may read old books in order to see how our knowledge "evolved" over time. They may even regard history as the gradual unfolding of the final, complete truth. If history is progressive, then to live at a later time is *ipso facto* to live in a more "advanced" age. In that case, one studies the works of earlier writers to see how their thought anticipated the thought of writers who, coming later in history, approached closer to the whole truth. One studies the books of earlier thinkers in order to see the progression of thought from earlier to later epochs. The earlier, and therefore less advanced thinker will be regarded as worthy of study for having stated the truth, albeit in a less developed form. For example, one might study Plato to see how he anticipated certain insights of Sigmund Freud.

The radical historicist, however, is prohibited from doing this, because he rejects the possibility of describing history as progressive. From his point of view, the writings of earlier authors may indeed be said to express things of which the authors themselves, being in thrall to the spirit of their times, were not entirely aware; but it makes no sense to describe the intellectual history of mankind as evolving toward the full expression of a final truth. Intellectual history may then be regarded as a glittering, albeit ultimately meaningless display, from which one is free to pick and choose at will, according to one's taste or "values." If one takes the more radical view, the motive for studying old books is no longer to validate the "progress" of knowledge up to the present time. The motive is rather to understand the manner in which historical conditions have influenced thought from age to age; or, it is to contemplate the variety of human thought and "cultures" which have existed in history.[14]

In this case, the history of thought becomes "interesting," in somewhat the same way that a curio shop or a museum is interesting. One regards the writings of earlier thinkers as artifacts, worthy of study for what they can tell us about how people lived and thought then; but no sensible historicist would ever consider seriously reading the books of Plato or John Locke or the Bible as though they contained the most important truths about the most important subjects, just as no sensible

---

[14] In the case of "deconstructionism," the text becomes merely an opportunity for displaying one's skill as an interpreter. There is no text as such, only interpretations of texts.

person would consider attempting to employ a museum artifact in his daily life.[15]

The radical critique of America's past seems to have combined the progressive and the historicist views in the following way. On the one hand, there is progress in moral understanding. The radical critics believe that they *are* morally more enlightened than their forebears, particularly those who founded this country. The radical critics believe that they see with full clarity what our founders discerned only obscurely, namely, that the political views of the Founders express only "class interests," which is to say their economic interests. The radicals, having benefited from the progress of history, understand, as the founders did not, the real truth about equality and freedom, namely, that they are thoroughly *politicized* terms, whose meanings are decisively shaped by economic interests. Therefore, the contemporary radical understanding of liberty and equality, having freed itself from "ideology" by coming to the truth that political life is fundamentally economic, has grasped the egalitarian essence of genuine democracy. Thus, the present has indeed genuinely progressed in moral understanding.

On the other hand, our forebears were, from epoch to epoch, merely the children of their time, prevented by class interests or their assumption of racial superiority, from seeing the true ground of their understanding of liberal democracy. In the past, there was no real progress in moral understanding from age to age, precisely because the

---

[15] This understanding of the past underlies many current educational fads, like "multiculturalism" and "valuing differences." These fads claim to embody the true nature of egalitarian democracy. They claim to be the authentic expression of democratic tolerance: one who is genuinely tolerant in the true spirit of liberal democracy will reject the view that there is only one culture, or at the least only a very few cultures. The true egalitarian will reject as unenlightened the view according to which one speaks of *the* cultivated human being. Those who advocate multiculturalism and valuing differences, however, are mistaken in their belief that they are merely being good democrats. Liberal democracy is based upon the view that there is a permanent human nature, which may be cultivated or destroyed, nurtured or perverted, by a given society. Multiculturalism, by contrast, is based on principles which are antithetical to the principles of liberal democracy. There are, of course, those multiculturalists who are more candid. They freely admit that multiculturalism is an attack upon Western culture, and upon liberal democracy in particular.

decisive discovery of the overwhelming power of economic interests had not yet been made.[16]

The radical historicist critique would, however, seem to have proved too much. The radical historicist critique is itself rooted in the political and philosophical tradition of the West. It grew in the same soil with the very principles of modern liberal democracy which it criticizes. The radical critique is the offspring of the teachings of Karl Marx and Friedrich Nietzsche. These thinkers were both powerful critics of liberal democracy. Both thinkers, however, accepted some of the premises of modern thought on which liberal democracy crucially depends. Therefore, the contemporary radical critique of liberal democracy, as the offspring of Marx and Nietzsche, also shares with liberal democracy certain important assumptions. If it is possible to understand the radical critique and the teachings of its founders on their own terms, and not merely as cultural artifacts, then it is *ipso facto* possible to do the same for the intellectual foundations of liberal democracy.[17]

To study these foundations seriously, however, one must take seriously the view that rejects both the progressive and historicist understandings of history and human nature. One sees this most immediately in the Declaration's reference to "the laws of nature and nature's God," or in the many discussions of human nature contained in *The Federalist*. To study the Declaration or *The Federalist* without begging the question, one must suspend temporarily one's acceptance of the historicist premise, and try to understand these writings on their own terms. This means, however, setting aside temporarily the belief in the superiority of the contemporary vantage point. It means calling into

---

16 Clearly this discovery had to await the coming of Karl Marx. In our discussion of Marx below, we shall see how he was obliged to demonstrate that history culminated in *his* comprehension of truths which had remained hidden to all previous thinkers.

17 This attitude toward old books is the ruling opinion in many of our colleges and universities. It is the simplistic version of a powerful philosophic teaching which was worked out during the past century and-a-half, not only by Marx and Nietzsche, but Martin Heidegger. Because of its sense of superiority to the past, the prevailing view is blind to its own history. It does not know that, not only Marx, but also Nietzsche and Heidegger are its teachers. It is the attitude of one who has climbed a ladder and then kicked the ladder away. It believes its condescension towards the past to be the highest sophistication of reason; but, because its own principles prevent it from taking old books seriously, it is relieved of any obligation to study its own intellectual roots. It thus shows itself to be characterized by a facile sense of superiority, claiming at best only the advantage of hindsight.

question the belief in the superiority of the contemporary vantage point.

We must therefore try to understand our intellectual forebears on their own terms. This conclusion is reinforced by the following practical consideration: our own happiness and moral well-being as a free people, seems to depend decisively upon the kind of country we live in and the principles it stands upon. We thus have an even more compelling motive for returning to the study of old books with an unqualified resolve to understand them on their own terms.

It is unnecessary here to undertake an elaborate theoretical refutation of historicism. Instead, we may simply note that historicism is itself largely responsible for our current predicament, our current diffidence about the moral decency of capitalism and liberal democracy. Historicism is part of the problem, not part of the solution. We obviously cannot find a solution without searching for it; but historicism, convinced of the equal validity of all solutions, obstructs the search for solutions. There is no *reason*, according to radical historicism, to prefer one solution to another, and thus there can be no motive to undertake the search.

Historicism is thus dogmatic, in the pejorative sense of being close-minded, despite its protestations to the contrary, that it is tolerant and "inclusive." Therefore, we cannot call our current predicament into question without calling historicism into question.

### III

In order to answer the question, What is liberal democracy? we return to the beginning:

> When, in the course of human events, it becomes necessary for one people to dissolve the political bands which have connected them with one another, and to assume, among the powers of the earth, the separate and equal station to which the laws of nature and of nature's God entitle them, a decent respect to the opinions of mankind requires that they should declare the causes which impel them to the separation. We hold these truths to be self-evident: that all men are created equal; that they are endowed by their Creator with certain unalienable rights; that among these are life, liberty, and the pursuit of happiness. That, to secure these rights, governments are instituted among men, deriving their just powers from the consent of the governed. That, whenever any form of government becomes destructive of these ends, it is the right of the people to alter or to abolish it and to institute new government, laying its foundation on such principles and organizing its powers in such form as to them shall seem most likely to effect their safety and happiness. Prudence,

indeed, will dictate that governments long established should not be changed for light and transient causes; and accordingly all experience hath shown that mankind are more disposed to suffer, while evils are sufferable, than to right themselves by abolishing the forms to which they are accustomed. But when a long train of abuses and usurpations, pursuing invariably the same object, evinces a design to reduce them under absolute despotism, it is their right, it is their duty, to throw off such government, and to provide new guards for their future security.[18]

It is, perhaps, difficult for us, living here and now, to read these words with the astonishment and thrill which those who first read them must have felt. The terms and phrases of the Declaration—"the laws of nature and nature's God," "self-evident truths," "all men are created equal," "the unalienable rights of life, liberty, and the pursuit of happiness," "consent of the governed," and so forth—are familiar to all reasonably well-educated Americans. It may be doubted, however, whether these words retain their power to move modern Americans as they once moved our ancestors; whether we fully understand their true significance; or whether we even believe that the things they refer to exist.

This is due partly to a natural human tendency: familiarity breeds, if not contempt, then at least comfortable complacency and good-natured condescension toward the greatness of past epochs. In his "Lyceum" speech, Lincoln described this tendency as follows:

> I do not mean to say, that the scenes of the revolution are now or ever will be entirely forgotten; but that like every thing else, they must fade upon the memory of the world, and grow more and more dim by the lapse of time. In history, we hope, they will be read of, and recounted, so long as the Bible shall be read;—but even granting that they will, their influence cannot be what it heretofore has been. Even then, they cannot be so universally known, nor so vividly felt, as they were by the generation [that fought the revolution] . . .

Lincoln went on to describe the disappearance of the "living history," that is, the death of the generation of those who fought in America's revolutionary war, and its effect upon the perpetuation of America's institutions:

> They were the pillars of the temple of liberty; and now, that they have crumbled away, that temple must fall, unless we, their descendants, supply their places with other pillars, hewn from the solid quarry of sober reason. Passion has helped us; but can do so no more. It will in future be

---

18 "The Declaration of Independence," in *The People Shall Judge*, 201.

our enemy. Reason, cold, calculating, unimpassioned reason, must furnish all the material for our future support and defence.—Let those materials be molded into general intelligence, sound morality, and, in particular, a reverence for the constitution and laws . . .

Moreover, because of certain modern opinions, which we discussed in the opening section of this chapter, we are disinclined any longer to feel the urgency of such issues as the existence of the laws of nature and nature's God. For example, most current usage of the term "rights" corrupts or distorts the meaning that term originally had for the American Founders, a meaning which they had learned primarily from the English philosopher, John Locke.

According to Locke, rights are above all else things which human beings have simply because they are human. Today, however, one regularly hears phrases like "women's rights," "minority rights," "gay rights," and so forth, which suggest that the rights you have depend upon the group you belong to; whereas, according to the Founders and to Locke, every human being, simply by being human, has the same natural rights as everyone else. This is not to say that no human being is ever denied the legitimate exercise of his rights, nor did the Founders or Locke assert this. Rather, they asserted that rights, insofar as they are natural, belong primarily and immediately to human beings as such, without regard to considerations like race, class, or gender.[19]

It is also likely that we now take it for granted that the principle of the natural rights of individual human beings provides the only legitimate foundation for government; but the Founders did not take this for granted. Indeed, some of them had grave doubts concerning the adequacy of this principle for founding a republic such as ours. In their opinion, the principle that individual rights are primary is inimical to the inculcation of public-spiritedness. How is it possible to derive a notion of the common good from the principle that individual rights are primary; and how is it possible to persuade people of the necessity and goodness of dedicating oneself to procuring the common good, especially given that such dedication may require self-sacrifice, for example, in time of war? Would it not be better to found our republic on the principle that duty and self-sacrifice are more necessary, not to mention higher and more noble, than rights?

---

[19] It is practically impossible today to discuss our founding documents without getting bogged down in discussions of this triad, which may be regarded as having become, in some circles at any rate, the new Holy Trinity.

Because of these and similar considerations, our task is to describe the conception of human nature upon which our founding principles are based. This task may be made more definite by raising the following questions: What is the understanding of human nature, upon which our founding is based, such that the natural and unalienable *rights* of individual human beings are the primary and sole legitimating principle of government? What is human nature such that rights and not duties are fundamental to good government? What connects human nature and rights? We are, in effect, asking to be persuaded of the truth of the proposition, said by the Declaration to be self-evident, that all human beings are created equal, and have been equally endowed with the unalienable rights of life, liberty, and the pursuit of happiness.

A close reading of the Declaration shows that *the argument of the Declaration itself* compels us to confront the question of human nature, as it was raised and answered by the Founders; but the Founders' understanding in turn was decisively shaped by the teaching of John Locke. Accordingly, our discussion begins with an analysis of the Declaration, and then turns to an examination of Locke's teaching on human nature, as he presented that teaching in two of his works, the *Essay Concerning Human Understanding* and the *Two Treatises of Government*.

## IV

It is rare in human history for a people to begin its life as a nation as did "we, the people of the United States," by proclaiming to the world *as universally true* the principles upon which that nation is to be established. The normal course of things seems rather for a nation to emerge as the result of war, necessity, chance, or the happy circumstance of certain congenial groups of human beings living in proximity to one another. Rational deliberation based upon an appeal to universally true principles usually has little to do with the founding of a nation. Indeed, a moment's reflection on the great nations in human history shows that their beginnings are often told in myth and legend, or resulted from caprice, chance, or necessity.

This fact was noted by Publius, near the beginning of *The Federalist*:

> It has been frequently remarked that it seems to have been reserved to the people of this country, by their conduct and example, to decide the important question whether societies of men are really capable or not of establishing good government from reflection and choice, or whether they are forever destined to depend for their political constitutions on

accident and force. If there be any truth in the remark, the crisis at which we are arrived may with propriety be regarded as the era in which that decision is to be made; and a wrong election of the part we shall act may, in this view, *deserve to be considered as the general misfortune of mankind.*[20] [emphasis added]

According to Publius, the possibilities available to mankind for establishing good government are accident and force, on the one hand, and reflection and choice, on the other. Can human beings take charge of their political destiny, or are they forever subject to forces which they cannot control? It appears to be the destiny of "the people of this country" to decide whether human beings can, in a deliberate and reasoned way, found a civil society; and the "wrong election" by the American people "deserves to be considered as the general misfortune of mankind."

One can understand why the wrong choice of government by the American people might be regarded as a misfortune for *us*; but why would it also be a misfortune for all mankind? The answer is that the American republic claims to be founded upon principles that are asserted as self-evidently and universally true, and not upon certain accidents, happy or otherwise, of time and place. The self-evident truths which form our founding principles are propositions about human nature; that is, they claim to be truths about what it means to be a human being, irrespective of accidents of birth, sex, race, degree of talent, national history, and so forth. We do not base ourselves as a nation on any alleged superiority of race, ancestry, or divine election. Quite the opposite, we justify our claim to independent status by appeal to principles that unite us with all mankind. We are no better, but neither are we any worse than any other people. Would it not, therefore, be better to live in a world of nations established on these humane and egalitarian principles, than in a world in which the nations are divided against one another, by their respective claims of national superiority or ethnic pride?

Another remarkable fact about the founding of the American republic was its philosophical character. The public debates over ratification of the Constitution were singular, both for their intensity and profundity, and for the elevated philosophic plane upon which they were held. These debates and public discussions concerned the great themes of politics: the division between rulers and ruled; the distribu-

---

[20] *The Federalist*, ed. J. E. Cook, no. 1 (Middletown: Wesleyan University Press, 1961), 3.

tion of wealth, power, and honor; the reconciliation of the need for local autonomy with the strength and security derived from a larger political union; and, the greatest, most comprehensive theme, namely, the relation between human nature and political society.

This great theme is announced by the Declaration: "the laws of nature and nature's God." The Declaration states, albeit in lapidary fashion, certain first principles of a philosophical teaching concerning human nature in relation to civil society. These principles, said to be universally and self-evidently true, set limits to government. They show how governments must be instituted in order to be legitimate, that is, so as to flow from and conform to the principles of human nature. It is conformity with the principles of human nature, in particular, the principle of "the consent of the governed," which distinguishes just from unjust governmental power. Human nature, whatever it may turn out to be, evidently is such that legitimate government requires the consent of the governed. Accordingly, it is necessary to discover what, according to the Founders, human nature is, such that the consent of the governed is the legitimating principle of government. Human nature, and, by implication, nature as a whole, is the standard according to which the argument of the Declaration proceeds. What is the "philosophy of human nature and nature as a whole" upon which the Declaration stands?

In 1822, John Adams, commenting upon Jefferson's authorship of the Declaration, asserted that "there is not an idea in [the Declaration], but what had been hackneyed in Congress for two years before." Jefferson did not take Adams to be criticizing a defect in the Declaration, and thus admitted the truth of his assertion: "Of that I am not to be the judge. Richard H. Lee charged it as copied from Locke's treatise on Government . . . I know only that I turned to neither book nor pamphlet while writing it. I did not consider it as any part of my charge to invent new ideas altogether and to offer no sentiment which had never been expressed before." In writing to Lee in 1825, Jefferson said that the important thing was

> to place before mankind the common sense of the subject, in terms so plain and firm as to command their assent . . . Neither aiming at original-ity of principles or sentiments, nor yet copied from any particular and previous writing, it was intended to be an expression of the American mind . . . All its authority rests then on the harmonizing sentiments of the day, whether expressed in conversation, in letters, printed essays, or the elementary books of public right, as Aristotle, Cicero, Locke, Sidney, etc.

In writing the Declaration, Jefferson was striving, not to originate a novel doctrine, but to express or represent accurately the "American mind." In Jefferson's view, therefore, absence of originality in the Declaration was not a defect but a virtue.

Moreover, Jefferson's intention was to commend the Declaration to the common sense of mankind, "in terms so plain and firm as to command their assent." This phrase recalls the Declaration's appeal to certain truths, which "we hold" to be "self-evident," and helps clarify the meaning of the term "self-evident." A self-evidently true proposition is one which "commands" the assent of the intellect by the "plain and firm" meaning of its terms. The philosophical literature, which Jefferson and many of the other Founders evidently knew well, often used the term "self-evidently true" of propositions whose truth was seen to be guaranteed by the meaning of the terms they contained. Once you understand the meaning of the terms of such a proposition, you cannot help but see that the proposition is true. "The whole is greater than the part" is such a proposition. You cannot fail to see that it is true, once you have understood what is meant by the terms "whole," "part," and "greater than."

The Declaration thus asserts that the propositions "All men are created equal," and "All men have been endowed by their Creator with certain unalienable rights," are self-evidently true: once one has understood the meanings of the terms "men," "equal," and "rights," one cannot help but see that these propositions must be true. To grasp their truth, one need not appeal to any special or privileged experience. Any reasonably intelligent human being may see for himself that "All men are created equal" is true, in the same way that he can see for himself that "The whole is greater than the part" is true, by first grasping the meanings of the terms of the proposition. Such a proposition, says Publius, "contain[s] an internal evidence, which antecedent to all reflection or combination commands the assent of the mind."

Publius continues by asserting that "[w]here it produces not this effect [i.e., the immediate assent of the mind], it must proceed either from some defect or disorder in the organs of perception, or from the influence of some strong interest or passion, or prejudice." That is, one who fails to assent immediately to the proposition that the whole is greater than the part is like one who, because of defective vision, cannot see that the sky is blue, or who, out of perverse obstinacy, refuses to admit that it is blue. The difficulty, says Publius, with making an analogy between the self-evident truths of mathematics and those of the science of politics or morals is that the human passions are not aroused by mathematics, as they are by politics. No one goes to war over the definition of a right triangle: "The objects of geometrical inquiry are so entirely abstracted from those pursuits which stir up and put in motion the unruly passions of the human heart, that mankind without difficulty adopts not only the more simple theorems of the science, but even those abstruse paradoxes, which however they may appear susceptible of demonstration, are at variance with the natural conceptions [of] the mind . . ." The unphilosophical mind will readily assent to the infinite divisibility of a line finite in length, although this is "not less incomprehensible to common sense, than any of those mysteries in religion, against which the batteries of infidelity have been so industriously leveled."

In matters pertaining to morals or politics, human beings are "found far less tractable." Intractability carried to a certain degree is useful in that it protects us from "error and imposition"; but, this intractability can be carried to the point of obstinacy. While it is true that the principles of political or moral knowledge do not have the same degree of certainty as the principles of mathematics, they nevertheless have, on account of their greater importance for human life, a greater claim upon our conduct. If we quarrel over these principles, it is more often because our own passions obscure our understanding than because of any obscurity in the principles themselves. The reciprocal influence of our reason and passion, which Publius cites in *Federalist* #10 as the inherent cause of political faction or division, affects our willingness or ability to assent to whatever self-evident moral or political truths there may be. Because our passions are immediately engaged by issues of politics and morals, we must try all the harder to suspend those passions in matters of political reflection or deliberation.[21]

Because human nature is always and everywhere the same, the meanings of the terms in "All men are created equal" remain constant and stable, regardless of change of time and place. Furthermore, however greatly the human condition may differ from individual to individual, all human beings are equal in the respect of being equally human. This is not a trivial remark. In the politically relevant respect, being equally human means being equally endowed with rights. Finally, to understand what human nature is, and what is meant by "rights," is to see immediately that human beings as such have rights which are by their nature "unalienable."

---

21 *The Federalist*, no. 31.

What connects democracy as a principle of ruling and being ruled, with the American version of democracy, specifically "liberal" democracy? What unites the principle of rule by the people with the principle of unalienable rights? Democracy means literally rule by the people, or rule by the majority of the people. The majority rules in a democracy because rule is necessary, and unanimity is impossible. Decisions must be made and actions must be taken. Unanimity is impossible; but majority rule approximates most closely to unanimity.

In a democracy, all human beings, or all citizens, are equal to one another in the sense that no one of them may rightly claim more power than anyone else. Democracy regards all individual human beings as equal in the politically relevant sense that no one may legitimately rule over another without the other's consent. Each individual is naturally *one* individual, and each individual is naturally one indivisible or whole individual. Democracy therefore understands equality, in the politically relevant sense, in terms both of numerical equality, and integrity. Each citizen is therefore the equal of every other in having a voice in ruling and being ruled; and each citizen has a personal integrity or wholeness which is equal to, and commands the respect of every other citizen. Those things which are part of the integral wholeness of each may not, therefore, be taken from any human being without violating his personal integrity. This is the partial explanation of what is meant by "*unalienable* rights." Therefore, the majority rules, but the principle of majority rule may not violate the natural unity and integrity of each citizen. Majority rule may not contravene the unalienable rights of any citizen.

In a liberal democracy, majority rule is connected with the principle of the unalienable rights of all by the qualifier "liberal." Liberal democracy is rule by the people, and is thus majoritarian; but this by itself does not indicate the principles for which the majority stands. It says nothing about what principle, if any, ought to govern or guide the majority.

The Declaration of Independence answers this question. On the one hand, "all men are created equal." This is the principle of democracy. On the other, the natural equality of all extends beyond simple numerical equality, according to which each human being is the same as any other, in respect of being a political unit. It extends to what we referred to above as the natural integrity of each human being. Our Declaration states this integrity in terms of being equally endowed with certain unalienable rights. To call these rights "unalienable" is to say that the natural integrity of each human being precludes being deprived of one's rights. One does not *have* rights as things adventitious or external to one's humanity. Rather, one's rights are as unalienable as one's humanity: to be human *is* to have rights.

It is the principal task of government to secure these rights. Government derives its "just powers" from the consent of the governed. Liberal democracy is popular rule, and thus majoritarian; but the majority is guided or ruled by the principle of the primacy of individual rights and liberty. In a liberal democracy, the majority rules in behalf of protecting or securing individual rights.

It is necessary to say one further word about the meaning of the term "liberal." "Liberal," insofar as it qualifies "democracy," means one thing; "liberal*ism* means something different. To call democracy "liberal" is to imply that some democracies are not "liberal." Democracy is not necessarily liberal. "Liberalism," on the other hand, is now used to describe a set of political policies, opinions, and sentiments found within liberal democracy. As such, "liberalism" is understood in contrast with "conservatism." Despite their differences, "liberalism" and "conservatism" both presuppose liberal democracy. Liberals and conservatives alike support liberal democracy. The meaning of the term "liberal," evidently must contain something to which both sides can agree.[22]

"Liberalism" and "conservatism" are themselves both phenomena of liberal democracy. They both presuppose liberal democracy, and are thus both "liberal," in the non-partisan meaning of that term. What liberals and conservatives hold in common is that which unites them into a political community. It is a shared conception of the common good.

The word "liberal" means both "generous, open-handed, unsparing in the distribution of one's wealth," as well as "open-minded, tolerant of individual differences"; but it also means "favorable to individual liberty." Liberalism thus appears to combine two potentially conflicting tendencies, namely, generosity, or the concern for the well-being of others, and individualism, or concern for the protection of individual rights and liberties. The relevant difference between liberals and conservatives thus appears to be that each side champions one sense of the term "liberal," as though that sense were its only meaning.

---

[22] It has become increasingly difficult to discern what is common to liberals and conservatives. Indeed, taking one's cue from both the 1988 and 1992 presidential campaigns, one may say that, whereas candidates for political office willingly admit in public that they support liberal democracy, they are reluctant to call themselves "liberal," preferring instead terms such as "progressive," or "centrist."

It would seem, though, that liberal democracy is liberal in various ways. Somehow these ways go together to make up true "liberalism," the liberalism of liberal democracy. Accordingly, it appears necessary to search the very principles of liberal democracy itself, namely, the primacy of individual rights and liberties, for the source of what unites and what divides liberals and conservatives.[23] Somehow, American liberal democracy combines, or is intended to combine, individualism with tolerance and generosity.

We have noted that the Declaration of Independence makes no appeal to any special divine revelation as the source of its first principles. Rather, the Declaration bases its argument on self-evident truths. No special revelation is required to know the truths upon which the Declaration appeals to "the opinions of mankind." If a proposition is self-evidently true, its truth need not have been revealed to men by God for them to know it as true. In terms of a traditional philosophical distinction well-known to educated people of Jefferson's day, the theology of the Declaration initially presents itself as "natural," not "revealed." Knowledge of the principles and truths of natural theology does not depend upon any special revelation from God. This knowledge is in principle available to be discovered by the unaided human intellect, that is, without benefit of divine revelation.

The God appealed to by the Declaration is, accordingly, the God of nature, or the ruling principle of nature. Nature is not chaos. Nature is an ordered whole, functioning according to rational principles which are sometimes called the laws of nature. The basis of our political system thus is neither arbitrary or capricious, nor is it a projection of the human will. Rather, our system of government has cosmic support. It is "the laws of nature and nature's God" which *entitle* the people of the United States to assume their "separate and equal station" among the nations.

This does not by itself imply that the Declaration denies the possibility of revelation, or that the Declaration is based upon principles inimical to revealed religion. Rather, it means that the Declaration, in appealing to "a candid world," does not claim a special pre-eminence

---

[23] There is, of course, another possible cause of the current divisions between liberals and conservatives, which is that what is now called "liberalism" is based upon a distortion, if not a radical transformation, of an earlier meaning of "liberalism," which was more congenial to the principles of liberal democracy. Taking one's bearing from those policies and causes embraced by contemporary liberals, one may question whether the current meaning of "liberalism" can be distinguished from "socialism."

for the people of the United States based upon their having been chosen by God to teach the world the proper ends of government. Instead, the Declaration justifies the course of action taken by the American people, by appealing for the reasoned assent of mankind to certain universal truths about human nature: man has a nature, and he is a part of the larger natural whole; and both are subject to "the laws of nature and nature's God."

What government accords best with human nature? We recall Jefferson's remark, quoted above. The Declaration "was intended to be an expression of the American mind . . . All its authority rests then on the harmonizing sentiments of the day, whether expressed in conversation, in letters, printed essays, or the elementary books of public right, as Aristotle, Cicero, Locke, Sidney, etc." It seems reasonable to assume that the sentiments expressed in conversation, and so forth, were themselves decisively shaped by the "elementary books of public right"; and this assumption receives support from even the most cursory reading of the essays, correspondence, and speeches of the day, especially those of men like Jefferson, Madison, and Hamilton. It was the remarkable good fortune of the United States that so many brilliant, well-educated, and public-spirited men presided over its founding; and their education in the tradition of Western thought, extending from Aristotle to Locke, was itself fundamental to their work as Founders.

On the other hand, anyone at all familiar with the Western intellectual tradition knows that it is not a seamless whole. It contains profound disagreements, precisely over the meaning of such terms as "nature" and "human nature," and the relation of human nature to political society. For example, Aristotle and Locke disagree fundamentally concerning the way that human nature leads to, or is otherwise connected with political society. Aristotle says that man is a "political animal." Man naturally seeks, or is led by a natural desire to seek, not only the society of other human beings, but society of a particular kind. Human beings by nature desire to live in political or civil society, a society of rulers and ruled, living in accordance with law and a shared conception of justice. Only in and through political society, says Aristotle, can human beings become fully human.

Locke, on the other hand, appears to teach that men naturally and primarily seek only their own preservation; that it is their concern for self-preservation which *compels* human beings to establish civil society. Absent the constraints of force present in civil society, the desire to preserve oneself will dominate over all other considerations: men do not naturally seek a society in which the common good takes precedence over the private good of each. Civil society, says Locke, with its laws, police, and security, is desired, not for its own sake, but because it protects men from one another. Thomas Hobbes, whose thought was modified by Locke, was even more emphatic: by nature, apart from the constraints and protection of civil society, human life is the "war of all against all."

Furthermore, modern political thought, and the Declaration in pai..icular, holds that "rights" are more fundamental to human nature than "duties." Writers like Plato and Aristotle teach that the principal work of the statesman is to make the citizens virtuous, where virtue, duty, and civic well-being are understood somehow to entail one another. This is particularly true in the case of the preeminent civic virtue, namely, justice. The Declaration teaches that the best government is that which is limited to securing individual rights, leaving it to individual citizens to decide for themselves, within the limits set by the laws, which way of life is best, and how best to obtain it. The principles of virtue or duty will be important to such a society, to be sure; but it will not be thought that the primary object of government is to make its citizens as virtuous as possible. In particular, justice will be regarded primarily as a negative principle restraining one's treatment of others, and not as a positive prescription.

The ancient philosophers, particularly Plato, are famous for teaching that, in the best case, the rule of the wise is superior to all other forms of political rule. Wisdom is the necessary and sufficient condition of the right to rule. Or, to state the point so as not to confuse the ancient understanding of natural right with the modern, the ancients taught that it is right by nature for the wise to rule. The Declaration of Independence, by contrast, asserts it as self-evidently true that political rule is legitimate only if it rules by the consent of the governed, without explicitly requiring the governed to be wise. It was partly for this reason that the classics gave at best only qualified approval to democracy. Wisdom is rare, and tends to flourish only in quiet and seclusion. Wisdom resides in the still, small voice, not in the heedless clamor of public debate. For all practical purposes, the rule of law is superior to the rule of men.

There was a second, and what may be called an economic reason for the classical reservations against democracy. Democracy bases its claim to be the best form of political rule by appeal to the principle of equality. Each human being is politically the equal of every other. Therefore, the many, and not the few, should rule. In practice, however, democracy almost inevitably entails the rule by the poor, for the simple reason that wealth is scarce and the competition for it fierce. Thus it happens that the poor, being driven by necessity, are more concerned with getting wealth than with ruling; but ruling in a political community requires the rulers to have a care for the general good. The poor, however, have not sufficient means or leisure for the education and study necessary to acquiring political wisdom, which includes knowledge of and dedication to the general good. For the same reason, the many will be reluctant to devote the time necessary to public service. In addition, the many will envy the wealth of the few, and will try to take it for themselves. The many will be vulnerable to demagogues. The wealthy few will fear the many poor and will seek ways to disenfranchise them. Democracies will be unstable and short-lived. In a democracy, concern for one's own material well-being will predominate, and public spiritedness will be rare. The common good will be little more than the bare aggregate of all the individual private goods.

By contrast, the classic exposition and defense of the Constitution, *The Federalist*, appears to teach a prudent reserve concerning the capacity of human wisdom for ruling, as may be seen from the following:

> When we pass from the works of nature, in which all the delineations are perfectly accurate, and appear to be otherwise only from the imperfection of the eye which surveys them, to the institutions of man, in which the obscurity arises as well from the object itself, as from the organ by which it is contemplated; *we must perceive the necessity of moderating still farther our expectations and hope from the efforts of human sagacity.* Experience has instructed us that no skill in the science of Government has yet been able to discriminate and define, with sufficient certainty, its three great provinces, the Legislative, Executive and Judiciary . . . Questions daily occur in the course of practice, which prove the obscurity which reigns in these subjects, and which puzzle the greatest adepts in political science.[24] [emphasis added]

From this admittedly brief statement of their disagreement, the traditions represented in Jefferson's statement respectively by Aristotle and Locke, would appear to differ from one another as desire differs from compulsion: either human beings naturally desire to live in political society, or they are compelled by harsh necessity to seek protection in it. Immediately, we are forced to wonder whether Jefferson was aware of this disagreement, not to mention others, which exists between the great minds of the philosophical tradition to which he refers. Perhaps the "harmonizing sentiments of the day," insofar as they

---

24 *The Federalist*, no. 37, 235.

were oblivious to these disagreements, were self-contradictory rather than harmonizing. Perhaps the Declaration of Independence, precisely as "an expression of the American mind," is incoherent or self-contradictory.

There is another possibility, which both the Declaration and the passages quoted from Jefferson suggest: perhaps our intellectual foundations contain both classical and modern (not to mention biblical) elements, standing, to be sure, in tension with one another, but not necessarily in self-vitiating contradiction. Indeed, tension need not always be a symptom of ill health. Tension may also be a sign of a vitality, perhaps rambunctious, but nevertheless vigorous. In this case, the two poles of this tension are represented by the terms "rights" and "duty."

To see a possible indication of this tension, consider the final paragraph of the Declaration:

> We, therefore, the Representatives of the United States of America, in General Congress assembled, appealing to the Supreme Judge of the world for the rectitude of our intentions, do, in the name, and by the authority of the good people of these colonies, solemnly publish and declare, That these United Colonies are, and of right ought to be, free and independent states . . . And for the support of this declaration, with a firm reliance on the protection of Divine Providence, *we mutually pledge to each other our lives, our fortunes, and our sacred honor.*" [emphasis added]

The Declaration began by asserting as self-evidently true the propositions that all human beings are endowed with the unalienable rights to "life, liberty, and the pursuit of happiness"; and that "to secure these rights governments are instituted among men, deriving their just powers from the consent of the governed." It concludes, however, with the public and solemn pledge by the representatives to the General Congress of their willingness to sacrifice, "for the support of this declaration," their lives, fortunes, and "sacred honor."

In the writings of Locke, upon which much of the Founders' thought depends, "the pursuit of happiness" means primarily the acquisition of property or fortune. One sees here, however, that the representatives are willing to sacrifice precisely those things to which, according to the self-evident truths announced at the beginning of the Declaration, they have an unalienable claim or right, and for the securing of which governments are instituted.

A moment's reflection shows that both the initial list of unalienable rights, and the concluding list of goods which the Founders pledge in support of the Declaration, rank their respective elements hierarchically;

but, the initial hierarchy, "life, liberty, and the pursuit of happiness," does not coincide with the climactic hierarchy, "life, fortune, and sacred honor." Considering the first hierarchy, one sees that life is required for, but does not by itself entail, liberty. One may choose to cling to life even in a condition of abject servitude or misery. Similarly with liberty. Only those who are free may choose to pursue happiness as they understand happiness; but liberty alone does not prevent one from squandering one's chances for happiness by living in self-pity or profligacy, or in a manner which destroys one's capacity for using one's freedom well.

The first hierarchy, the hierarchy of rights, culminates in the right to the *pursuit* of happiness. Each of the first two rights in the list is evidently necessary to the one following it, and is somehow fulfilled or completed by its successor; but the right to the pursuit of happiness evidently does not itself culminate in a further, and presumably higher, or more comprehensive, right. In particular, there is no mention of a "right to happiness," or of any obligation on the part of government either to guarantee happiness or to give positive content to the meaning of happiness. The Declaration appears to teach that each human being naturally has the right to pursue happiness as he understands it, limited, of course, by the legitimate exercise by every other human being of his right to do the same.

The Declaration next states as self-evidently true the proposition "that to secure these rights, governments are instituted among men, deriving their just powers from the consent of the governed." What, if anything, connects the right to the pursuit of happiness with both the institution of government for the purpose of securing rights, and the consent of the governed as the criterion for distinguishing just from unjust power?

The connection is this: in the state of nature, that is, the state of human life outside civil society, the right to the pursuit of happiness is unrestrained, and the unrestrained pursuit of happiness makes rights insecure. If no restraints are placed upon the individual pursuit of happiness, then, for example, one who believes that the life of the tyrant holds the prospect of the greatest happiness may claim tyranny as his right, if only he is sufficiently powerful and ruthless to obtain it. That is, in the condition of mankind apart from the security of government and the rule of law, our rights are perilously insecure. Obviously, if the right to the pursuit of happiness is not secure, then neither are the rights to life and liberty.

Furthermore, in order to secure rights, a government must have power; but power may be used well or badly. If a government intends to use its power well, can it rightly dispense with the consent of the governed? May not the intention to use its power for the benefit of the people, even for the purpose of securing the rights of the governed, exempt a government from the obligation of obtaining the consent of the governed to legitimate its power to rule? Suppose a people, reckless of their best interests, who do not know how dangerously insecure their rights are in the state of nature. In this case, would it not be better for such a people to be ruled—even if it were *without* their consent—by those whose only concern is to secure their rights? In that case, would not a benevolent dictatorship be a legitimate form of government?

The answer, according to the argument of the Declaration, is emphatically in the negative, for the following reason. The natural equality of rights implies that no one is by nature the ruler over anyone else. Therefore, good intentions not withstanding, no human being may rule over another without the latter's consent. Furthermore, no one may be said to have consented to being ruled despotically, because the principle of the consent of the governed is founded upon the natural equality of all human beings. Consent, as *the* legitimating principle of government's power, may not be given to a form of government that destroys the very equality upon which consent is based. Consent is not merely a formal criterion of legitimacy, but a substantive one; and its substance is the natural equality of all human beings.

Therefore, the institution of government for the purpose of securing the right to happiness, and the consent of the governed are connected as follows. Rights are insecure apart from the rule of law, because the initial hierarchy of *natural* rights, namely, those rights which human beings have in the state of nature, culminates in the unlimited right to the *pursuit* of happiness. The rule of law is therefore necessary so that civil order and justice may prevail; but the just establishment of these requires that the consent of the governed be obtained.

The climactic hierarchy of goods differs from the initial one in that fortune and sacred honor replace liberty and the pursuit of happiness. It is their sense of what is honorable which leads the Founders to put aside self-concern in behalf of the common good. The defense of our system of government, or, the act of proclaiming the independence of a nation founded upon the universal truths of human equality and liberty, commends itself to their sense of what is honorable or noble. To defend the system of government devoted to securing one's rights to life and fortune, the representatives pledge their own lives and fortunes.

They are compensated for doing so by the nobility of their pledge. Virtue is its own reward.

Virtue is of necessity its own reward, if only for the negative reason that one may be required to sacrifice everything else, including life itself if need be, in the cause of virtue. On the other hand, it is the sacred character of one's honor, or its nobility, which gives honor its self-sufficiency as a motive for action, and moves one to be willing to sacrifice everything in its behalf.

The Declaration's initial hierarchy, of the rights of life, liberty, and the pursuit of happiness, thus necessarily culminates in the second hierarchy, which itself culminates in sacred honor, or self-sacrifice in behalf of the common good; and this fact adumbrates what we earlier referred to as *the* great challenge to a republic based upon the principle of the primacy of individual rights, namely, how to inculcate a devotion to the common good. This may be stated paradoxically: the nature of individual rights implies that self-rule, via the consent of the governed, is the only legitimate form of government; but the *defense* of the principle of self-rule requires the inculcation of those human qualities, honor and self-sacrifice, which transcend self-concern. Our form of government is not based upon the obligation to make its citizens virtuous; but, our form of government is impossible without virtue.

## V

Publius announces "a new science of politics," which is superior to classical political thought in the greater clarity and precision of its comprehension of the nature of republican government:

> The science of politics . . . like most other sciences has received great improvement. The efficacy of various principles is now well understood, which were either not known at all, or imperfectly known to the ancients. The regular distribution of power into distinct departments—the introduction of legislative balances and checks—the institution of courts composed of judges, holding their offices during good behaviour—the representation of the people in the legislature by deputies of their own elections—these are either wholly new discoveries or have made their principal progress toward perfection in modern times. *They are means, and powerful means, by which the excellencies of republican government may be retained and its imperfections lessened or avoided.*[25] [emphasis added]

What are the excellencies and imperfections of republican government? The provisional answer to this question is that the excellencies

---

25 *The Federalist*, no. 9, 51.

and imperfections of republican government must be understood in the light of certain natural human tendencies. Republican government, as a form of self-rule via "the representation of the people in the legislature by deputies of their own elections," commends itself to our natural equality and liberty; whereas "the introduction of legislative balances and checks" will mitigate the obnoxious tendency of human nature towards self-love and the desire to have one's own way, irrespective of the desires or rights of others.

What about provisions for the inculcation of public-spiritedness? At first glance, *The Federalist* appears to say little about this. For example, in *Federalist #51*, we read:

> . . . *what is government itself but the greatest of all reflections on human nature?* If men were angels, no government would be necessary. If angels were to govern men, neither external nor internal controls on government would be necessary. In framing a government which is to be administered by men over men, the great difficulty is this: You must first enable the government to control the governed; and in the next place, oblige it to control itself. A dependence on the people is no doubt the primary control on the government; but experience has taught mankind the necessity of auxiliary precautions. *[The] policy of supplying by opposite and rival interests, the defect of better motives, might be traced through the whole system of human affairs, private as well as public. We see it particularly displayed in all the subordinate distributions of power; where the constant aim is to divide and arrange the several offices in such a manner as that each may be a check on the other; that the private interest of every individual, may be a sentinel over the public rights.* These inventions of prudence cannot be less requisite in the distribution of the supreme powers of the state. [emphasis added]

Men are not angels; therefore government is necessary. Angels do not govern men; therefore both external and internal controls on government are necessary. Evidently, angels do not suffer "the defect of better motives," which characterizes human beings. Angelic beings are motivated only by the love of God, and the selfless concern for the welfare of all creation, which is the consequence of the love for the Creator of all things.

Human nature, by unflattering contrast, comes to sight primarily as standing in need of government. Human beings evidently do not love the good, or the final good; rather, they love themselves, or, they love themselves first. Even if human beings love the final, or comprehensive good, the weakness of their nature will prevail, and self-interest will predominate over the concern for the welfare of the whole. Human nature is fundamentally characterized by dividedness, by a division between self-interest, which is immediate and strong, and duty, or selfless devotion to the common good, which, insofar as it is a conclusion of reason, is always less compelling. The reasoned and reasonable concern for the good of all is always less powerful in human affairs than self-interest.

In human affairs, the policy which Publius recommends seems Machiavellian, namely, to "[supply] by opposite and rival interests the defect of better motives." In human affairs, for the most part it is imprudent to depend upon the good or generous motives of human beings. Rather, the prudent course, particularly in distributing power, is to arrange matters so that private interest "may be a sentinel over the public rights." The implication is that self-interest, the concern for one's own good, is that element in human nature which necessitates government; but, in a properly organized government, self-interest may be enlisted in behalf of government. Although public-spirited men exist, they are rare. The public-spirited ones will dedicate themselves to the common good out of a concern for the common good; but most men will prove intractable to the reasonable teaching that the good of the whole precedes the good of the individual. Most men will promote the common good only indirectly, by intending primarily to protect their self-interest against the encroachments of others.

Elsewhere in *The Federalist*, we find passages like the following: "men are ambitious, vindictive and rapacious"; the "latent causes of faction are . . . sown in the nature of man"; "the propensity of mankind to fall into mutual animosities [is so strong] that where no substantial occasion presents itself, the most frivolous and fanciful distinctions have been sufficient to kindle their unfriendly passions, and excite their most violent conflicts"; "Why has government been instituted at all? Because the passions of men will not conform to the dictates of reason and justice, without constraint."; "As long as the connection subsists between [man's] reason and his self-love, his opinions and his passions will have a reciprocal influence on each other; and the former will be the objects to which the latter will attach themselves."; "To judge from the history of mankind, we shall be compelled to conclude that, the fiery and destructive passions of war, reign in the human breast, with much more powerful sway, than the mild and beneficent sentiments of peace; and that to model our political systems upon speculations of lasting tranquility, is to calculate on the weaker springs of the human character." "No man is allowed to be a judge in his own cause; because his interest would certainly bias his judgment, and, not improbably, corrupt his integrity."

In sum, Publius clearly teaches that the fundamental fact of human nature is the reciprocal influence of human reason and self-love; that reason may teach justice and peace as the true good of humankind, but men's passionate regard for their private interests will always cloud their judgment, with what destructive effects history demonstrates only too abundantly. Human beings are motivated more powerfully by self-interest and love of their own, than by love for their fellow human beings, or for the common good. Human beings are naturally quarrelsome and prone to fight each other over trifles. Although endowed with reason, a capacity that enables the human mind to grasp the great universal truths of the Declaration, human beings are for the most part deaf to the counsel of reason. Private interest will generally prevail over reason and the counsel of wisdom.

On the other hand, in *Federalist #57*, Publius also says:

> As there is a degree of depravity in mankind which requires a certain degree of circumspection and distrust: So there are other qualities in human nature, which justify a certain portion of esteem and confidence. *Republican government presupposes the existence of these qualities in a higher degree than any other form.* Were the pictures which have been drawn by political jealousy of some among us, faithful likenesses of the human character, the inference would be that there is not sufficient virtue among men for self-government; and that nothing less than the chains of despotism can restrain them from destroying and devouring one another. [#55; emphasis added]
>
> The aim of every political constitution is, or ought to be, first to obtain for rulers men who possess most wisdom to discern, and most virtue to pursue, the common good of the society; and in the next place, to take the most effectual precautions for keeping them virtuous, whilst they continue to hold their public trust.

Human nature therefore combines two elements, neither of which can be reduced to the other. These two elements are reason and self-love. Self-love seeks its own good; reason seeks justice, the common good. In practice, reason is subordinated to self-interest, and thus becomes calculation; but, through extraordinary effort, reason occasionally transcends self-interest in favor of the common good. Although a few rare individuals exist who are capable of making this effort, it is generally difficult to find a motive sufficient to incite human beings to make it.

Therefore, political science must discover the means of supplying the "defect of better motives"; and it is this discovery which, according to Publius, distinguishes the modern understanding of republican democracy from the ancient. Despite this discovery, republican government cannot dispense with certain virtues. The citizens of a republic must be inculcated with those qualities and habits of character necessary for self-rule. The peculiar form taken by our republic, namely representative democracy, as contrasted with participatory democracy, makes possible a democracy of much greater extent than the ancients thought possible, and thus renders inevitable a certain distance between ordinary citizens and their government. On the other hand, it is precisely this distance which makes necessary the virtues associated with self-rule. The citizens of a representative democracy must not confuse distance from government with indifference to the common welfare.

Publius teaches that however human beings may differ in respect of natural ability, they are equal in being composed of the two elements, reason and self-love. This fundamental fact determines the human possibilities. Men seek their own good, but they also seek justice. Government emerges in response to these two things. In concert with others, men are able to satisfy their needs and protect their interests. In communities, the power of individual human beings is augmented. Moreover, together men are better able to protect themselves against the depredations of others, who would otherwise deprive them of their goods.

On the other hand, men are rational. They have a capacity for transcending their own private and particular good, a capacity for laying hold of universal truth and the common good. They have a capacity for wisdom, or for seeking wisdom. Human beings understand somehow that wisdom is good, that wisdom satisfies a human need or longing, just as food, clothing, shelter, and safety do. Accordingly, men are driven by harsh necessity to covenant with one another for the sake of establishing political societies, because alone they are weak and vulnerable; they are, nevertheless, dissatisfied with mere survival. They must have justice as well.

Human nature is motivated by a conception of its higher capacities, for nobility, self-sacrifice, and devotion to the common good. Human equality is such that the only legitimate rule is self-rule; but human nature is also such that self-rule must appeal to a principle that transcends self-interest. The form of government which appears to meet these requirements best is one based upon the principle of self-legislation. It is unnecessary and impossible, however, for all citizens to be involved in actually making and executing the laws. The principle of the consent of the governed indicates the way to establish self-government on a large scale. Self-government is possible through representative government. Representative government will be just only if it is based upon the consent of the governed, if it is constructed so as to restrain the representatives of the people, to prevent them from contravening the great principle of the consent of the governed.

The consent of the governed must be complemented by wisdom; but wisdom is a rare gift, possessed by only a few. A substitute for wisdom is thus necessary. This substitute is the great principle that all men are created equal. If the people are taught that natural human equality, in the sense that no human being by nature may rule over another, is the basis of the consent of the governed, they will possess, not wisdom, but the enlightenment necessary to a people that will govern itself.

The people will consent to be governed, but not because they are persuaded that their rulers are always wiser than they are. They will consent because they understand that rule is necessary, given the influence of self-interest; and, that no one may rule another without his consent. Accordingly, the legitimacy of the rulers, their political authority, derives only from the consent of the governed. Thus, the cause of wisdom will be served as well as is practicable by the system of representation, which will in turn, Publius believes, refine and enlarge the views of the public.[26]

Publius teaches that human nature is such that all legitimate government is dedicated to securing the natural and unalienable rights of human beings, and that duties are subordinate to and derived from rights. To claim something as one's right is to assert that one's claim upon that thing is justified. A natural right is, therefore, not an arbitrary or idiosyncratic claim to whatever one pleases. It is not an expression of one's personal whim, wish, or caprice. It is, rather, an expression of, and rooted in one's nature as a human being, without reference to any government, society, or civilization. Civil rights, or, the rights one has in civil society, are derived by modification of natural rights.

We began this chapter by asking, What is liberal democracy? We saw that not every democracy is liberal. Not every democracy is devoted, not merely to equality, but to liberty as well. Liberal democracy champions both political equality and individual liberty. In liberal democracy, equality and liberty meet in the principle that all men are equally free, or equally endowed with certain rights. Liberal democracy is a system of self-government, in our case, by means of the scheme of representative government. Being devoted to liberty as a political good,

---

[26] This account relies upon Harry Jaffa's excellent discussions of this issue, in *Crisis of the House Divided* and *How to Think about the American Revolution*.

liberal democracy leaves it to individual citizens to decide for themselves, within certain limits, in what their happiness shall consist. Whereas the ancient political philosophers regarded liberty as a condition of moral virtue, the proponents of modern liberal democracy regard liberty as a kind of virtue, or good: liberty is good in itself, apart from the use one makes of it. Liberty is worth defending, with one's life, if necessary. Human beings will be more firmly attached to defending liberty if they are allowed to decide for themselves what their happiness shall entail, than if they are forced to accept another's understanding of happiness, even if that other should happen to be wise.

Publius learned many of the foregoing lessons from John Locke. We, therefore, now turn to a statement of Locke's teaching, as it appears in his *Two Treatises of Government*, and the *Essay Concerning Human Understanding.*

# CHAPTER THREE

# John Locke and Natural Rights

## I

Whether one intends to criticize or defend America's version of liberal democracy, one must first encounter the writings of John Locke. In them, one finds the authoritative philosophic teaching concerning human nature and political life which, for better or worse, most profoundly affected the founding of the American system.[1]

Locke stands out as one of the great thinkers in that period of Western civilization, the seventeenth and eighteenth centuries, which came to be called "The Enlightenment." The great or characteristic achievement of the Enlightenment was, as the German philosopher, Immanuel Kant, put it, to liberate man to "make use of his understanding without direction from another." According to Kant, the motto of the Enlightenment was "Dare to know! Have courage to use your own reason." Think for yourself.

Our Declaration of Independence may be said to be one of the great fruits of the Enlightenment. It proclaims to a "candid world," certain propositions said to be self-evidently and universally true. Our founding as a nation is based upon these truths, and submits them to the reasoned consideration of all human beings. Our founding is thus eminently rational, and is an exemplary product of confidence in the enlightened mind's ability to think for itself. Indeed, what Kant called the "public use of reason" was, perhaps, never more prominent in the founding of a nation than in the case of the United States; and we have, in our preceding remarks on the philosophical teaching of the Declaration of Independence, attempted to give some sense of the

---

[1] This statement must be qualified. Locke's teaching is decisive for our founding; but it is not the only influence on our founding. One must also mention the thought of Rousseau; and, as we saw above, Thomas Jefferson, in referring to the "harmonizing sentiments of the day," mentions also the books of Aristotle, among others. Lincoln's frequent references to the Bible must also be recalled.

extent to which the public debate and discussion of principles, frequently conducted on a high intellectual plane, shaped our founding.

In particular, *The Federalist* must stand forth as a classic example of what Kant described as the use of reason "which a person makes of it as a scholar before the reading public." There have been, to be sure, other instances in the history of political thought of a philosophical writer addressing himself to the task of persuading his readers to undertake a certain course of action, or to adopt a particular form of government, or to rule in a certain way. *The Federalist*, however, is distinguished, both by being addressed to a people at large, who are themselves engaged in deliberating upon and ratifying a constitution, and by its frank manner of appealing to the reasoned judgment of its readers as fellow citizens. The very fact that the *Federalist* was first published in the popular press seems to distinguish it from other classic political treatises.

The public nature of *The Federalist*, and the debate it intended to provoke, however, were both consistent with the principles and spirit of The Enlightenment. Moreover, the "resolution and courage" to use one's own reason, to which Kant appealed in his essay, "What Is Enlightenment?" is immediately evident in both the Declaration and *The Federalist*, as is the confidence in the tendency of free public debate to arrive at an enlightened view of the nature and proper ends of political life.

The Declaration speaks, not merely to the citizens of the "good people of these colonies," but to mankind as a whole, to whom it says, in effect, "Come, let us reason together." It is motivated by a "decent respect to the opinions of mankind" to "let facts be submitted to a candid world." *The Federalist* declares that "it seems to have been reserved to the people of this country, by their conduct and example, to decide the important question, whether societies of men are really capable or not, of establishing good government from reflection and choice." It is, therefore, no exaggeration to say that our founding was in part a test of the Enlightenment's bold confidence in the freedom to think for oneself, and in the politically salutary tendencies of reasoned public debate. Our founding would answer the question whether human beings were capable of establishing government through reflection and choice, or whether political institutions depended decisively for their establishment on chance or necessity.[2]

---

2 When we reflect upon this nation's great good fortune in having so many highly intelligent men, both well educated and dedicated to the public good, as its founders, we may wonder whether our founding entirely escaped the

When one turns from *The Federalist*, which certainly must be regarded as having called every man to his vocation for thinking for himself concerning high political matters, to search for the "self-liberator who then liberated others,"[3] one encounters Locke. It is in Locke's writings, particularly his *Essay Concerning Human Understanding* and *Two Treatises of Civil Government*, where one finds the teaching on human nature and political society which authoritatively shaped the principles of the American founding. The diligent reader of these two books may come to see for himself what natural rights are, how they are grounded in human nature, and how they may be transformed into civil rights by being secured by government.

As we noted above, Richard H. Lee charged that Thomas Jefferson had copied the Declaration from "Locke's treatise on government . . ." The Declaration itself alludes to Locke, by the phrase "life, liberty, and the pursuit of happiness." This phrase evokes, but does not exactly quote, Locke's *Second Treatise of Government*, the book from which , according to Lee, Jefferson copied in writing the Declaration.

Whatever the truth of Lee's charge (and, as we have seen, Jefferson admitted that, if he *had* copied from Locke, he did so insofar as Locke's writings were part of the "harmonizing sentiment of the day"), when one turns to the *Second Treatise*, one finds phrases such as "life, health, liberty, or possessions"; or, "men . . . must be allowed to pursue their happiness, nay cannot be hindered"; and, "Nature . . . has put into man a desire of happiness . . ." Comparing the Declaration and the *Second Treatise* with *The Federalist*, # 10, one finds Publius asserting that the "protection of [the faculties of men from which the rights of property originate] is *the first object* of government."

Comparison of these with similar passages shows that, according to the understanding of rights which is original to our founding, the right to the pursuit of happiness and the right of property are inseparable, if indeed they are not identical. It is not unreasonable, therefore, to wonder whether, the noble rhetoric of our Declaration does anything more than enshrine man's unlimited desire to acquire material wealth, and to encourage, if it does not justify, selfishness. How can a society based upon the identification of the right to pursue happiness with the right

---

effects of chance or necessity. There is, of course, a third possibility, namely providence, to which many of the Founders referred in reflecting upon the birth of the United States.

[3] Taken from Immanuel Kant, "What Is Enlightenment?" *Foundations of the Metaphysics of Morals* (New York: Bobbs-Merrill, Library of Liberal Arts), 85ff.

to own property be anything other than individualistic and materialistic?

These questions express one of the legitimate concerns which must be addressed by any serious critique of the American system of liberal democracy and capitalism. One need not share the Left's antipathy for democratic capitalism in order to wonder whether a society such as ours can indeed inculcate both a genuine dedication to the public good, as well as a general aspiration to those human ends which are naturally higher or nobler than the unlimited acquisition of material wealth. Surveying American society at the end of the twentieth century, one must be dismayed by the vulgarity of its popular culture, the unedifying spectacle of the often petty and vicious character of its public life, and the apparent inability of its citizens to agree upon a common, uniting purpose. Do these qualities not, after all, flow inevitably from our principles? That is, must not one conclude that the only adequate critique of American society is a radical critique which culminates, not in reform, but revolution?

Perhaps, then, there is some basis in our founding principles themselves for sympathy with some of the sentiments which may motivate the radical critique of democratic capitalism. On the other hand, one must not conclude too quickly that writers of the competence of Locke and Adam Smith simply ignored or were otherwise oblivious to those dimensions of human life which transcend mere survival or the accumulation of wealth, or that they were insensible of the defects of a political or economic system erected upon their teachings.

Nor should one simply turn away from the intellectual traditions of the American system, hoping to find in its greatest twentieth century rival, socialism, *the* remedy for its defects, if not complete satisfaction for our desire for political justice, assuming for the moment that our desire for political justice can be perfectly satisfied. As we have observed elsewhere, socialism has retained its moral appeal despite its almost universal repudiation by those who have actually lived under socialist regimes. Socialism, however, is itself as much a product of modern Western political thought as are liberal democracy and capitalism, and shares with them certain important assumptions about human beings and political life. At the very least, one must admit that socialism and modern liberal democracy both repudiate ancient political thought, as well as the Thomistic natural law tradition, which tried to synthesize the political teaching of Aristotle and the doctrines of the Roman Catholic Church.[4]

In rejecting democratic capitalism for socialism, one may find that one has gone from the frying pan to the fire. Indeed, those who disparage American society for its vulgarity, crass materialism, and spiritual deadness, will find informed critics who have attributed the very same qualities to life in the former Soviet Union, while denying to it the one saving grace which graces life in America, namely religious liberty.

It must always be borne in mind that human nature, in its capacities for both good and evil, is *the* guiding principle of our founding. Human beings, acting together in political society, are capable of only so much good; but history appears to teach us that the human capacity for cruelty is virtually without limit. To praise and encourage the good while restraining or reducing cruelty and selfishness is thus the duty of all. If our system, despite whatever other imperfections it may possess, enables us to meet these two obligations better than any other of which we know, it ought, if only for that reason, to command both our respect and our allegiance.

## II

Returning, therefore, to the prominence given to property rights by both Locke, as well as the Declaration and *The Federalist*, we hope to find in Locke's writings the articulation of that understanding of human nature in which the right of property and the right of the pursuit of happiness coalesce: the right of property is, or sums up the fundamental natural right. Beginning from Locke's teaching on property

---

[4] It is important to distinguish between the two terms, "natural rights" and "natural law." "Natural rights" is the term used by Locke, Adam Smith, and many of the American Founders, to designate the most important and fundamental fact about human nature in relation to political society, namely certain justified claims upon basic goods, that we have merely as humans. In our tradition, rights precede duties, as we can see in the Declaration of Independence. It is because human beings have natural and unalienable rights that government may justly be required to observe the principles of limited government and the consent of the governed. "Natural law" is the term used to indicate those *duties* we have simply as humans. The doctrine of natural law is closely associated with what we call "conscience." When we refer to the conscience, we mean something in us that prescribes or forbids certain actions. The conscience is our inner moral voice, whose binding moral force is sometimes thought to take precedence over man-made laws. See below for further discussion of the difference between natural law and natural right.

and its origin, we are led finally to see how all natural human rights, including the right of property, are rooted in our very nature as human beings; but the special prominence Locke gives to the right of property indicates the direction we are to look in understanding the origin of natural rights, and the manner in which they are transformed into civil rights in and by political society.

Locke belongs to a group of political thinkers of the first rank, among whom one also finds Machiavelli and Thomas Hobbes, who radically transformed the Western understanding of the basis of political life, and thus founded a distinctively modern political philosophy. They achieved this transformation by replacing what medieval thinkers in the West (the most influential being Thomas Aquinas) had called "natural law," with "natural right," or "natural rights," the plural form indicating more truly the import of the modern understanding.

What is the difference between natural law and natural rights? Leo Strauss, writing about the political philosophy of Hobbes, has described this difference as follows:

> Traditional natural law is primarily and mainly an objective 'rule and measure,' a binding order prior to, and independent of, the human will, while modern natural law is, or tends to be, primarily and mainly a series of 'rights,' of subjective claims, originating in the human will . . . [T]he essence of modern natural law and all its essential implications are nowhere more clearly seen than in [the doctrine of Thomas Hobbes.] For Hobbes obviously starts, not, as the great tradition did, from natural 'law,' i.e., from an objective order, but from natural 'right,' i.e., from an absolutely justified subjective claim which, far from being dependent on any previous law, order, or obligation, is itself the origin of all law, order, or obligation. [5]

It is one of Locke's great achievements to have shown how the subjective claim, from which rights originate, is "absolutely justified." That is, although rights are subjective in origin, they are not therefore arbitrary. They originate in the human will; but, they do not vary according to individual caprice or idiosyncrasy. Moreover, originating in the *will*, that is, in a faculty belonging only to rational beings, rights are to be distinguished from the natural appetites and inclinations which men may have in common with the sub-rational animals. No claim, justified or not, can be said to originate from the appetites or inclinations; but a right is most emphatically a claim upon something as one's own. The

---

[5] Leo Strauss, preface to *The Political Philosophy of Thomas Hobbes* (Chicago: University of Chicago Press, 1952), vii-viii.

ends or purposes of human life may be given by the passions; but reason, by calculating the indispensable means to those ends, is the source of our rights or claims upon those means.

Clearly, if, as the old natural law tradition believed, the ground of obligation and virtue is an objective order, existing prior to and independently of the human will , one must inquire into that order to discern as well as one can the basis of virtue or political justice. According to the great tradition from which Locke departed, the objective order was understood to be either nature, or the revealed word of God. God did not reveal His Law to all mankind, but only to some; but, according to the Thomistic tradition, there are laws, knowable as such, which are binding upon all human beings simply as rational. These laws are apprehended by the conscience, and are apprehended *as* imposing obligations, without any special assistance from revelation. According to Thomas, although the Divine Law is necessary to complete the laws imposed by the conscience, the latter do not conflict with the former.

If, however, the ground of obligation is thought to be a justified *subjective* claim, it is likewise necessary to inquire into the "subjective order," to discern the basis of that justification. In his discussion of the human soul, understood as the *self*, Locke articulates that basis. The *Second Treatise of Civil Government* presents the famous Lockean doctrines of natural right and the state of nature; but a close consideration of those doctrines compels the reader to turn to the *Essay Concerning Human Understanding*, where one finds the account of the human soul as self, an account which supplies the necessary foundation of Locke's political teaching.

Near the beginning of his *Second Treatise*, Locke asserts:

> To understand political power aright, and derive it from its original, we must consider what state all men are naturally in, and that is, a state of perfect freedom, to order their actions, and dispose of their possessions, and persons as they think fit, within the bounds of the law of nature, without asking leave, or depending upon the will of any other man. A state also of perfect equality, wherein all the power and jurisdiction is reciprocal, no one having more than another: there being nothing more evident, than that creatures of the same species and rank promiscuously born to all the same advantages of nature, and the use of the same faculties, should also be equal one amongst another without subordination or subjection . . . [6]

6 John Locke, *Second Treatise of Government*, ed. Peter Laslett (New York: Cambridge University Press), 269.

We note Locke's assertion that man, in his natural state, already has possessions, or, at least he has the right to own possessions. The right of property is not the creation of civil government, but precedes civil government. That is, Locke teaches that the right of ownership has a natural basis in man's original condition, as he exists in the state of nature.

This is one great point of disagreement between modern liberalism and socialism. Marx taught that the conditions of production in society determine who may own property and who is prohibited from acquiring it. Locke emphatically denies this. For example, Locke defines political power as follows:

> [Political power is] a right of making laws with penalties of death, and consequently all less penalties, *for the regulating and preserving of property*, and of employing the force of the community, in the execution of such laws, and in defence of the commonwealth from foreign injury, and all this only for the public good. [emphasis added]

That is, the legislative function has the right of "regulating and preserving," but not of creating property; neither is the right of property merely a creature of the positive law.

In his definition, Locke immediately connects political power with certain other rights: the right to the legislative or law-making function; the right to punish, even to the point of taking the life of the one punished; and all this for the sake of "regulating and preserving property." That is, in some cases, the very right to life itself may be forfeited for the sake of protecting property. Moreover, after the protection of property, there follow, in order of presentation, the rights of "employing the force of the community" to execute the laws, and defending the commonwealth against foreign enemies. "[A]nd all this," Locke adds, "only for the public good."

Thus, in following the order in which Locke states his definition of political power, we see that he begins from the right to impose capital punishment in the defence of property and ends with the public good. What specifically connects the right of the legislative power to impose capital punishment, with the public good? To answer this question, it is necessary to follow Locke in his derivation of political power "from its original," namely, the human condition outside political society, the state of nature.

The thoughtful reader, however, attempting to extract Locke's teaching concerning the state of nature from the *Second Treatise*, quickly encounters difficulties. Locke does not present his teaching on natural right and the state of nature straightforwardly, but in a manner which seems confusing if not self-contradictory.

For example, in the chapter entitled "On the State of Nature," Locke refers to "*the great law of nature*, Who so sheddeth man's blood, by man shall his blood be shed." He illustrates this law with the example of Cain, who "was so fully convinced that every one had a right to destroy such a criminal [as himself], that after the murder of his brother, he cries out, Every one that findeth me, shall slay me; *so plain was it writ in the hearts of all mankind*." [emphasis added]

Two paragraphs later, however, Locke acknowledges that his teaching, according to which everyone in the state of nature has the executive power of the law of nature, is a "strange doctrine." He tacitly agrees with those who object to his doctrine that "it is unreasonable for men to be judges in their own causes," as they perforce would be if each man had the executive power of the law of nature: "self-love will make men partial to themselves and their friends," and excessively harsh in dealing with their enemies.

"I easily grant," continues Locke,

> that civil government is the proper remedy for the inconveniencies of the state of nature, which must certainly be great, where men may be judges in their own case since 'tis easily to be imagined *that he who was so unjust as to do his brother an injury, will scarce be so just as to condemn himself for it* . . . [ emphasis added]

Locke thus admits that the great law of nature, which he had just described as being written so plainly "in the hearts of all mankind," is not written so plainly that it will compel Cain to condemn himself for murdering his brother. Self-love will cause Cain to show partiality for himself, or to exempt himself from "the great law of nature." If Cain has a conscience, self-love nevertheless easily overpowers it. Locke gives the reader ample reason to doubt whether he believed there is such a thing as the conscience. That is, Locke's reading of Genesis indicates his rejection of the Thomistic natural law tradition.

Moreover, Locke omits from his account of the story of Cain and Abel any mention of God's intervention on Cain's behalf. According to Genesis, the Lord says "Whoever kills Cain will suffer a seven-fold revenge." Even if the great law of nature is written plainly in the hearts of men, the Bible teaches that the Lord God may abrogate it where He so desires. Thus, whereas Genesis teaches that it is God's compassion and mercy that protect Cain from other men and the revenge sanctioned by the law of nature, Locke looks to civil government to remedy the "inconveniencies" of man's pre-political condition.[7]

We choose this example to illustrate the following point: Locke's manner of writing is meant to conceal the fact that his teaching is not entirely respectable. Locke rejected the classic and venerable tradition of natural law teaching, originated by Thomas Aquinas and carried on by writers like Richard Hooker. Instead, Locke teaches that the rights of individual human beings are more fundamental than duties, that the free pursuit of self-interest is more likely to bind men to civil society than are any exhortations to civic virtue, and that any ill effects resulting from emancipating the desire for the unlimited acquisition of material wealth ought to be endured for the sake of the security and comfort accruing to society as a result. Locke feels compelled to assimilate his thought to that of writers like Hooker, to give respectability to his own teaching; however, his teaching contradicts Hooker's teaching, as we demonstrate below.

By "the state of nature," Locke does not necessarily mean some condition of the human race which actually existed in its pre-history but disappeared long ago. Indeed, later in the *Second Treatise*, we learn that Locke teaches that all independent nations are in a state of nature relative to one another:

> 'Tis often asked as a mighty objection, where are or ever were there any men in such a state of nature? To which it may suffice as an answer at present that, since all princes and rulers of independent governments all through the world are in a state of nature, *it is plain the world never was, nor ever will be, without numbers of men in that state.*[8] [emphasis added]

It is not to man's nature, taken to mean his end or purpose, that we are to look to understand political power correctly; rather, we are to consider man's beginning, by which Locke means man's condition outside civil society. Locke thus implicitly denies a principle of ancient political

---

[7] The Bible's teaching on civil government as a remedy for the harshness of man's state outside civil society is partly indicated by the following: Cain, the first murderer, is the founder of the first city; but it is only through the protection of the Lord that he is spared and allowed to become the founder. Lamech, Cain's descendant, boasts that "I have killed a man for wounding me, a young man for striking me. If Cain is avenged sevenfold, truly Lamech seventy-seven fold." Lamech boasts that his justice is mightier than God's justice, whereas it is in fact a perversion of God's justice, an expression of man's pride in his own might and alleged self-sufficiency. Man is not content to be self-sufficient; rather, he seeks to outdo God, or to become godlike himself.

[8] Locke, *Second Treatise*, 276.

thought, namely, that "nature" means "end" or "purpose," something to which man is drawn by desire. Locke replaces this meaning of nature, with a teaching according to which nature is something from which man seeks to protect himself.

To understand man's beginning more clearly, one must ask why independent governments are in a state of nature relative to each other. Locke writes:

> Men living together according to reason, without a common superior on earth with authority to judge between them, *is properly the state of nature* (280). [italics are in the original]

The state of nature, according to Locke, is properly contrasted with civil society:

> Those who are united into one body and have a common established law and judicature to appeal to, with authority to decide controversies between them and punish offenders, are in civil society one with another; but those who have no such common appeal, I mean on earth, are still in the state of nature, each being, where there is no other, judge for himself, and executioner; which is, as I have before shew'd it, the perfect *state of nature* (272).

The state of nature and the state of civil society are therefore distinguished from one another by the absence or presence of a common judge with authority to enforce the law.

In the state of nature, however,

> [m]an being born . . . with a title to perfect freedom, and an uncontroled enjoyment of all the rights and privileges of the law of nature, equally with any other man, or number of men in the world, hath by nature a power, *not only to preserve his property, that is, his life, liberty and estate*, against the injuries and attempts of other men; but to judge of, and punish the breaches of that law in others, *as he is persuaded the offence deserves*, even with death it self, in crimes where the heinousness of the fact, *in his opinion*, requires it. But because no political society can be, nor subsist without having in it self the power to preserve the property, and in order thereunto punish the offences of all those of that society; there, and there only is political society, where every one of the members hath quitted this natural power, resign'd it up into the hands of the community in all cases that exclude him not from appealing for protection to the law established by it. And thus all private judgment of every particular member being excluded, the community comes to be umpire, by settled standing rules, indifferent and the same to all parties . . . (286) [emphases added]

Here Locke appears to expand the sense of the term "property," to include "life, liberty, and estate." This is, perhaps, unexpected. We tend to think of property only in terms of material possessions. Here, however, Locke says that one's life and liberty are as much one's property as is one's "estate." Locke must be understood, therefore, as teaching that one's material property is as much a part of one's natural person as are one's life and liberty. One's natural right to one's material possessions is as unalienable as are one's rights to life and liberty. This natural right evidently is preserved when one enters civil society, because Locke asserts that no such society "can be, nor subsist without having in itself the power to preserve property." This part of Locke's teaching may therefore be summed up by saying that one's material goods are an unalienable part of one's person, both natural and civil.

We note also in this passage that Locke teaches that a human being has not only the right to preserve his property in the state of nature, but also the right to "judge of, and punish the breaches of [the law of nature] in others, as he is persuaded the offence deserves, even with death itself, in crimes where the heinousness of the fact, *in his opinion*, requires it." [emphasis added] Outside civil society, then, human beings are both judges and executors of that "law of nature" which prohibits one from taking the property of another.

On the other hand, we are surprised to find Locke stating that, in judging and punishing others for breaches of the natural law which protects property, one acts "as he is persuaded the offence deserves, even with death itself," if, *in his opinion*, it is deserved. Whence arises this apparently absolute right of ownership in the state of nature? Apart from civil society and its laws, what justifies my claim of ownership upon a thing? And what justifies my acting as judge and meting out punishment to others?

The reason for describing the right of property in the state of nature as "absolute" is that Locke appears to teach that, in the state of nature, there is a law of nature which protects property; but each human being may judge and punish transgressions of that law as he sees fit. Moreover, each human being punishes "the breaches of that law *in others*"; but who judges the judge? The question inevitably arises, who adjudicates when I have appropriated the goods of another, but defend my action on the grounds of self-interest? In the state of nature, then, it appears that each man will be the judge in his own cause; and, given the great power of self-interest, he will always find grounds for excusing in himself what he condemns in others. It is for this reason, therefore, that we have called the natural right of property "absolute."

The natural justification for property rights in the state of nature is, therefore, what Locke calls "the law of nature," and the natural law commands respect for the property of others. On the other hand, there being no common sovereign in the state of nature, each man will be judge in his own case, and will therefore be inclined to be harsh with others and lenient with himself, even in those cases where he takes the property of others. The natural law will have no binding force. The state of nature appears unable to provide society with the normative standard of impartial justice necessary for its existence.

Indeed, Locke concedes this. He writes:

> The state of nature has a law of nature to govern it, which obliges every one: and *reason, which is that law,* teaches all mankind, *who will but consult it,* that being all equal and independent, *no one ought to harm another* in his life, health, liberty, or possessions . . . Every one as he is bound to preserve himself, and not to quit his station willfully; so by the like reason *when his own preservation comes not into competition,* ought he, as much as he can, to preserve the rest of mankind, and may not unless it be to do justice on an offender, take away, or impair the life, or what tends to the preservation of the life, the liberty, health, limb or goods of another (271). [emphases added]

Reason teaches everyone "who will but consult it" that we ought not harm anyone in his "life, health, liberty, or possessions." We note that reason does not compel or incite us to consult it: not everyone will consult reason. Perhaps only a very few will consult reason. Moreover, reason does not teach the obligation of charity or philanthropy. It teaches that justice means, first of all, leaving others alone. The primary teaching of the law of nature, or reason, is *negative*: harm no one; but because this teaching is evident only to those who "will but consult" reason, it may be questioned whether this law of nature will be widely known, much less observed in the state of nature.

The question regarding the status of the law of nature in the state of nature is thus two-fold: i) what guarantees that the law of nature will be promulgated in the state of nature (which it must be, according to Locke, if it is to be a law, because all law must be promulgated in order to have the status of law)?; ii) what guarantees that the law of nature will be enforced in the state of nature?

Locke adds that reason also has a positive teaching: we have a duty to preserve our fellow men. This positive obligation, however, is qualified. I am to preserve my fellow men so long as my own preservation "comes not into competition." What does reason require when my own preservation *does* "come into competition" with my duty to preserve others? We see from the above passage that Locke admits that "to do justice on an offender" of the law of nature, one may "take away, or impair the life, or what tends to the preservation of the life, the liberty, health, limb or goods of another."

We are compelled, in the light of Locke's teaching, to ask the following question: in a society based upon the principle of individualism understood in Locke's sense, to what standard of justice will one appeal, beyond one's own judgment of what is required for one's preservation, to decide questions of competing interest? That is, how can conflicts of private interest be adjudicated reasonably, by appeal to an objective principle, if reason itself teaches that my judgment alone may legitimately determine what conduces to my own preservation?

This point may be restated. In the state of nature, the law of nature, which is reason, teaches the duty of refraining from harming others, to those who will consult reason; but, as we noted above, why should one consult reason? What interest can one have, as compelling or immediate as the interest in one's own preservation, for consulting reason? There may indeed be a duty to consult reason which, Locke asserts, is the law of nature; but what will motivate one to overcome one's natural desire to preserve oneself, and to consult reason in those cases where the good of others may require it? This question is particularly urgent, given that Locke asserts that reason, which is the law of nature, itself prescribes the duty of preserving others, *when this does not conflict with one's own preservation*; but is it likely that there will ever be a case where one could not, on the basis of self-interest, plausibly argue that one's duty to preserve others conflicts with, and, therefore, may be superseded by one's duty to preserve oneself?

Locke, in effect, concedes the difficulty we have raised. He writes:

To this *strange doctrine*, viz. that in the state of nature, every one has the executive power of the law of nature, I doubt not but it will be objected, that it is unreasonable for men to be judges in their own cases, that self-love will make men partial to themselves and their friends. And on the other side, that ill nature, passion and revenge will carry them too far in punishing others. *And hence nothing but confusion and disorder will follow*, and that therefore God certainly appointed government to restrain the partiality and violence of men. I easily grant, that civil government is the proper remedy for the *inconveniencies of the state of nature, which certainly must be very great, where men may be judges in their own case* . . . but I shall desire those who make this objection, to remember that absolute monarchs are but men, and if government is to be the remedy of those evils, *which necessarily follow from men's being judges in their own causes, and the state of nature is therefore not to be endured*, I desire to know what kind of government that is, and how much better it is than the state of nature, where one man commanding a multitude, has the liberty to be judge in his own case, and may do to all his subjects whatever he pleases, without the least liberty to any one to question or control those who execute his pleasure? And in whatsoever he doth, whether led by reason, mistake, or passion, must be submitted to (275)? [emphases added]

We note that Locke grants that the "inconveniencies" of the state of nature must certainly be very great when men are allowed to be judges in their own causes. Indeed, he concedes to his imaginary critic the strangeness of his doctrine that, in the state of nature, each man has i) the executive power of the law of nature, which commands that everyone preserve himself, as well as all other human beings, when to do so does not interfere with his own preservation; and, ii) the right to judge in all cases of possible conflict between his own interests and those of another.

Locke does not appeal to the state of nature as a halcyon age of sweet reason and harmony, which can be the positive standard for establishing political society. Rather, the state of nature is a state of chaos and peril, from which all reasonable human beings flee as quickly as they can, in order to seek security in civil society. Locke's correction of the ancient political philosophers is this: to learn the truth about political society, you must first study what man above all else seeks to avoid. Nature, contrary to what the ancients taught, is that which man flees, not that which he pursues. The motive for consulting reason is that, although it is subordinate to the ends proposed by the passions, reason can calculate, or determine the means for attaining those ends. Reason will not try to correct the passions. In particular, reason will not thwart the most fundamental passion, the fear of death, and the consequent desire to preserve oneself. Reason will always be instrumental to that passion.

One might be tempted to equate the state of nature as Locke describes it, with the Bible's description of man's state of innocence before the Fall. Although Locke might otherwise welcome such a comparison, giving as it does a color of respectability to a teaching which Locke himself admits is "strange," one would nevertheless be wrong to identify Locke' description of man in the state of nature with the account in Genesis of pre-lapsarian man. Indeed, Locke himself, in describing the state of nature, intentionally writes so as to blur the distinction the Bible clearly makes between man's condition before and after the Fall.

In his chapter, "Of Property," Locke raises the question "how any one should ever come to have a property in anything." He is compelled to ask this question, because natural reason and revelation appear to agree in denying the right of private property. That is, natural reason teaches that each human being has the right to his preservation, and consequently to those natural goods necessary to his preservation. Revelation teaches, for example in Psalm 115, that God has "given the earth to the sons of men." How, then, can anyone justify appropriating to himself as his sole possession that which God has given to all in common; or how may one rightly claim as his sole possession, "without any express compact of all the commoners," that to which all have an equal right?

Briefly stated, Locke's answer to this question, which we discuss below in more detail, is that each man has a "property in his own person," to which no one has a right but himself. Those things upon which man labors are his, labor being but an extension of his body. The right of property originates in man's labor. Why does man's labor upon a piece of ground, for example give him a property right in that ground? Because, says Locke, nature, unimproved by man's labor, is virtually worthless. Unimproved land "would scarcely be worth anything"; "t'is labour then which puts the greatest part of value upon land."

Furthermore, "nature and earth furnished only the almost worthless materials" for labor. The value of things is their usefulness to us: "labour makes the far greatest part of the value of things, we enjoy in this world . . . (297-298)" If, without my labor, a thing is virtually useless, then, if I add value, or utility to it by expending my labor upon it, I make it my property. Below, we consider Locke's reasons for asserting that unimproved nature is virtually worthless. Here, we note that the right of ownership belongs to the one who "creates value," value being understood to mean "utility."

In demonstrating that reason and revelation concur regarding the origin of the right to own property in labor, Locke blurs the Biblical distinction between the status of man's work before and after the Fall. Genesis teaches that, before the Fall, man was placed in the Garden of Eden "to till it and keep it," that is, to be its steward; but after the Fall, God says to Adam:

> cursed is the ground because of you; in toil you shall eat of it all the days of your life; thorns and thistles it shall bring forth to you; and you shall eat the plants of the field. In the sweat of your face you shall eat bread till you return to the ground, for out of it you were taken; your are dust, and to dust you shall return.

Thus, after the Fall, work is the pre-eminent sign of man's disobedience and consequent mortality. Work is a sign of man's neediness and dependence. Work produces toil and sweat, but property is not mentioned.

Locke, however, writes:

> . . . the chief matter of property being *now* not the fruits of the earth, and the beasts that subsist on it, but the earth itself . . . I think it is plain, that property in that too is acquired as the former. As much land as a man tills, plants, improves, cultivates, and can use the product of, so much is his property. He by his labour does as it were, inclose it from the common. Nor will it invalidate his right to say, every body else has an equal title to it; and therefore he cannot appropriate, he cannot inclose, without the consent of all his fellow-commoners, all mankind. God, when he gave the world in common to mankind, *commanded man also to labour, and the penury of his condition required it of him*. God and his reason commanded him to subdue the earth, i.e., improve it for the benefit of life, and therein lay out something upon it that was his on, his labour. He that in obedience to this command of God, subdued, tilled and sowed any part of it, thereby annexed to it something that was his property, which another had no title to, nor could without injury take from him (290-291). [emphasis added]

In the Biblical story, the "penury of man's condition" compels him to eat his bread "in the sweat of his face." God curses both man and the ground from which he was made, on account of man's disobedience. The curse is of cosmic dimension. Prior to the Fall, man was called to be steward of God's creation. He was commanded by God to be fruitful and multiply, to fill and subdue the earth; but man was not at enmity with the created order. His diet was vegetarian and simple. Locke, however, collapses the distinction between God's command to man prior to the Fall, and man's penurious condition after the Fall, and cites them jointly as the origin of man's labor, and the right of property in the produce of his labor.

Locke's purpose in blurring this distinction, as we observed above, is that he still feels himself compelled to justify both the institution of private property as well as the unlimited acquisition of material wealth. Neither has any basis in the teaching of Genesis. Indeed, both are rejected by Genesis. These doctrines have not yet become respectable. Locke must make them respectable, so that political life can be made peaceful and secure. So, he says that God and man's reason "commanded him to subdue the earth." Reason and revelation agree that labor is necessary to "improve [the earth] for the benefit of life", as well as to acquire property. If one obeys God, one acquires property, which cannot "without injury" be taken away.

Locke concedes that the state of nature, as he has described it, is a state of "confusion and disorder"; but he does so, not to qualify or retract his teaching, but to deny that monarchy is the solution to the political problem set by the existence of the state of nature. In other words, the negative reason for preferring democratic rule over monarchic is that the latter is no improvement over the state of nature. In a monarchy, only one man may be the judge in his own cause; but this is enough to reintroduce precisely those uncertainties which human beings sought to escape by establishing civil society in the first place. This is Locke's correction of the teaching of Thomas Hobbes, who maintained that the state of nature is the "war of all against all," and that the only legitimate government is absolute monarchy. Locke argues that absolute monarchy is no better than the state of nature.

Locke admits that, precisely because of the confusion and disorder which inevitably exist in the state of nature, where each man is judge in his own case, the state of nature is "not to be endured." Evidently, then, human beings are by nature inclined to flee the state of nature; but to what? The state of nature seems unable to supply a positive goal to direct mankind to his natural political end.

The state of nature, then, is that state in which one's property, meaning one's natural person, or life, liberty, and estate, is insecure. The insecurity of one's person is the direct consequence, however, of the unlimited character of one's right of self-preservation. That is, precisely because each human being's right of self-preservation is unlimited, the rights of all are insecure. In order to understand this part of Locke's teaching adequately, we must inquire still further into his teaching concerning rights and the origin of property.

We have seen that, although Locke asserts that we have a duty to preserve all mankind, he qualifies his assertion by adding, "Every one as he is bound to preserve himself, and not to quit his station willfully; so by the like reason when his own preservation comes not into competition, ought he, as much as he can, to preserve the rest of mankind." A careful reading of this passage shows that Locke says that everyone is *bound* to preserve himself, but *ought* to preserve the rest of mankind. One's attachment to one's own preservation (and therefore to one's own property), differs from one's attachment to the preservation of others, in the same way that being bound by necessity differs from being obliged by law. They differ as necessity differs from duty. Locke therefore appears to teach that natural necessity takes precedence over whatever duties are prescribed by the natural law.[9] Man is driven by natural necessity more forcibly than he is obliged by the law of nature. Indeed, the law of nature may merely be another name for natural necessity.

To see this more clearly, we turn to Locke's *Essay Concerning Human Understanding*. One of the great objects of that book is to demonstrate that there are no "innate principles," either speculative or practical, in the mind. It is important to understand what Locke means by "innate principles in the mind." An innate principle is a truth of reason, something one apprehends solely with one's intellect. An innate principle is not acquired through experience, but is rather "stamped upon the mind of man, which the soul receives in its very first being, and brings into the world with it."

These innate principles may be either speculative or practical. That is, they are truths either about the way things are, or the way human beings act or ought to act. To call them principles is to say that they are so fundamental that they cannot be deduced from any prior truth. To call them innate is to say that they are as irreducibly a part of us as human beings as is our ability to breathe or grow. We do not acquire them; rather, we possess them.

An example of a speculative truth is the assertion that "it is impossible for the same thing both to be and not be." Such a principle is fundamental to all reasoning about anything. It cannot be deduced from any higher or more comprehensive principle. An example of a practical principle is the assertion that one ought to honor one's contractual obligations, and in general, treat others justly. It is important to stress that Locke does not say that these principles are false. Rather, he says that they are not innate. We do not possess them; rather, we acquire them.

---

9 In Chapter II of the *Second Treatise*, Locke appears to cite the authority of Richard Hooker, the great Anglican divine and staunch defender of Thomistic natural law, to support his own assertion that men in the state of nature are equal; that is, no one is by nature subjected to the rule of any other. He quotes a passage from Hooker's *Ecclesiastical Polity*, in which Hooker deduces from the natural equality of men the duties of justice and charity. Locke, however, deduces from natural equality only that men have a duty not to harm one another in their "life, health, liberty, or possessions." He deduces no positive duty towards others; and, as we have seen, he qualifies the duty one has of preserving the rest of mankind, by adding "when his own preservation comes not in competition." This further indicates how far from traditional natural law teaching Locke is: the right of self-preservation takes precedence over all duties.

If there are no innate practical principles, it follows that there are no innate natural duties, which is to say that there is no such thing as the conscience. Why? Because a duty is rationally *deduced* as an obligation from a general moral rule; and no such rule, according to Locke, is innate. It does not follow, however, that there is no innate natural right, for the simple reason that natural rights do not originate from reason.

To say that natural rights are not rational is to say that they are not based upon principles discerned or apprehended by reason. That is, Locke teaches that natural right is based on something that is both non-rational, as well as something more fundamental, in the sense of being more efficacious or more reliable than law. This turns out to be "a desire for happiness, and an aversion to misery," implanted in man by nature. These two things, says Locke, "indeed are innate practical principles," which, "as practical principles ought, do continue constantly to operate and influence all our actions without ceasing [and which] may be observed in all persons and all ages, steady and universal."

Locke thus appears to contradict himself, by both affirming and denying that there are innate practical principles. The contradiction disappears, however, when one recalls that Locke's point is that human action is *fundamentally* determined, not by rational principles, but by the passions, specifically, the desire for happiness and the aversion to misery. These passions, then, are the basis of natural rights, and particularly the right to the pursuit of happiness. Why? Because, as Locke says, "men . . . must be allowed to pursue their happiness, *nay, cannot be hindered.*"

The original and principal meaning of "rights" is this: to say that one has a right to something is to say that one has a justified claim upon that thing; but, one's claim is justified precisely insofar as it "*must* be allowed," because "it *cannot* be hindered." Natural right originates from precisely those ineluctably compelling natural desires, for life, liberty, and property, from which all human action immediately springs. Now desire, according to Locke, is a species of anxiety. In its mode of operation, therefore, desire more closely resembles compulsion, than it resembles desire as it is traditionally understood, namely, a yearning to be satisfied by something sought after as good.

Natural rights appear to originate, not in the dictates of reason or the commandments of God, but in the very same natural necessity which governs, not only mankind, but nature as a whole. It is partly for this reason that the Declaration justifies the people of the United States in assuming "among the powers of the earth" their rightful "separate and equal station," by appealing to "the laws of nature and nature's

God." To repeat: according to the original understanding of the meaning of the term "natural rights," one has a natural right to or claim upon life, liberty, and property, because, being human, one cannot be prevented from pursuing them.

Locke teaches that natural necessity compels human beings to be concerned above all else with their own preservation. From this fundamental fact flow the rights to life, and to those things necessary to life, namely liberty and property. Because the desire for self-preservation is the fundamental fact about human nature, the right to life is the fundamental right. Although men are distinguished from the other animals by the possession of reason, it is not reason that acts as the practical principle in human nature. Locke asserts that practical principles are those which:

> do continue constantly to operate and influence all our actions without ceasing; these may be observed in all persons and all ages, steady and universal; but these are the inclinations of the appetite to the good, not impressions of truth on the understanding.[10]

We note that Locke distinguishes the good from the true. The understanding, or reason, does not discern the good as true, but only as desired by the appetites. This teaching anticipates the contemporary view that the good is not rational, or knowable by reason. This is the foundation of the view that values are relative or subjective. Reason does indeed discover the means necessary to the satisfaction of one's fundamental needs; but it is the passions, and not reason, which supply the ends of human life. The passions, being concerned with pleasure and pain, are the ineluctably powerful motives of human action. This is because the human person is essentially a *self*, and, as such, is concerned, above all other things, with preserving itself. Why is it that being a self necessarily entails that the desire to preserve oneself takes precedence over the intellect as well as all other passions? Locke answers this question in his *Essay Concerning Human Understanding*.

In order to understand fully Locke's answer to this question, we must separate rights from things which are sometimes mistakenly called "rights." As we have seen, rights are first of all to be distinguished from duties. Rights are not duties. Duties may be based on rights, or the exercise of one's rights may impose duties, but the two terms mean fundamentally different things.[11]

---

[10] Locke, *Essay Concerning Human Understanding*, bk. I, ch. iii, no. 3.

[11] One may say, without much exaggeration, that the difference between the view that rights are fundamental, and the view that duties are fundamental is

Whereas a right expresses my justified claim upon something, a duty imposes an obligation upon me. It makes a claim upon me as a moral agent. The commandment to love my neighbor as myself imposes a duty upon me; and, it must be added, the commandment imposes this duty upon me without simultaneously granting me the right to expect my neighbor to reciprocate my love towards him. I am simply commanded to love my neighbor as myself; which is to say, I am commanded always to will or otherwise promote the good of others. By contrast, I may indeed have the right to expect that my neighbor will refrain from taking what belongs to me; but I have no right to expect him to love me.

Rights must also be distinguished from privileges. "Privilege" literally means "private law." In Roman antiquity, it meant a special ordinance having reference to a particular individual. In general, a privilege is, according to the *Oxford English Dictionary*, a "right, advantage, or immunity, granted to or enjoyed by a person, or a body or class of persons, beyond the common advantages of others; an exemption in a particular case from certain burdens or liabilities." Rights, on the other hand, belong to all human beings simply as human. Rights are no respecters of persons.[12]

This leads us to consider the difference between "natural rights" and "civil rights," because the latter term has often been used as though it meant "minority rights." The Declaration specifically mentions certain rights as "unalienable," as having been bestowed on us by "nature's

---

the difference between modern political thought, on the one hand, and the political teaching of both the Bible and classical antiquity, on the other.

12 Accordingly, it makes no sense to talk about "women's rights," or "minority rights," or "gay rights," as though there were rights unique to women, minorities, or homosexuals. Women do not have rights as women; rather, they have rights as human beings. Thus, for example, Article XIX of the Bill of Rights does not *give* women the right to vote; indeed, no mention of gender appears in the language of the Article. Rather, it makes explicit what was already present in the Constitution, namely, that no *citizen* may be *denied* the right to vote on the basis of sex. Neither do Articles XIV and XV give black Americans the rights to equal protection under the laws and to vote. Neither Article refers to "minorities" or "Negroes" or "blacks." Instead, they refer to "all persons born or naturalized in the United States," "citizens," and "any person." The language clearly refers to an antecedently existing right, and explicitly prohibits any interference with the legitimate exercise of that right. We do not have rights because we are *entitled* to them, on account of our belonging to a particular gender or race. We have them, simply because we are citizens.

God," namely, "life, liberty, and the pursuit of happiness." It is to *"secure these rights that governments are instituted among men."* [emphasis added] These rights antedate civil society. They are not created or granted by civil society; nor do they come into existence upon the establishment of civil society. The enjoyment of these rights is, instead, made more secure in civil society.

More secure than what? More secure than in "the state of nature," that is, the condition of human society prior to the establishment of civil society. It must be added that, if government can create rights, it can also take them away. Thus, giving government the power to create rights perforce makes rights *insecure*; whereas, the legitimate task for which governments are instituted is to secure rights.

We distinguish, then, between the rights we have merely as human, apart from any reference to our being members of a political community, and the rights we have as members of such a community. The latter are less extensive than the former, but they are derived from the former. Our rights in the state of nature are insecure because they are unlimited. Every human being in the state of nature, says Locke, "hath a right to punish [an] offender, and be executioner of the law of nature," a law which prescribes the preservation of mankind. Our rights can be secured, however, by government of a certain kind, namely limited government. Absolute monarchy is no less insecure than the state of nature, because no limits are set to the power of the executive. Therefore, the task of securing rights demands a kind of government in which the governed, by their consent, both agree to be ruled, and set limits to the power of the rulers.

Thus men give up the state of nature, which is a state of chaos, along with their unconditioned right to be executor of the law of nature. They mutually consent to limit, and thus secure, their rights under the rule of civil government. Accordingly, our unalienable rights to life, liberty, and the pursuit of happiness are now circumscribed, as the consequence of our mutual consent. A citizen *may* be deprived of his civil rights to life, liberty, or property, but not without due process of law, or just compensation.[13]

Therefore, civil rights include both natural rights, now limited and secured, as well as those rights ancillary to the limiting and securing of

---

[13] We note, in passing, that this means that the death penalty, whatever else may be said about it, is not unconstitutional. It also calls into question such current practices as appropriating private land as "wetlands," without compensation, as well as the *de facto* appropriation of private property through rent control.

natural rights, for example the rights of due process and universal suffrage. The "civil rights movement" is thus a movement to ensure the secure enjoyment of the rights of *citizens* to those who, for reasons of racial bigotry, have been denied the legitimate exercise of what is rightfully theirs. It is, in fact, a movement in behalf of the rights of citizenship. It is not a movement in behalf of minority rights. As we saw above, Lincoln argued during his debates with Stephen A. Douglas, that if the civil rights of one group are insecure, then the civil rights of all are insecure. If I may deny certain people the legitimate exercise of their civil rights because of their race, why may they not do the same to me, as soon as they are able?[14]

According to Locke, human beings are driven to enter civil society; yet we have also seen that Locke teaches that what fundamentally motivates human action is desire. This suggests that one is drawn, rather than compelled, to one's natural good. Below we take up an analysis of Locke's special understanding of desire as a species of anxiety. Here we note the primary cause of men's entering into society with one another. What, specifically, could motivate human beings to part with the unconditioned freedom they enjoy in the state of nature, and agree to subject themselves to the dominion of others? Locke raises and answers this question as follows:

> If man in the state of nature be so free, as has been said; if he be absolute lord of his own person and possessions, equal to the greatest, and subject to no body, why will he part with his freedom? Why will he give up this empire, and subject himself to the dominion and control of any other power? To which 'tis obvious to answer, that though in the state of nature he hath such a right, *yet the enjoyment of it is very uncertain,* and constantly exposed to the invasion of others. For all being kings as much as he, every man his equal, *and the greater part no strict observers of equity and justice*, the enjoyment of the property he has in this state is very unsafe, very unsecure. This makes him willing to quit this condition, which however free, is full of fears and continual dangers. And 'tis not without reason, that he seeks out, and is willing to join in society with others who are already united, or have a mind to unite for the mutual preservation of their lives, liberties and estates, which I call by the general name, property. *The great and chief end therefore, of men's uniting into*

---

14 It is partly for this reason that one must view with trepidation the deterioration of the civil rights movement into a quest for power, as contrasted with justice.

*commonwealths, and putting themselves under government, is the preserva-*
*tion of their property.*[15] [emphases added]

Therefore, unconditioned freedom, without the peace and stability to enjoy it, is not as desirable as the limited enjoyment of freedom under the dominion of another. Apart from the security of civil law and the force required to keep it, most men are "no strict observers of equity and justice." Thus, every reasonable man will quit the state of nature, and agree to enter the state of civil society. The enlightenment which prevails in civil society will thus be based upon the mutual recognition of the ineluctable power of the desire for self-preservation, which operates with equal force in every human being, no matter what his station or condition. This is the original form of that equality which is natural to human beings.

We may confirm the foregoing reflections by recalling the triad of rights specifically named in the Declaration, "life, liberty, and the pursuit of happiness," and that each right in this triad presupposes the right that precedes it. The logic of this line of thought alone implies that the right to life is the most basic right. We would therefore expect to find Locke affirming that the desire for life, and therefore the right to life, is more fundamental than the desire for happiness, which he does: "[T]he first and strongest desire God planted in men, and wrought in the very principles of their nature, is that of self-preservation." Therefore, the first and strongest right is the right of self-preservation.

The passions being more powerful than reason as motives of human action, rights are more fundamental than duties. What is the specific relation of reason to rights? It is the relation of means to end. Reason does not guide man to his natural end by apprehending the good for man as man; rather, reason calculates what is "necessary and useful to [man's] being." It teaches man that "he that is master of himself and his own life has a right, too, to the means of preserving it." Reason teaches man that he has a right, not only to those things necessary to preserve himself, but as well to those things necessary to "the *comfortable* [emphasis added] preservation of [his] being."

Finally, as we noted above, reason teaches man that all human beings, however they may differ in other respects, are equally endowed with the desire for, and hence the right to, self-preservation. Or, as Locke writes:

> Though I have said above . . . *That all men are by nature equal,* I cannot be supposed to understand all sorts of *equality: age* or *virtue* may give

---

[15] Locke, *Second Treatise,* 350-351.

men a just precedency: *excellence of parts and merit* may place others above the common level: *birth* may subject some, and *alliance* or *benefits* others, to pay an observance to those to whom nature, gratitude or other respects may have made it due; and yet all this consists with the *equality*, which all men are in, in respect of jurisdiction or dominion one over another, which was the *equality* I there spoke of, as proper to the business in hand, being that *equal right* that every man has *to his natural freedom*, without being subjected to the will or authority of any other man.[16]

Human beings are thus equal in their right to whatever is necessary to their self-preservation; and it is here we find the natural basis for property. Or, as Locke says, "man's property in the creatures, was founded upon the right he had, to make use of those things, that were necessary or useful to his being," or, "to the comfortable preservation" of his being.

This answers the question, What is the natural basis of man's right to property? But, what makes something mine? What removes something from "the common store" of goods available to mankind as a whole, and gives me an exclusive claim to it? Clearly this question must be raised, for if all human beings are equally entitled to appropriate those things necessary to their survival and comfort, then it must be explained how one comes to have an *exclusive* right to the use of anything, which is what the term "property" entails.

Although man did not originally own property, he did have from the beginning the *right* to own property, because he had the right to whatever he deemed necessary to preserve himself. What, then, is the origin of actual ownership? It is man's labor. Labor is both the source of whatever value or utility natural materials acquire, as well as the "original" the title to property. Locke taught that nature, in her unimproved state, is virtually worthless. Nature is not "an actual plenty, but only a potential plenty."[17] It is man's labor which reduces nature's potentiality to actuality, and transforms natural things into useful things; and it is thus man's labor which is the source of value, where "value" means "utility." Therefore, property originated in the simple act of laboring, of mixing the activity of the one thing which every man may rightly claim as his own, namely his body, with the goods provide by nature.

---

[16] Ibid., 337.
[17] Robert Goldwin, "John Locke," in *History of Political Philosophy,* Third Edition, ed. Strauss and Cropsey (Chicago: University of Chicago Press, 1987), 489.

At first, Locke says that men had the right to gather whatever they wanted without asking the leave of any other man, as long as there was always "enough and as good" left over. In particular, Locke says, the amount men might legitimately gather was limited by what they could use over time without there being any spoilage or waste of what they had gathered. If, however, as Locke himself eventually admits, there is a superabundance of natural goods, then there is no need to limit what each man may take for himself; but it was Locke's tacit assumption of a natural superabundance which justified his assertion that the simple act of laboring for something makes it one's own. If, however, there is not a superabundance of goods (especially of perishable goods), then "not even labor can establish a right to a part of a whole, to the exclusion of all other men."[18]

It is for this reason that we have stressed the necessity of understanding the virtual worthlessness of nature in light of Locke's teaching concerning human desire, namely, that desire is a species of anxiety, oriented not towards satiety in the possession of its natural good, but towards the secure and comfortable possession of property. The origin of property is the origin of the right every man has to whatever he thinks may be required for his own preservation; but this is also the origin of the chaotic and dangerous condition of the state of nature. In the state of nature, the right to property exists, to be sure; but the security of one's property is imperiled, precisely because every one in that state is the judge of what his own preservation requires. The emancipation of acquisitiveness advocated by Locke derives from the indefinite nature of the anxiety over the future, which is itself the source of man's striving to acquire the means to ensure his peace and safety in the present. Thus, foremost among man's natural, unalienable rights is the right to acquire property.

### III

The *Second Treatise* teaches that the primary right, the right of self-preservation, derives from the primacy of the passion to preserve oneself. Why is the desire to preserve oneself the primary fact about human nature? The ancient philosophers taught that both the end and character of political life are determined by reference to a natural standard, namely the good for man as man. The good for man is what he truly desires as human. As an object of desire, the good for human beings

---

[18] Ibid., 490.

supplies a positive standard for human action, something that sets human life in motion by drawing men to it.

Locke, however, teaches that nature supplies only a negative, not a positive standard. Human nature being what it is, men are determined in their actions more by their desire to avoid pain, than their desire to seek the good; and the natural, that is, pre-political state of mankind is one of uncertainty, which is a painful state. In particular, this means that man's efforts to acquire property, those goods which he deems necessary, not merely for his preservation, but for his comfortable preservation, are motivated primarily by his desire to remove present uneasiness. *The right of property, therefore, is grounded in Locke's peculiar understanding of human desire as a species of anxiety.*

Anxiety has its source in the very nature of human consciousness itself. In the *Essay Concerning Human Understanding*, Locke defines desire as follows:

> *Desire*—The uneasiness a man finds himself in upon the absence of anything whose present enjoyment carries the idea of delight with it, is that we call desire; which is greater or less, as that uneasiness is the more or less vehement. Where, by the by, it may perhaps be of some use to remark, that the chief, if not the only spur to human industry and action, is uneasiness. For whatsoever good is proposed, if its absence carries no displeasure or pain with it, if a man be easy and content without it, there is no desire of it, nor endeavour after it . . . [19]

Locke then proceeds to discuss the sense in which man's will is free, and observes that "the motive for continuing in the same state or action, is only present satisfaction in it; the motive for change is always some uneasiness; nothing settles us upon the change of state, or upon any new action, but some uneasiness." Locke continues:

> [W]hat is it that determines the will in regard to our actions? . . . [it] is not, as is generally supposed, the greater good in view, but some (and for the most part the most pressing) uneasiness a man is at present under. This is that which successively determines the will, and sets us upon those actions we perform. This uneasiness we may call, as it is, desire; which is an uneasiness of the mind for want of some absent good . . . For desire being nothing but an uneasiness in the want of an absent good, in reference to any pain felt, ease is that absent good . . . Good and evil, present and absent, it is true, work upon the mind: but that which immediately determines the will, from time to time, to every voluntary action, is the uneasiness of desire, fixed on some absent good . . . (bk. II, ch. xi, #31)

---

[19] Locke, *Essay*, bk. II, ch. xx, no. 6.

Locke's teaching contradicts the traditional view, which holds that the greatest positive good determines the will. Not so, says Locke. A man may acknowledge the truth that moral virtue benefits its possessor in this world and the next;

> yet, till he hungers or thirsts after righteousness, till he feels an uneasiness in the want of it, his will will not be determined to any action in pursuit of this confessed greater good; but any other uneasiness he feels in himself shall take place, and carry his will to other actions (bk. II, ch. xi, #35).

Present uneasiness will always overcome absent good; and desire, which, we recall, is "an uneasiness of the mind for want of some absent good," is not directed to its specific good as supplying its proper satisfaction, but to the removal of uneasiness. Human beings are not motivated primarily by the positive desire *for* something; rather, they are primarily moved by the desire to be rid of their present uneasiness. Our fundamental motivation is to flee pain, not to pursue good. The good is understood negatively, as that which removes present uneasiness, and not positively, as that which satisfies a specific desire.

It follows that, as Locke says, "the removal of uneasiness is the first step to happiness." Why is it that present uneasiness determines the will, excluding the influence of any absent good? Because, says Locke, human beings are

> capable [of only] one determination of the will to one action at once . . . [W]hilst we are under any uneasiness, we cannot apprehend ourselves happy, or in the way to it; pain and uneasiness being by every one concluded and felt to be inconsistent with happiness, spoiling the relish even of those good things which we have; a little pain serving to mar all the pleasure we rejoiced in (bk. II, ch. xi, #36).

Therefore, as long as we suffer any pain or uneasiness, the removing of it will always take priority as a means to happiness.

Why does Locke insist that the contemplation of an absent good is unable to determine the will? Because "it is against the nature of things, that what is absent should operate where it is not." There is, in the language of the physics of Locke's day, no "action-at-a-distance."[20]

---

[20] The problem of action-at-a-distance arose for classical, or Newtonian mechanics, as the joint result of its "first law of motion," that is, the law of inertia, and its mathematical method. The first law of motion states that "ever body continues in its state of rest, or of uniform motion in a straight line, unless compelled to change that state by forces impressed upon it." Forces are "impressed" upon a moving body by direct contact; but what about the force of gravity? Newton agreed with Galileo that the curvilinear orbits of planets

Human action, like the motions of all bodies, must be understood as the result of the impact of one body upon another, and not of some principle which, like desire, is able to produce motion in us, even though the good desired is "at a distance" from us. It is true, Locke admits, that

> the idea of [some absent good] indeed may be in the mind, and viewed as present there; but nothing will be in the mind as a present good, able to counterbalance the removal of any uneasiness which we are under, till it raises our desire; and the uneasiness of that [namely, desire] has the prevalency in determining the will.[21]

You may, says Locke, set before a man a vision of the eternal and infinite joys of heaven, and he may even admit them to be desirable above all other things; but, if he is under some present uneasiness, he will infallibly attend to it first: "the infinitely greatest confessed good [is] often neglected, to satisfy the successive uneasinesses of our desires pursuing trifles."

Will you say, asks Locke, that all men desire to be happy, and are moved to act by that desire? Let it be granted; but, what can be meant by happiness "in its full extent," other than "the utmost pleasure we are capable of, and misery the utmost pain." You will object to this definition of happiness that it is hedonistic: happiness is pleasure, misery is pain. But surely human happiness is more than mere pleasure or the absence of pain. What justifies Locke in identifying happiness with pleasure, particularly when experience shows that the attainment of excellent or noble things, to which human beings obviously aspire, is

---

may be resolved mathematically, into the imparted rectilinear motion of the body and the deflecting pull of gravity. On the basis of these principles, Newton was able to formulate a law of force, with which he explained all natural motion, celestial and terrestrial. "Gravity," in this system, may indeed be understood as a mathematical relation between "attracting bodies"; but the attempt to give it a physical explanation leads to absurdities, once you have said that all motion is inertial, and that all change of motion is due to direct contact. Newton himself, in a famous letter, recognizes this absurdity: "That gravity should be innate, inherent and essential to matter, so that one body may act on another at a distance through a vacuum, without the mediation of anything else, by and through which their action and force may be conveyed from one to another, is to me so great an absurdity, that I believe no man who has in philosophical matters a competent faculty of thinking, can ever fall into it." Certainly, Locke would appear to fit the description of one having "a competent faculty of thinking" in philosophical matters.

21 Locke, *Essay*, bk. II, ch. xxi, no. 37.

frequently accompanied with much suffering and sacrifice; or that the forsaking of one's duty for pleasure is often followed by shame and guilt?

Furthermore, it is obvious that human beings are, for the most part, not able to attain happiness "in its full extent." Indeed, most sensible people will probably admit that you must, at least in this life, accept it that complete happiness is impossible. Perhaps human happiness contains an element of paradox. In order to be happy, or at least, reasonably happy, you must learn to live with a certain degree of unhappiness. Real happiness requires one to moderate one's expectations of life.

Locke readily admits this: "Happiness and misery are the names of two extremes, the utmost bounds whereof we know not." Quoting St. Paul, Locke describes complete happiness as that which "the eye hath not seen, ear hath not heard, nor hath it entered into the heart of man to conceive." We have no conception of complete happiness; but we do have "very lively impressions" of *some degree* of both happiness and misery. The "lowest degree of what can be called happiness is so much ease from all pain, and so much present pleasure, as without which any one cannot be content"; but the question remains unanswered, what justifies Locke in identifying happiness with pleasure?

Locke's answer to this is that we human beings, like all other living, sensate things, are subject to a certain natural necessity. Thus, pleasure and pain "are produced in us by the operation of certain objects, either on our minds or our bodies, and in different degrees . . ." Thus it happens that we tend to call "good" those things which are "apt" to produce pleasure, and "evil" those things which produce pain, and for no other reason than their tendency to produce either pleasure or pain. Furthermore, "good" and "evil" are comparative terms. If one object tends to produce pleasure to a degree greater than another, we call the first good in comparison to the second, and similarly with objects tending to produce pain: ". . . the cause of every less degree of pain, as well as every greater degree of pleasure, has the nature of good, and vice versa."

This fact of human nature has decisive implications for the good we desire, which we regard as conducing to our happiness. While it is true that all good is the proper object of desire in general, "yet all good, even seen, and confessed to be so, does not necessarily move every particular man's desire; but only that part, or so much of it as is considered and taken to make a necessary part of his happiness." So it is, says Locke, that all human beings do indeed desire happiness, and agree that the good is that which everyone desires; yet it is true of every man that, however much he may admit the goodness of a particular thing, he may nevertheless not be moved to desire it, if he thinks he can "make up [his] happiness without it."

It is not so with pain, however. Human beings are "always concerned for" pain; indeed, "they can feel no uneasiness without being moved." "Therefore," Locke concludes, "being uneasy in the want of whatever is judged necessary to their happiness, as soon as any good appears to make a part of their portion of happiness, they begin to desire it."

Locke concludes that those philosophers of old who referred to the greatest good, or the *summum bonum*, as the fully sufficient motive of human action, were mistaken:

> [T]he greater visible good does not always raise men's desires in proportion to the greatness it appears, and is acknowledged to have; though every little trouble moves us, and sets us on work to get rid of it . . . All present pain, whatever it be, makes a part of our present misery; but all absent good does not at any time make a necessary part of our present happiness, nor the absence of it make a part of our misery. If it did, we should be constantly and infinitely miserable; there being infinite degrees of happiness which are not in our possession. All uneasiness therefore being removed, a moderate portion of good serves at present to content men (bk. II, ch. xxi, #44).

One should not be misled by Locke's assertion that, when all uneasiness has been removed, "a moderate portion of good serves at present to content men"; for when is it ever the case that all uneasiness has been removed? We recall Locke's statement, quoted above, that "[h]appiness and misery are the names of two extremes, the utmost bounds whereof we know not." The natural condition of mankind is a state wherein pleasure and pain are mixed together; but, present pain will always overcome absent good as a motive for action. Therefore, human action is fundamentally an effort to remove pain and anxiety, a flight from evil, rather than a motion towards good. Therefore, it almost never occurs that a "moderate portion of good serves at present to content men."

Thus it is that the state of nature is a state of continual agitation and unrest, a state of anxiety over the uncertainty of life and the insecure condition of one's goods. In a word, the natural condition of men is one of misery; but the social contract, upon which civil society is based, holds out the promise of escape. Here we come to the great divide between modern and ancient political philosophy. Aristotle had said that all human beings by nature desire to live in political society.

As we noted above, the desire to live in political society means more than mere natural sociability. Human beings desire to live in communities united by a shared conception of justice, or the common good, a society necessarily divided into rulers and ruled. According to Aristotle, nature is an end, which, being known, can guide man to the life proper to a human being. Locke clearly disagrees. Nature does not serve as a positive guide to human goodness or happiness, but indicates what in nature is to be overcome or avoided, or, at the least, controlled.

In the longest chapter of his *Essay*, entitled "Of Power," Locke asserts that the greatest happiness "consists in the *having* those things which *produce* the greatest pleasures." [emphasis added] It is not the enjoyment of present pleasure, but the means of producing the greatest pleasures, both now and in the future, which are sought by man's acquisitiveness. Since you can never be sure that the present quantity of your wealth is sufficient for future contingencies, you are justified in acquiring as much wealth as you can, particularly, as Locke adds in *The Second Treatise*, once money has been invented.

We should add that Locke did not *encourage* the establishing of a society devoted to the inculcation of human avarice and greed. Instead, he, like Smith, maintained that the unlimited acquisition of wealth is compatible with, and indeed requires, civil society and its laws; and, like Smith, Locke argued that the unlimited acquisition of wealth is a source of wealth and stability to all in society. Locke tried to show how to construct a political society wherein human beings could be allowed, within limits, to do what comes naturally to them, and still live together in relative peace and harmony.

In his *Two Treatises of Government*, Locke says that God originally implanted in mankind the strong desire of preserving himself. In his *Essay*, however, Locke states that the root of the desire of self-preservation is this: to be a human being is to be a *self*, and to be a self *is* to be concerned with preserving oneself. Being a self and being self-concerned are one and the same thing. Locke writes:

> *Self depends on Consciousness.* [Locke's emphasis] Self is that conscious thinking thing, whatever substance made up of, (whether spiritual or material simple or compounded, it matters not), which is sensible or conscious of pleasure and pain, capable of happiness or misery, *and so is concerned for itself*, *as far as that consciousness extends* (bk. II, ch. xxvii, #17)." [emphasis added]

Moreover, the things of which one is conscious are what Locke calls "perceptions": the "thought or perception of the mind is . . . accompanied also with pleasure or pain." Pleasure and pain are what Locke calls "simple ideas," meaning that they cannot be known through definition, but only by immediate experience:

> For, to define [pleasure and pain] by the presence of good or evil, is no otherwise to make them known to us, than by making us reflect on what we feel in ourselves, upon the several and various operations of good and evil upon our minds . . . Things, then, are good or evil, only in reference to pleasure and pain. That we call good, which is apt to cause or increase pleasure, or diminish pain in us; or else to procure or preserve us in the possession of any other good or absence of any evil. And, on the contrary, we name that evil which is apt to produce or increase any pain or diminish any pleasure in us; or else procure us any evil or deprive us of any good . . . Pleasure and pain and that which causes them, good and evil, are the hinges on which our passions turn . . . (bk. II, ch. xx, no. 1) [emphasis added]

Therefore, to be a self is to be concerned for preserving oneself; insofar as one is concerned with increasing or preserving pleasure, and avoiding or removing pain, it is to be concerned above all with pleasure and pain. Human beings are by nature hedonistic. They identify good and evil with pleasure and pain.

It is nearly impossible to overestimate the effect on modern thought of the teaching that the human person is fundamentally a *self*—not a soul, not a spirit, but a self. Indeed, a brief survey of the principal works of modern philosophers shows that it is no exaggeration to say that the birth of modern philosophy and the birth of the self are coeval. According to the modern teaching, the self is that thing or principle according to which you are the person you are, and not another. The self is the locus of one's personal identity. Furthermore, the self is something that may be understood by itself, without reference to something else. The self stands alone. It is what it is by standing alone. It is not, as a self, essentially related to anything else—to other selves, to the world, or to God.

This does not mean that one who believes in the existence of selves must be a solipsist (one who doubts or denies the existence of other selves), a radical skeptic (in this case, one who doubts or denies the independent existence of something that corresponds to the world of our experience), or an atheist. It *does* mean that the self is the primary thing to which we refer to explain what and who we are.

Furthermore, modern philosophy typically accounts for human experience in terms of the self: what one experiences are first and foremost modifications of oneself.[22] Locke himself calls these modifications "ideas." In the Introduction to his *Essay*, Locke writes:

> . . . before I proceed on to what I have thought [on the subject of the human understanding], I must here in the entrance beg pardon of my reader for the frequent use of the word "idea," which he will find in the following treatise. It being that term which, I think, serves best to stand for whatsoever is the object of the understanding when a man thinks, I have used it to express whatever is meant by phantasm, notion, species, or whatever it is which the mind can be employed about in thinking; and I could not avoid frequently using it. I presume it will be easily granted me, that there are such ideas in men's minds; *everyone is conscious of them in himself, and men's words and actions will satisfy him that they are in others*. [emphasis added]

The critical thing to be grasped from Locke's statement is that "ideas" are "the object of the understanding when a man thinks," and that "ideas" are "*in* men's minds." That is, ideas, not things, are the *immediate* objects of the understanding when it thinks; and ideas are "in" men's minds. The self, as thinking, is immediately oriented, not to other human beings, the world of independently existing things, or God, but to its own ideas, that is, to modifications of itself.

The great advantage of the hypothesis that the human mind is immediately preoccupied, not with things outside it, but with ideas inside it, is that it allows us to avoid a question that vexed all the old philosophers: how can we ever be *certain* that our knowledge conforms to the way things *really* are in the world? The old philosophers had a simple, albeit unsettling answer to this question: we can't ever be certain. Therefore, they taught that it behooves us human beings to be moderate in the claims we make for our knowledge of the world. We should be skeptical about our knowledge, without, however, falling into radical skepticism.

Radical skepticism teaches that we have *no* reason to believe that the world is anything at all like our experience of it; but this teaching, said the ancients, is as unreasonable and extreme a view as is naive realism, the view that we see things exactly as they are. It *seems* to us that we see

---

[22] This immediately implies, of course, that one must somehow find a way to guarantee the objectivity of these modifications: certainty becomes the goal of modern philosophy precisely to the extent that the doctrine of the self is accepted. Furthermore, the phenomenon which is most characteristic of human experience, namely, the experience of being immediately and indubitably in contact with a world that is really there, remains inexplicable: how are modifications of the self transformed into the experience of a world?

things pretty much as they are, and that our sense experience of the world is, for the most part, reliable; but radical skepticism by definition can give no reason why we place this confidence in our senses. This confidence, however, is as much a datum for philosophical reflection as is the fact of error. Therefore, in rejecting this confidence out of hand, radical skepticism shows itself to be a form of dogmatism.

If, however, the mind is concerned immediately and essentially with its own *ideas*, things that are "in" the mind, then, as long as we confine ourselves to inquiries about those ideas, we shall be acting prudently. We may then have *certainty* about those subjects for which corresponding ideas exist in our minds, and may cease to trouble ourselves about topics for which no such ideas can be produced.

Locke makes the point in the following way:

> If by this inquiry into the nature of the understanding, I can discover the powers thereof, how far they reach, to what things they are in any degree proportionate, and where they fail us, I suppose it may be of use to prevail with the busy mind of man to be more cautious in meddling with things exceeding its comprehension; to stop when it is at the utmost extent of its tether; and to sit down in a quiet ignorance of those things which, upon examination, are found to be beyond the reach of our capacities. We should not then perhaps be so forward, out of an affectation of an universal knowledge, to raise questions, and perplex ourselves and others with disputes about things to which our understandings are not suited, and of which we cannot frame in our minds any clear or distinct perceptions, or whereof (as it has perhaps too often happened) we have not any notions at all. If we can find out how far the understanding can extend its view, how far it has faculties to attain certainty, and in what cases it can only judge and guess, we may learn to content ourselves with what is attainable by us in this state . . . For though the comprehension of our understandings comes exceeding short of the vast extent of things, yet we shall have cause enough to magnify the bountiful Author of our being, for that proportion and degree of knowledge he has bestowed on us, so far above all the rest of the inhabitants of this our mansion.[23]

The difference between Locke's view and the classical view is the difference between constantly questioning things, as a result of skepticism, even moderate skepticism, and sitting down "in quiet ignorance" before those subjects that are "beyond the reach of our capacities." It may not be too wide of the mark to say that Locke's hypothesis, that *ideas* are the object of the human understanding, is partially motivated

---

[23] Locke, *Essay*, Introduction.

by the desire to persuade men to cease from their skeptical agitations and to sit down in quiet ignorance.[24]

To return briefly to Locke's statement about the self, we note that *what* the self is, namely, a "conscious thinking thing," can be known independently of whether the self is "spiritual or material simple or compounded, it matters not." That is, it is not necessary to concern oneself over the age-old question, whether the human soul is spiritual or material; the important thing is that the self is a conscious thinking thing, which is "sensible or conscious of pleasure or pain." Evidently, that which is most immediate or vivid in the consciousness of the self are pleasure and pain. Being conscious of pleasure and pain, the self is *thus* capable of happiness or misery. This confirms what we have already seen, that Locke teaches that happiness and misery are to be understood in terms of the consciousness of pleasure and pain. Locke concludes from the immediacy of the self's consciousness of pleasure and pain that the self, as a conscious thinking thing, is "*concerned for itself* as far as [its] consciousness extends." [emphasis added] We therefore see that self-concern is rooted in the very being of the self.

## IV

When Locke admits that his teaching will sound "strange," perhaps he really means "repugnant." The "strangeness" of Locke's teaching is precisely this: the state of nature is not to be endured, but the civil society which best secures the rights of human beings against the chaos of the state of nature is that society which, as far as possible, and consistently with the security of the rights of all, *reproduces* the state of nature, albeit in a more secure and circumscribed form. The natural equality and liberty which belong to human beings in the state of nature, must be given free play in the civil society erected to protect human beings from the chaos which results from the unrestrained condition of natural equality and liberty. In such a society, however, self-interest will still predominate, and reason will be dedicated to its service.

---

24 We do not, of course, experience ideas *as* ideas. Rather, we experience them as the world, as something "there," independent and given. Our certainty that the world is there is immediate. Whence comes this certainty? Various answers to this question have been given by modern philosophers, some of which may be satisfactory. The main point here though is that one distinguishing characteristic of modern philosophy is its critique of "naive realism," or what may otherwise be called "common sense." The great originator of the peculiarly modern critique of common sense was René Descartes.

At this point, one may feel compelled to turn away from Locke in disgust or dismay; but, if one accepts Locke's view of human nature, one will find it difficult to reject his understanding of the origin, nature, and true purpose of political society. Locke holds a mirror up to human nature. What we see reflected therein is unflattering; but, if the reflection is true, should we not be grateful to Locke for having shown us how, despite natural human selfishness, we may nevertheless have a political society in which *some* happiness and security are possible?

On the other hand, perhaps Locke overlooked, or was otherwise oblivious to, a dimension of human life which cannot be ignored. One writer puts the point this way:

> . . . I am ambivalent on the question of whether to consider myself a Lockean. To put it too briefly and sweepingly, much of what we deplore in modern American life—the poverty of spirit, the excessive concern for comfort and convenience, the emphasis on self and selfishness—can be ascribed to Locke, sometimes to his true teaching, more often to a distortion of it. Much of what is most admirable in human nature, and most noble in social and political life, is slighted by Locke, or denied. I once described him as "a backwards Midas": golden things he touched turned to iron.[25]

If one admits that the fear of death, or a kind of pervasive anxiety for the future, takes precedence over all other human passions, must not one also admit that a political society, based upon the teaching that individualism and competition are unavoidable, will be superior to other forms of society, precisely because it gives full scope to the desire of self-preservation, while protecting the acquisition of property, as a fundamental human right? Can we be satisfied, though, with a communal life in which dedication to the common good, and the noble aspirations which such dedication elicits, will always be subordinated to protecting private interest? Can human beings be satisfied with a civil society that is, in the words of Thomas Paine, no better than a necessary evil?

In his famous revolutionary tract, *Common Sense*, Paine wrote:

> Some writers have so confused society with government as to leave little or no distinction between them, whereas they are not only different but

---

[25] Robert A. Goldwin, introduction to *Why Blacks, Women, and Jews Are Not Mentioned in the Constitution, and Other Unorthodox Views* (Washington: AEI Press, 1990), 4. One might leave it saying that Locke, rather than being a "backwards" Midas, is simply the modern incarnation of Midas. The "Midas touch" was, as we noted above, not a blessing but a curse.

have different origins. Society is produced by our wants and government by our wickedness; the former promotes happiness *positively* by uniting our affections, the latter *negatively* by restraining our vices. The one encourages intercourse, the other creates distinctions. The first is a patron, the last a punisher. Society in every state is a blessing, but government, even in its best state, is but a necessary evil . . . Government, like dress, is the badge of lost innocence; the palaces of kings are built upon the ruins of the bowers of paradise.[26]

Despite the noble rhetoric of the Declaration's peroration, will not exhortations to defend such a government, with one's "life, fortune, and sacred honor" if necessary, ring hollow?

To this Locke might reply, Well, you can't have it all. I have shown how human beings, despite their overpowering concern for their own preservation, may nevertheless unite in communities, and have peace, security, and prosperity. When you consider the alternative, this is not an achievement to be despised. If, in addition, you wish to instill in the people a concern for the common welfare, nothing prevents you. Enlighten the people. Teach them that their self-interest is served by the strength and decency of civil society, and that every reasonable person will therefore do what he can to promote the common good. As for *society*, will not men be freer to associate with whomsoever they please under mild and unintrusive government, than they would under any other form of government?

Or, to quote Goldwin again:

The paradox is that we also owe to Locke much of our enjoyment of the best fruits of modernity. Nations that have been taught by Locke are freer, more stable, more prosperous, more peaceable, and more successful in providing security for the rights of every individual. And Lockean nations—that is, nations whose first principles are liberty and equality of rights—never go to war against each other . . . [I]t is hard to be a Lockean and equally hard, for an American , not to be one.[27]

Locke teaches that the combination of calculating reason and self-love which defines human nature, gives the political problem its peculiar quality, and sets the limits to its solution. It is true that human beings desire both society and security. Human nature being what it is, the best possible solution to the political problem is limited government, based on the consent of the governed and the securing of rights. The

---

[26] "Common Sense," in *The People Shall Judge* (Chicago: University of Chicago Press, 1949), 1:182.
[27] Goldwin, *Blacks, Women, and Jews,* 4.

separation of human social existence into government, whose task is to secure and limit rights, and society, in which men may be left to pursue their happiness as they desire, *is* the best practicable solution.

This is the solution proposed by Locke, and adopted, at least in part, by the authors of the Declaration and Constitution: civil society secures natural rights, by limiting them in accordance with the rule of a government which itself is limited, deriving its just powers from the consent of the governed.

Natural rights are thus transformed into civil rights. Civil rights are derived from, but are not co-extensive with, natural rights. Civil rights are based upon the view that the rule of law is superior to the rule of individual human beings. It is the rule of law, manifested in part as the principle of due process, that simultaneously secures and limits our rights. As one writer puts it:

> Civil society exists to protect life, liberty, and property, but it does so precisely by wielding the power to deprive its members of life, liberty, and property. Those rights are more secure in civil society than in a state of nature, which is also to say they are more secure in a properly organized civil society than in a defective one, because they can be lost only in accordance with due process of law.[28]

In the state of nature, rights are unconditioned and therefore insecure; in civil society, they are secure because they are conditioned.[29] Justice in such a society comes to light primarily as peace and security; freedom means being left to do as one desires, commensurate with the rule of law; well-being is defined principally in material terms; and the pursuit of material well-being is in principle without natural limit.

As we have seen, Locke teaches that human freedom is, in its natural state, both negative and positive; but, in order of priority, freedom appears first as negative. Freedom is fundamentally freedom *from* being controlled by "the will of any other man." Within certain boundaries set by the "law of nature," however, men are free to do as they "see fit."

---

28 Nathan Tarcov, "American Constitutionalism and Individual Rights," in *How Does the Constitution Secure Rights?* ed. Goldwin and Schambra (Washington: The American Enterprise Institute, 1985), 102.

29 This point, fundamental for the understanding of our form of republican government, appears to have been largely forgotten in some contemporary political debates. Thus, for example, in the debate over abortion, the two extreme views, both "pro-life" and "pro-choice," overlook the possibility that the right to abortion, if such a right exists, cannot be unlimited because, as we saw above, no right secured under the Constitution is unlimited.

Thus, according to Locke, what freedom is *for* is, within limits, left to be determined by each human being.

With respect to its end, human freedom is essentially indeterminate. Nature supplies the materials for use by human freedom, but not the ends governing that use. The latter are supplied by human reason, calculating what is necessary to one's own and society's preservation. It is for this reason that we have the unalienable right to the pursuit of happiness, but not to happiness. Each man will be more firmly attached to the pursuit of his own interest if *he* is the one who defines that interest.

Equality, according to Locke, is connected with freedom in that each human being is equally free from being subjected to the will of another. There is "nothing more evident, than that creatures of the same species and rank promiscuously born to all the same advantages of nature, and the use of the same faculties, should also be equal one amongst another without subordination or subjection . . ." There is no natural superiority among human beings which could justify any man in ruling over another without his consent; and Locke denies that God, "the lord and master" of all men, has "by any manifest declaration of his will set one above another."

The Founders, basing themselves on Locke's understanding of natural equality, as well as his rejection of revelation as the source of the right to rule, thus adapted Locke's understanding of liberty and equality to the purposes of the Declaration and Constitution. In particular, the negative character of the Constitution's language, as well as its manner of setting limits to the powers of government, and securing rights, is made necessary by the conception of government as a negative, and not a positive institution. As such, government reflects the compromise from which civil society begins, namely the agreement among human beings to surrender their several rights to be the executors of the law of nature, as well as to be judge in their own causes, to one common authority having the power to enforce the law. The legitimacy of such a common authority, however, presupposes its having been instituted by the consent of the governed; and its unintrusive nature reflects its dependency on that consent.

This understanding of government, whatever its strengths, appears insufficient to inspire the signatories of the Declaration with the willingness to sacrifice their lives, fortunes, and sacred honor, "for the support of this declaration." Neither does it seem capable of eliciting the noble passion, manly rhetoric, and power of argument which infuse *The Federalist*. Above, we noted that *The Federalist* asserts that republican government, more than any other form of government, requires a virtuous, that is, public-spirited, people. We also saw that Publius teaches the necessity of supplementing a reliance upon the virtue of the people, with certain prudential provisions in the structure of government itself, whereby self-interest may be enlisted to co-operate with virtue in behalf of the public good. Thus enlightened, self-interest will not be suppressed or overcome; rather, it will be made tractable, having been persuaded that dedication to the common good also benefits self-interest.

## V

Alexis de Tocqueville treats this subject in *Democracy In America*, in a chapter entitled, "How the Americans Combat Individualism by the Principle of Self-Interest Rightly Understood." In this chapter, Tocqueville discusses, in an explicit and general way, a theme which runs throughout his book, namely, the opinion that prevails in America, that "man serves himself in serving his fellow creatures and that his private interest is to do good."

In earlier, aristocratic ages, says Tocqueville, it is probable that human beings were no more virtuous than in other ages, "but they were incessantly talking of the beauties of virtue, and its utility was only studied in secret."

That is, in aristocratic ages, it was considered vulgar, if not imprudent, openly to discuss the *utility* of virtue. In aristocratic ages, men were more effectually motivated by a lofty sense of duty. They were "fond of professing that it is praiseworthy to forget oneself and that good should be done without hope of reward, as it is by the Deity himself." The austere beauty of self-sacrifice was the only true and worthy source of the love of duty. To speak of the utility of virtue would be unwittingly to invite men to begin to calculate how to subvert the common good for their own selfish ends.

But, says Tocqueville, it is different now "that the imagination takes less lofty flights, and every man's thoughts are centered in himself." Moralists no longer exhort men to sacrifice their interests to the common good; rather, they

> content themselves with inquiring whether the personal advantage of each member of the community does not consist in working for the good of all; and when they have hit upon some point on which private interest and public interest meet and amalgamate, they are eager to bring it into

notice . . . [I]t is held as a truth that man serves himself in serving his fellow creatures and that his private interest is to do good.[30]

One may lament the demise of the noble principle of self-abnegation in behalf of the good of all; and indeed, says Tocqueville, Americans themselves, despite their protestations to the contrary, "are sometimes seen to give way to those disinterested and spontaneous impulses that are natural to man."

In general, however, the principle of self-interest rightly understood governs the opinions of most Americans. It comports better with the practical side of the American character. If this principle does not aim high, its aim is nevertheless true. In a society based upon the principle of self-interest rightly understood, one will seldom find "great acts of self-sacrifice"; but one will find "daily small acts of self-denial." Thus, this principle by itself "cannot suffice to make a man virtuous; but it disciplines a number of persons in habits of regularity, temperance, moderation, foresight, self-command; and if it does not lead men straight to virtue by the will, it gradually draws them in that direction by their habits."

In democratic times, it is futile to expect or hope for the return of altruism; but one ought not despair:

> If the principle of interest rightly understood were to sway the whole moral world, extraordinary virtues would doubtless be more rare; but . . . gross depravity would then also be less common. The principle of interest rightly understood perhaps prevents men from rising far above the level of mankind, but a great number of other men, who were falling far below it, are caught and restrained by it. Observe some few individuals, they are lowered by it; survey mankind, they are raised (121).

It is the duty of all thoughtful defenders of democracy to promote as well as they can the acceptance of the principle of self-interest rightly understood, for it is the "chief remaining security" against the destructive excesses of individualism. Even if the principle is judged to be "incomplete" regarding man's highest moral possibilities, "it must nevertheless be adopted as necessary." There is a great difference between selfishness pure and simple, and enlightened selfishness. Tocqueville observes that "[e]ach American knows when to sacrifice some of his private interests to save the rest."

Tocqueville, writing during the first half of the nineteenth century, stated his firm conviction that the spread of democracy and the growth

---

[30] Alexis de Tocqueville, *Democracy In America*, ed. Henry Reeve (New York: Alfred A. Knopf, 1976), 2: 121.

of equality are "providential facts." This phenomenon has all the characteristics of the work of providence: it is "universal, it is lasting, it constantly eludes all human interference, and all events as well as men contribute to its progress." Furthermore,

> [n]o power on earth can prevent the increasing equality of conditions from inclining the human mind to seek out what is useful or from leading every member of the community to be wrapped up in himself. It must therefore be expected that personal interest will become more than ever the principal if not the sole spring of men's actions; but it remains to be seen how each man will understand his personal interest. If the members of a community, as they become more equal, become more ignorant and coarse, it is difficult to foresee to what pitch of stupid excesses their selfishness may lead them; and no one can foretell into what disgrace and wretchedness they would plunge themselves lest they should have to sacrifice something of their own well-being to the prosperity of their fellow creatures (123ff.).

The genius of the American system, says Tocqueville, consists in its having captured and expressed most successfully the spirit of democracy. The noble passions and tastes of the aristocratic age are, perhaps lamentably, now past; but we may rejoice that the cruelty, instability, and rigid class divisions which characterized that age have also disappeared. The tendency of democracy is toward stability, comfort, material well-being, and equality of condition. If men now undertake fewer brilliant, daring enterprises, they also no longer embark on crusades, or go to war over religious differences. The tendency of democracy is toward reason and sobriety, and away from the old zeal for high, rare, and noble things.[31]

What virtues are necessary to the citizens of a country like the one Tocqueville describes? They will be those virtues necessary for self-rule under that system of representative government, which, says Publius, distinguishes our *democratic* republic from all previous republics. They will be the homely virtues of sobriety, thrift, hard work, and a due regard for one's own interest, to be sure; but they will also include a sense of fair play, and a decent concern for the well-being and interests of others, even to the point of occasionally subordinating one's own self-interest, if necessary, to the general welfare.

Publius writes, in *The Federalist*, #55:

---

31 In confirmation of Tocqueville's argument, let it be recalled that, in the twentieth century, the most bellicose and restless political regimes—namely, Nazi Germany and the Soviet Union—have been characterized by the rejection of the solid, bourgeois qualities which he praises in democracy.

As there is a degree of depravity in mankind which requires a certain degree of circumspection and distrust: So there are certain qualities in human nature, which justify a certain portion of esteem and confidence. Republican government presupposes the existence of these qualities in a higher degree than in any other form. Were the pictures which have been drawn by the political jealousy of some among us, faithful likenesses of the human character, the inference would be that *there is not sufficient virtue among men for self-government*; and that nothing less than the chains of despotism can restrain them from destroying and devouring each other. [emphasis added]

The American form of republican government, by its representative nature, indicates the Founders' faith that there *is* "sufficient virtue among men for self-government." The American character is not merely self-regarding. Men can, with the necessary institutional precautions, be trusted to represent the best interests of their fellow citizens. Neither are men merely driven by the spirit of acquisitiveness. They do indeed seek to acquire material wealth, but not to the point of extinguishing their capacity to admire and aspire to nobility and self-sacrifice. If the ancients regarded liberty as the condition of virtue, Americans tend to regard liberty *as* a virtue, that is, something good and desirable in itself. Liberty, thus understood, can stand as something worthy of noble self-sacrifice.

Republican freedom, thus understood, is not merely open-ended or licentious. Rather, the freedom necessary for self-rule requires a certain dignity, or sense of self-worth, for it is informed by the consciousness that self-restraint is the necessary condition of self-rule. It rests upon the recognition that I ought to be ashamed if I must rely on others to do for me what only I can do for myself; or that I have only myself to blame if, through lack of self-control, I miss opportunities for advancement. Merely indeterminate freedom cannot be distinguished from enslavement to the passions; and all liberation from the tyranny of the passions is of necessity self-liberation. The freedom *for* self-rule is the freedom of a people mature enough for self-rule. In its mature state, freedom cannot be separated from the consciousness that one's self-respect obliges one to respect the best interests of others.

The Declaration of Independence, deferring to this principle, acknowledges that the people of the United States are obliged, by "a decent respect for the opinions of mankind," to "declare the causes which impel" them to separate themselves from England. This language is echoed by *The Federalist*, #11, in a discussion of the national character of the United States, and the importance of such a character for eliciting "the esteem of foreign powers."

> [A] sensibility to the opinion of the world . . . is perhaps not less necessary *in order to merit, than it is to obtain, its respect and confidence*. An attention to the judgment of other nations is important to every government for two reasons: The one is, that independently of the merits of any particular plan or measure, it is desirable on various accounts, that it should appear to other nations as the offspring of a wise and honorable policy: The second is, that in doubtful cases, particularly where the national councils may be warped by some strong passion, or momentary interest, the presumed or known opinion of the impartial world, may be the best guide that can be followed. What has not America lost by her want of character with foreign nations? And how many errors and follies would she not have avoided, *if the justice and propriety of her measures had in every instance been previously tried by the light in which they would probably appear to the unbiased part of mankind*? [emphasis added]

We desire, not only the respect and confidence of the world, but also to be worthy of that respect and confidence. Moreover, we believe it to be a council of prudence that our national policies not only serve our interests, but display "justice and propriety" in the eyes of the "unbiased part of mankind." Accordingly, we need not view as incompatible the impartiality required by justice and propriety, on the one hand, and a due regard for our national interest, on the other. We shall not "shrink too timidly from the display of a partisanship which, on one side or the other, it would be insensate not to feel"; and, we shall regard it as the "true obligation of impartiality . . . that [one] should conceal no fact which, in his own mind, tells against his views."[32]

Thus, our national character seems to have been achieved through a *modification* of Locke's teaching. We acknowledge that the genesis of civil society contains an element of compulsion, and that a sober regard for self-interest and individual material well-being is indispensable. Yet, if a nation erected upon these principles is not an altogether edifying spectacle, it is nevertheless a secure haven.

If one's attachment to America is less ardent and immediate than that felt by the patriots of the ancient republics, it may still be more stable and enduring, being based upon assent to certain universal truths about human nature. We appeal to the permanent essence of nature and nature's God for the rectitude of our intentions, not to the vagaries of time and place, nor to special revelation, nor to a dubious sense of ethnic superiority. The source of our decency and sobriety, namely, our

---

32 Lord Charnwood, ed., *Abraham Lincoln* (New York: Henry Holt and Company, 1917), 2.

attachment to the principle of self-interest rightly understood, is also the cause of our enlightenment.

The principle of self-interest rightly understood enables us, on the one hand, to assert without embarrassment or contradiction, that the first object of government is to secure property rights; and, on the other, to insist that the "justice and propriety" of our policies be able to withstand the scrutiny of the "unbiased part of mankind." Accordingly, the Preamble of our Constitution is able to proclaim without hypocrisy that it was "ordained and established" to "establish justice," and to "promote the general welfare."

Publius thus appeals to a principle similar to what Adam Smith called the "impartial spectator," as a check on self-interest. Indeed, another great source of America's modification of Locke's teaching, is Adam Smith. In his first book, *The Theory of Moral Sentiments*, Smith demonstrates how a concern for the well-being of others may consist in human nature with the concern for one's own well-being. The mechanism by which this is achieved is the passion that Smith calls "sympathy," the natural human capacity for pity or compassion with the joys and sorrows of others. Man's natural gregariousness thus includes both self-concern, as well as sympathy for others. Smith's great correction of Locke, therefore, is that concern for others, being rooted in a passion, will be equally efficacious with the passion of self-interest. Dedication to the common good, therefore, does not depend entirely upon a calculation of reason, and will not inevitably be sacrificed to self-interest when the two conflict.

In his other great work, *The Wealth of Nations*, Smith evolves a system of economy, based, to be sure, upon the principle of self-interest, but one nevertheless compatible with the principle of sympathy. Taken together, these two books show how "economic man," the calculating, self-interested Lockean citizen, may be transformed into a man who is at once self-regarding and sociable. Accordingly, we now turn to a consideration of Smith's teaching, as he sets it forth in *The Theory of Moral Sentiments* and *The Wealth of Nations*.

# CHAPTER FOUR

# *Adam Smith*

I

Before beginning our discussion of the teaching of Adam Smith, we must first consider the contemporary understanding of capitalism, because the intellectual provenance of the contemporary understanding obstructs the effort to uncover the original understanding.

"Capitalism" is now generally used to designate that economic system devoted primarily to protecting capital and the interests of the owners of capital, or to creating and increasing capital by means of profits. Capital is accumulated wealth, the main purpose of which is to create more wealth for its owners, in the form of profits. This understanding of capitalism comes from Karl Marx, whose political teaching is primarily a critique of capitalism.

According to Marx, all political communities are divided into classes, and classes are defined primarily by their relation to the prevailing economic system, or to the prevailing material conditions in a political society. The material conditions in any given political society are the most important characteristic of that society. The economic facts of civil life are the most important for understanding the ends and social hierarchy of any political society.

In a capitalist society, so Marx taught, the most important classes are the capitalists and the workers. The owners of capital seek to promote their own material well being at the expense of the workers or producers. The value of goods results from the labor of the producers; but, the capitalists, although they produce nothing, claim a portion of the selling price of goods for themselves, in the form of profits. Thus, capitalist society is characterized primarily as a struggle between the owners of capital and the means of production, and the workers.

The only satisfactory and stable resolution to this struggle is the elimination of the private ownership of capital. No compromise or reform is possible. While it is true that members of the working class occasionally become owners of capital, this is not in their best interests. No one's best interests are served by the perpetuation of a capitalist economy. The workers may indeed wish to preserve the capitalist system in the belief that they too will someday become wealthy through owning capital; but, they are deluded in believing this to be in their interests. By perpetuating this belief, the capitalists and their lackeys keep the workers in thrall to the material interests of the capitalists.

Adam Smith also taught that capitalists exploit workers, in the sense that, although productive labor creates value, the capitalists claim a portion of the selling price of goods as their own, as a reward for having put their capital at risk in the first place. However, Smith disagrees with Marx's contention that the only resolution of the struggle between the capitalists and the workers is revolution and the abolition of private ownership of the means of production. According to Adam Smith, the wealth created by capitalists is spread throughout a society without the capitalists necessarily intending it. That is, the capitalists, by pursuing only their own material well being, promote the material well being of society as a whole. Marx denies this. He teaches that there are no classes without class struggle; and, each class struggles to overcome or destroy its opposing classes. There can be no compromise. As long as the private ownership of capital exists, human beings will continue to be divided, or, to use Marx's term, alienated, both from themselves and from their fellow human beings.

It is ironic that the very term most often used to designate our system of economy comes from the teaching of its most relentless critic, and not from the thinker who is credited with having discovered it. Adam Smith never uses the term "capitalism." Instead, he refers to his system of economy as the "system of natural liberty." By reflecting upon this difference of terms, one may begin to see more clearly the nature of the quarrel between Marx and Smith, and thus may begin to liberate oneself from the effects of Marx's influence on the current understanding of capitalism. One will then be prepared to understand Smith on his own terms.

Whereas Smith employs terms like "nature" and "liberty," which appear to apply to each human being simply as human without reference to a particular form of society, Marx refers to "capitalism" and "capitalists," terms which apply to some human beings but not to others, thus recalling Marx's teaching that human society is divided into classes; and, because the owners of capital are inevitably the oppressors of those who do not own capital, the term "capitalism" alludes to the inherent injustice of that system, and to the struggle between those who own capital and those who do not.

Capitalism, in Marx's account, appears essentially as a "point of view," or, to use the term invented or at least made famous by Marx, as an "ideology." An ideology is a set of opinions or manner of thinking characteristic of a particular class of human beings, but not of all human beings as such. Moreover, an ideology, although it may present itself as a universal or permanent truth about the human condition, in fact reflects only the "class interests" of those holding that opinion, where classes are determined fundamentally by economic interests.

An ideology, however, is not a lie. Most ideologues honestly believe that they are attempting to be dispassionate and non-partisan in their theoretical views; but, behind their backs, their material interests get the better of their theoretical interests. Dispassionate theoretical reason is in thrall to material interests. Marx proposed the daring thesis that all political and economic teachings prior to his, including that of Smith[1], are ideologies.

Marx also teaches that capitalism, as an ideology, depends upon certain "historical conditions," specifically those economic conditions and modes production which exist at a given time. As an "ism," capitalism thus refers to a set of conditions which are essentially transient. Therefore, it is a mistake, says Marx, to treat those categories which merely reflect capitalist practice, as though they referred to permanent, unchanging realities of economic life. Smith believed he had discovered certain permanent truths about man's social and economic condition, truths which depend upon the existence of unchanging things, like "nature," "human nature," and "liberty"; but Marx charged that Smith's teaching was itself only an ideology. As such, it depended essentially on the fact that Smith's own unacknowledged if not unconscious interest in maintaining the status quo prevented him from questioning the validity of the categories he used to analyze political economy.

---

[1] In effect, Marx charges that Smith is merely an apologist for capitalism. Though Marx distinguishes between its classical and vulgar forms, political economy is in his opinion a bourgeois science, which "first sprang into being during the period of manufacture." Engels, in his Preface to the English edition of *Capital*, writes, "Political economy has generally been content to take, just as they were, the terms of commercial and industrial life, and to operate with them, entirely failing to see that by so doing, it confined itself within the narrow circle of ideas expressed by those terms . . . [Thus] even classical Political Economy never went beyond the received notions of profits and rents, never examined this unpaid part of the product (called by Marx surplus-product) in its integrity as a whole, and therefore never arrived at a clear comprehension, either of its origin and nature, or of the laws that regulate the subsequent distribution of its value."

In particular, Marx asserted, Smith did not question the morality of *profit*. Without too much exaggeration, one may say that the fundamental disagreement between Smith and Marx concerns the moral status or legitimacy of profit. If all the value of commodities, or goods produced for exchange, comes from labor, as Smith apparently admitted, then, asked Marx, should not the one who labors to make the commodity receive whatever price is paid for that commodity? What justifies the owner of the "means of production," the capitalist, in taking a part of that price for himself as profit?

Smith's partial answer to this question appears in *The Wealth of Nations*:

> In exchanging the complete manufacture either for money, for labor, or for other goods, over and above what may be sufficient to pay the price of the materials, and the wages of the workmen, something must be given for the profits of the undertaker of the work who hazards his stock in this adventure. The value which the workmen add to the materials, therefore, resolves itself in this case into two parts, of which the one pays their wages, the other the profits of their employer upon the whole stock of materials and wages which he advanced. *He could have no interest to employ them, unless he expected from the sale of their work something more than what was sufficient to replace his stock to him; and he could have no interest to employ a great stock rather than a small one, unless his profits were to bear some proportion to the extent of his stock.* [2] [emphasis added]

That is, absent any interest on the part of the owner of capital, or, absent his expectation of getting back a sum of money in excess of the amount necessary to replenish his stock, the laborers would have no work. Moreover, it is his expectation that his profits will be proportional to the amount of stock he employs, which induces the owner of capital to risk a greater stock.

In this passage, therefore, Smith appears to be relatively unconcerned about the very question which exercised Marx so greatly, namely the question of the moral justification of profit. Even the casual reader of *The Wealth of Nations* will notice Smith's relative complacency regarding the moral status of profit. Smith's unconcern becomes even more perplexing when one recalls that, according to his "labor theory of value," all value of commodities, that is, goods produced for exchange, is due to labor. Should not all the price of the sale of the commodity therefore go to the laborer?

---

[2] Adam Smith, *The Wealth of Nations*, ed. Edward Canaan (Norman Berg, 1976), 48 (hereafter cited as *WON*).

In apparent disregard for this consequence of his own theory of value, Smith seems to imply in this passage that, were it not for his expectation of profit, the owner of capital would not employ it, and the laborer would have no work. Given that others were employed by the capitalist as the consequence of his decision, perhaps one ought to be grateful that the owner of capital *did* put his capital at risk, even if he was motivated to do so by his expectation of making a profit. At any rate, the sense of this passage appears to be that, whatever one may think of the capitalist's motives, a tangible benefit accrues to others in society on account of those motives, however questionable they might be morally. Perhaps one ought to be willing to live with an element of moral irregularity, in exchange for the resulting addition to the general wealth of the society.

Smith thus appears indifferent to the motive of the entrepreneur; that is, he appears to be unconcerned with the morality of profit. Does this mean that his system, the system of natural liberty, is either immoral or amoral?

There is, however, another possibility. Perhaps Smith believed that "the profit motive" is rooted in something permanent in human nature, some ineradicable human concern for acquiring the means of preserving one's life, or for the improvement of one's material well-being. To be sure, Smith would not thereby be prevented from believing that human nature also includes other permanent concerns. The profit motive need not be the only or even the dominant motive. If, however, the profit motive *is* founded upon some permanent and irrepressible passion in human nature, then perhaps it would be more prudent and humane to accommodate or channel that passion, to mitigate its harmful tendencies while encouraging its beneficial ones, rather than to suppress it. In that case, it would be better to establish a system of economy that allowed human acquisitiveness a certain degree of freedom and scope, consistent with a respect for the rule of law. If in addition the system of economy were such that others benefited from the capitalist's desire to profit from the employment of his stock, then so much the better. The benefits accruing to society from such a system might very well outweigh the disadvantages; and means might also be found partially to mitigate those disadvantages.

It is indeed from this perspective that one must view Smith's teaching. Although the initial question raised above concerned the moral status of profit, it now appears that there is a prior question, namely, the question concerning the existence and specific character of human nature, which must be addressed, before one can judge Smith's teaching. It is all very well to condemn capitalism because of the alleged immorality of profit.[3] If, however, Smith is right about human nature, perhaps one ought to be willing allow certain economic improprieties to exist if the resulting benefits to society outweigh them.

Moreover, given the specific character of human nature, perhaps one would do immeasurably greater harm in trying to eliminate those improprieties than in allowing them to exist. After all, any system of economy, even one managed with the intention of achieving an equitable distribution of wealth, would still have to be managed by human beings. Would the managers, however compassionate their intentions, be any less susceptible to the attractions of economic gain than would the owners of capital? One must conclude that any critique, including Marx's, which does not show that Smith is mistaken about human nature, fails to engage the question of the morality of profit at its most fundamental level.

Obviously, one could agree with Smith's analysis of human nature, but disagree with his conclusion, namely, that the system of natural liberty is the best economic system. One might then say that, precisely because human beings are by nature acquisitive and self-interested, it is necessary to regulate the economy to ensure that some do not get richer than they need to be while others become poorer than they should be. This is the requirement of simple justice. That is, the quarrel between Marx and Smith could proceed on their common acceptance of Smith's understanding of human nature. In that case, the question becomes, Is justice better served by an economic teaching which encourages a nation and its people to increase their wealth without limit; or, is it more just to subordinate the acquisition of wealth to a policy aimed at remedying the inequitable distribution of wealth?[4]

Even formulated in this manner, however, the question may still fail to do justice to the subtlety of Smith's teaching, for the following reason: Smith believed he had hit upon a way of helping solve what is perhaps *the* political problem, namely, that of reconciling self-interest with the concern for the well-being of others, a concern which is necessary for there to be a political community. As we have seen, the Founders and the author of *The Federalist* believed that this problem is especially

---

[3] The question of the immorality of profit is obviously not the same as the question whether some profits are gotten immoraly.
[4] The third possibility, the one taught by writers like Aristotle, is that a political society ought to inculcate its citizens with certain virtues, among them temperance, and liberality, the virtue of moderating one's desire for getting wealth while being generous in giving of one's own substance.

acute in a republic based upon the principle of the primacy of the natural rights of individual human beings. They also believed, however, that one must find a way to moderate self-interest and make it tractable to a concern for the common welfare. This is to be achieved, not by forcibly subordinating self-interest to duty, but by *enlightening* self-interest. To enlighten self-interest, you must show that an attachment to the common good is congenial to or promotes self-interest.

Smith's solution to this problem is fully in the conciliatory spirit characteristic of modern political thought, in that it seeks a way to avoid opposing interest by duty. His solution is based upon the two fundamental human passions, self-interest or the desire for material gain, and sympathy. According to Smith, these two passions are the roots of human sociability, and thus of human society.

Smith's project, therefore, is to show how sympathy, a sociable passion, can mitigate the less desirable effects of acquisitiveness or the desire for material gain, which is itself an unsociable passion, without having recourse to duty. Smith's reason for playing the passions against one another in this way is not cynical. He is not indifferent to considerations of duty. Neither does he believe that human beings are indifferent to duty. Rather, Smith believes that, for the most part, human beings are more likely to be motivated by their passions and desires than by reason.[5] Accordingly, one must look to the passions themselves for the source of human society. Moreover, human society will, in the best case, aim at satisfying man's natural gregariousness, as well as his desire for security and material well-being.

For example, while one might acknowledge that, in order to comply with the rational requirements of justice, it is necessary to eliminate disparities of wealth from society, one might nevertheless be wary of producing in society those divisions that inevitably result when one takes from some so that others might have. Those from whom one takes will resent it, and those to whom one gives may come to regard it as their just due. It is not difficult to imagine the resentment, mutual hostility, and indolence which would likely result from such a policy. In that case, it is conceivable that more, and not less division and resentment would result, than in a system where all were guaranteed only the freedom and opportunity to acquire wealth, even at the expense of the occasional unequal distribution of wealth. In the latter system, the sympathy which, says Smith, human beings naturally have for one

---

5 Of course, one *may* decide to obey reason; but Smith's point is in part that, for most of us most of the time, it requires considerably more effort of will to obey reason and resist our inclinations, than to do the reverse.

another's suffering, would more likely have greater salutary effect. In the former system, where duty would always be externally imposed and enforced, resentment would get the better of sympathy.[6]

We conclude our initial discussion of the meaning of the term "capitalism" by suggesting a further point of connection between capitalism and liberal democracy. Publius argues in *Federalist* #10 that the causes of faction in political society are inherent to human nature: as long as human beings are free and their reason fallible, there will always be factions. In particular, there will always be economic factions. The "first object" of government is to protect those "faculties of men from which the rights of property originate." By protecting "different and unequal faculties of acquiring property," government ensures the "possession of different degrees and kinds of property." And, "from the influence of these on the sentiments and views of the respective proprietors, ensues a division of society into different interests and parties." Human beings are prone to form themselves into factions of different kinds; but, "the most common and durable source of factions, has been the various and unequal distribution of property." Contradicting Marx's view that the opposition of economic classes is overcome by the dialectical movement of history, Publius asserts that "[t]hose who hold, and those who are without property, have ever formed distinct interests in society." Political liberty and economic liberty cannot be separated; and, where liberty exists, there also will exist the unequal distribution of property. Is the unequal distribution of property unjust? No, not in principle: Publius says at the end of *Federalist* #10 that the equal division of property is a "wicked project." You deserve to keep what you earn, even if you earn more than someone else. Disparity of wealth can be eliminated only by eliminating liberty. The injustice that results from encouraging economic factions to proliferate will be considerably less than that which results from attempts to regulate an economy.

We have argued that Marx was able to criticize what he called "capitalism" only by denying the two principles on which Smith had based his teaching, namely, nature and liberty. Did Marx thereby refute Smith? The reader of Marx must determine whether Marx *demonstrated* that Smith's principles are false, or whether Marx merely *disagreed* with Smith. This means that one must determine whether Marx succeeded in showing that the "bourgeois" categories of liberty

---

[6] Indeed, polls tend to show that Americans do not resent the wealthy, as long as they believe them to have earned their wealth.

and nature were indeed superseded by what he called "the dialectic of history."

Marx may be said to have discovered, if he did not invent, "history," in the distinctively modern sense of that term. History is not merely what happened in the past, nor is it merely an account of what happened in the past. According to Marx, history doesn't just happen. Neither is history "made." Human beings make history, but history also remakes human nature.

By "history," Marx therefore obviously does not mean what was once meant by history. Historians like Thucydides and Gibbon wrote about certain great events in human affairs, in order to discern and transmit lessons about human nature, lessons which are universally true. The great historians taught that human history, despite its great variety, is unified by the permanence of human nature. The more things change, the more they stay the same. History, according to Marx, has its own internal logic, its own laws. The name Marx gives to the process of history, and the laws of its unfolding, is "dialectic." Any stage in history contains within itself, and finally gives rise to, its own negation or destruction; but the negation of any stage of history is not its annihilation. Something is preserved, but elevated to a higher level. For example, capitalism, although it is doomed to pass from the scene, contains the seed of the truly rational society, a society based upon the principle, "from each according to his ability, to each according to his need." Marx believed that history culminates in the rational society.

History, according to Marx, is a species of change or motion. All things, human and non-human, are, says Marx, in motion or flux. Nothing simply *is*, not even God. God does not exist, except as the projection of human consciousness or imagination. The economic injustice and misery of our lives here and now causes us to yearn for a God, or some permanent realm, where things simply *are*. Human life, however, is subject to the law of motion which governs all change. Like all other motion, human life as change results from *contradiction*. Each thing "exists" only dialectically, by becoming its opposite, and by "negating" that very opposite.

Human history is itself a dialectical process. History unfolds in accordance with the permanent laws of this dialectical process. What is the specific cause of this unfolding in the case of history? It is the "mode of production" which prevails in a given society. One writer describes the dialectic of history and its cause as follows:

> Because the primary phenomenon is the material conditions of production, the Marxist doctrine of history is called dialectical materialism, to

distinguish it from the idealist dialectic of Hegel which asserted the primary phenomenon to be the self-dependent reason as the source of historical change. As a theory of human life, dialectical materialism asserts that the ground of all development in society and understanding is contradiction in the order of production. The most massive of such contradictions is the conflict between classes in society. By subsuming the opposition of class interests under the apparatus of dialectic, Marxism seeks to show that the conflict cannot be resolved through compromises or mutual accommodations but only by a 'negation of the negation,' *i.e.*, by revolutionary changes in which the existing classes are annihilated and replaced by a synthesis 'on a higher level.' . . . The contradiction [in human society] between existent social relations and the emergent mode of production, *i.e.*, clash between the established and the embryonic dominant classes, is the source of 'all collisions in history.'[7]

It is absolutely essential to note this, for the following reason. Despite their professed belief in "history," socialists have not been convinced by the historical failure of Marxism, that the principles of socialism are theoretically unsound. For them, the moral ideal of socialism remains intact. By their continued loyalty to the moral ideal of socialism in the face of its historical failure, the socialists appear to testify to their belief in the existence of a realm of theoretical truth existing independently of historical, that is, material conditions.[8] This fact suggests that, contrary to Marx's teaching, the defenders of socialism believe that human thought and rationality are not merely reflections of existing material conditions: thought is not simply reducible to matter. Accordingly, one must continue to engage the socialists on theoretical grounds. The fight between Smith and Marx is a fight over moral principles.

The great gulf separating liberal democracy and capitalism from

---

[7] Joseph Cropsey, "Karl Marx," in *The History of Political Philosophy*, Third Edition, ed. Strauss and Cropsey (Chicago: University of Chicago Press, 1987), 812-813.

[8] The other possibility is that the continued loyalty of the socialists indicates a belief in the triumph of the *will* over adversity, all evidence to the contrary notwithstanding. In this case, however, the socialists reject a fundamental teaching of Marx, namely that the dialectical movement of history is in the direction of and culminates in the overcoming of all class distinctions in the society where the means of production are owned by all. According to Marx, it is history which "justifies" the end; whereas the undying loyalty of the socialists would seem to imply that they have replaced history by the triumph of the will. In that case, Nazism and Communism are seen to have a common root.

socialism is represented by the very terms Smith employs to name his system, "nature" and "liberty." Marx denies that there is such a thing as "nature," unless by "nature" one means only "matter." The natural world, according to Marx, is merely material, stuff to be worked on and transformed, to be used and shaped, having in itself no shape or form, end or purpose.

In particular, Marx rejects the view that human nature determines the good for man, and thus the good for human beings living in political society. Human life is driven by man's animal needs, which are themselves determined by conditions external to man's reason, conditions which are only material. Accordingly, Marx also rejects the belief that there exists a realm of human freedom, essentially undetermined by the material conditions of history.

It is essential to Marx's critique of capitalism not only to deny the existence of nature as containing some end or good for human beings, but to *demonstrate* that nature is overcome or replaced by "history." As a process unfolding in accordance with its own internal logic, history culminates in the eventual transformation of political society into a "classless," and therefore, Marx concludes, truly free and just society. *According to Marx, the belief in nature is itself an ideology.* The failure to demonstrate the overcoming of nature by history would thus, at the very least, amount to a begging of the question in Marx's critique of capitalism, insofar as capitalism itself asserts the existence of a permanent natural order.

Marx denies the existence of "human nature," some enduring thing in human beings which makes us all human, recognizable to one another as human, no matter where or when we happen to exist. According to the old fashioned view, styles and manners may change, technology may advance in unimaginable ways, but human nature stays the same. The old view taught that it is only by understanding human nature that one can discern man's purpose, the end that guides action to the attainment of human happiness. Marx denies this. Man's "nature" is really the *result* of history, which is itself driven by existing material conditions.

Returning to our discussion of Marx's critique of capitalism, we note that, although capitalist production does encourage men to employ their productive abilities in accordance with the needs of other men, the form of this use under capitalism is *exploitation*. Ability is made to serve need; but the desire for material gain forces men to produce beyond what is required merely for the satisfaction of needs. Men of ambition and ability get rich by exploiting the needs of other men.

Goods are produced, not for the sake of the one truly rational end of production, namely, satisfying human needs. Instead, goods are produced for the sake of exchange for profit. In the final, socialist society, production will allow the abilities of men scope; but production will be altruistic, that is, guided only by the real, as opposed to imagined or artificial needs. Thus, ability and need, linked in capitalistic society by greed and exploitation, will be linked by the purely rational consideration of genuine needs, and their satisfaction.

We have said that, according to Marx, man's history is determined by the material conditions of his society, or by the mode and ownership of the means of production that predominate in a given historical epoch. Man's nature is the result of the pressure of his animal needs, and the means of production he employs in different epochs to satisfy those needs. The sign of man's humanity is conscious production for the purpose of satisfying his needs, precisely because he is primarily determined by those needs. Human nature is thus indistinguishable from the nature of any other animal.

Similarly, man's "liberty" is determined by the given historical conditions. Only in the final society, the post-revolutionary Marxist society from which all class struggle will have disappeared, will man be truly free, and thus truly moral. Human freedom is fully achieved only at the end of history, in the culmination of the dialectical struggle between conflicting class interests.[9]

## II

Compassion, or one particular meaning of that term, is now thought to be *the* great political virtue: society has a duty to be compassionate. As recently as 1960, however, an American President could exhort Americans to "ask not what your country can do for you, but what you can do for your country." Now, however, almost every contender for political office seems to base his appeal to the electorate on

---

[9] We note in passing an apparent difficulty in Marx's teaching. Man, like all other animals, is determined by his material needs. His consciousness and rationality are derivative, not fundamental. On the other hand, human production is characterized by rational intention. Man plans his production and his projects; but, to emphasize man's rationality would contradict Marx's teaching that consciousness depends *fundamentally* on its ambient material conditions and the existing means of production. It is therefore open to question whether Marx was able, without contradicting himself, to deny the existence of a human nature which transcends the material conditions of the moment. See Cropsey, "Karl Marx," 803.

his superior compassion for the disadvantaged, the victims of society's alleged indifference, if not outright hostility. Government is, by implication, thought to be the principal agent of compassion.

It may, therefore, surprise some to learn that Adam Smith, the founder of that system of political economy thought by some to be characterized principally by its lack of compassion, had himself reflected deeply on the nature of human compassion, or as he called it, "sympathy." Moreover, Smith had, in his first book, *The Theory of Moral Sentiments*, sought to understand all of human morality in terms of the natural capacity of human beings to sympathize with the suffering of others.

To be sure, by "sympathy," Smith did not mean exactly the same thing that is now meant by the term "compassion." Sympathy is, writes Smith, "the emotion we feel for the misery of others, when we either see it, or are made to conceive it in a very lively manner."[10] Whereas "compassion" now means something like "active benevolence," or "charity," Smith used the term "sympathy" in its more literal meaning of "feeling with" another human being. Moreover, compassion, as it is now understood, is selective. Unlike sympathy, compassion does not spontaneously extend to other human beings, regardless of their station in society. Instead, compassion is reserved for certain groups of disadvantaged human beings, the "victims" of society.

It is important to stress these differences in meaning. The contemporary use of "compassion" includes a sense of *duty*, not to the less fortunate as such, but to the victims of society's injustice; whereas for Smith, sympathy, being literally a feeling, did not by itself impose any moral obligation, and extended to human beings merely as human. Sympathy is both humanizing and sociable, whereas, in its contemporary sense, compassion is condescending and divisive. Smith's great achievement was to show how sympathy lies at the base of our sense of moral propriety, and thus makes moral life possible.

One should refrain from concluding, therefore, that Smith's teaching may be separated into two unrelated parts, namely, *The Theory of Moral Sentiments*, which treats of the altruistic dimension of human actions, and *The Wealth of Nations*, which treats of the egoistic side. This would be fundamentally to misunderstand Smith's guiding intention, which is precisely to show how the *division* between altruism and egoism, or, to use older words, duty, and the passions or inclinations associated with self-interest, may be overcome. This project, in general,

---

10 Adam Smith, *The Theory of Moral Sentiments*, ed. Raphael and MacFie, (New York: Oxford University Press, 1976), 9 (hereafter cited as *TOMS*).

guided the efforts of the great political thinkers of modernity to whom the American Founders looked as their teachers. In particular, this is the project of Adam Smith and his great predecessor, John Locke. It is, fundamentally, a *moral* project.

Gertrude Himmelfarb makes this point well:

> The basic themes of the *Wealth of Nations* are too familiar to need elaboration: the division of labor making for increased productivity and thus the increased "opulence" of all society; the fundamental facts of human nature—self-interest (or "self-love") . . . One subject that did not appear in the chapter titles or sub-heads was poverty. Yet this was as much a theme of the book as wealth itself. Indeed, it may be argued that if the *Wealth of Nations* was less than novel in its theories of money, trade, or value, it was genuinely revolutionary in its attitude toward the poor. It was not, however, revolutionary in the sense which is often supposed: the demoralization of the economy resulting from the doctrine of *laissez faire*, the demoralization of man implied in the image of "economic man," and the demoralization of the poor who found themselves at the mercy of forces over which they had no control—over which, according to the new political economy, no one had any control. This is a common reading of the *Wealth of Nations*, but not a just one. For it supposes that Smith's idea of a market economy was devoid of moral purpose, that his concept of human nature was mechanistic and reductivist, and that his attitude towards the poor was indifferent or callous. Above all it fails to take account of the fact that Smith was a moral philosopher, by conviction as well as profession. As Professor of Moral Philosophy at the University of Glasgow and the celebrated author of *The Theory of Moral Sentiments*, he could hardly have thought it his mission to preside over the dissolution of moral philosophy. [11]

Smith's concern for morality is immediately apparent in the opening paragraph of *The Theory of Moral Sentiments*:

> *How selfish soever man may be supposed*, there are evidently some principles in his nature, which interest him in the fortune of others, and render their happiness necessary to him, *though he derives nothing from it except the pleasure of seeing it*. Of this kind is pity or compassion, the emotion which we feel for the misery of others, when we either see it, or are made to conceive it in a very lively manner. That we often derive sorrow from the sorrow of others, is a matter of fact too obvious to require any instances to prove it; for this sentiment, like all the other original passions of human nature, is by no means confined to the virtuous and humane,

---

[11] Gertrude Himmelfarb, "Adam Smith: Political Economy as Moral Philosophy," *The St. John's Review* Winter-Spring (1983): 5.

though they perhaps may feel it with the most exquisite sensibility. The greatest ruffian, the most hardened violator of the laws of society, is not altogether without it.[12] [emphasis added]

Smith agreed with his great modern predecessors, that self-interest decisively influences human action; but self-interest is not the only fundamental passion in human nature. Sympathy, which, unlike self-interest, is essentially a sociable passion, is the other. Accordingly, the student of Adam Smith is obliged to understand how, in Smith's view, the system of morality elaborated in *The Theory of Moral Sentiments* fits with the system of economy set forth in *The Wealth of Nations*.

Neither the founders of the American republic, nor their great teachers, John Locke and Adam Smith, seemed very much concerned with compassion in its modern meaning[13]; and they most emphatically rejected the radical egalitarianism, now thought by some to be the essence of liberal democracy. They believed that the politically relevant sense of equality is what Locke called equality of "jurisdiction," according to which no one human being is naturally the ruler of another. Furthermore, they believed that each human being is the equal of any other with respect to his naturally endowed rights. They drew the conclusion that each human being is, in this sense, the political equal of any other human being, and has the right to "the equal protection of the laws" in civil society. Beyond this carefully specified sense of equality, both the Founders and their teachers insisted that certain inequalities must be tolerated in a civil society, either because those inequalities are natural, or because they are the result of differing degrees of ability and effort, or because the cost of eliminating them is too high.

Indeed, as we saw above, one crucial premise in the argument of *Federalist* #10, which gives the American solution to the problem of

---

[12] Smith, *TOMS*, 9.

[13] Indeed, in *The Theory of Moral Sentiments*, Smith refers to "those whining and melancholy moralists, who are perpetually reproaching us with our happiness, while so many of our brethren are in misery, who regard as impious the natural joy of prosperity, which does not think of the many wretched that are at every instant labouring under all sorts of calamities, in the languor of poverty, in the agony of disease, in the horrors of death, under the insults and oppression of their enemies. Commiseration for those miseries which we never saw, which we never heard of, but which we may be assured are at all times infesting such numbers of our fellow-creatures, ought, they think, to damp the pleasures of the fortunate, and to render a certain melancholy dejection habitual to all men." This passage may remind one of the way in which good economic news is frequently reported by the major news media.

political faction, is that equal economic opportunity inevitably results in disparities of wealth. Smith's great discovery was that free market economies mitigate this disparity more effectively and more fairly than any managed economy could, precisely because the forces at work in such economies are "impersonal," in the sense of not being controlled by the greed, manipulation, or caprice of any one individual human being. Furthermore, because in a free market economy, any man may compete with any other, each human being becomes, at least potentially, the economic equal of any other. Thus, the system of natural liberty is the natural complement to a political system which sees equality principally in terms of equal rights and equal opportunities.

Because of the success of the radical critique of capitalism, the principles and virtues which were part of the original understanding of liberal democracy and capitalism have been discarded, and new ones have taken their place; but the new principles and virtues are alien to the original understanding of democracy and capitalism. Therefore, democracy and capitalism are now criticized in accordance with standards which contradict their original intention. Compassion and equality, as they are now understood, in fact violate the requirements of the principle of justice upon which the American republic was founded.

### III

The great tradition of political thought in which Locke and Smith stood holds that justice has to do with the common, as contrasted with the private, good. The common good is that one good thing—virtue, peace and security, equal participation in ruling and being ruled—in which all citizens may share, a good which is itself not diminished by being shared in: there is always enough to go round. By definition, then, the common good is that good for which there can be no competition. By sharing in the common good, a collection of individual human beings is transformed into a community. In this sense, laws are called just which, as Aristotle says, "aim at the common advantage." Laws which aim only at the private advantage of a particular group are unjust. It is just, therefore, that the law be no respecter of persons. Therefore, one point of contact between justice and equality is that all are equal before the law.

This understanding of justice considers, therefore, the good, not of oneself alone, but of others as well. Justice, in contrast with individual virtues such as courage or temperance, is understood to be essentially concerned with one's actions which affect the well-being of others. Being concerned with what is due another, justice thus involves the notion of duty or obligation. As Thomas Aquinas writes, "To each one is due what is his own," and "it evidently pertains to justice that a man give another his due." Accordingly "justice *alone*, of all the virtues, implies the notion of duty."[14] [emphasis added] Thus, when one treats others justly, when one gives to another his due, one does no more than duty requires.

One great debate in the history of Western political thought concerned the sufficiency of justice, understood in the foregoing sense, for establishing a good society. Immanuel Kant, for example, believed that if perfect justice, in the sense of each one giving the other his due, could be achieved, then a collection of individual human beings would be transformed into a perfect harmony of freely acting and willing citizens. Aquinas disagreed with this view, believing instead that justice is necessary to a good society, but not sufficient. He writes, "Peace is the *work of justice* indirectly, in so far as justice removes the obstacles to peace; but it is the *work of charity* directly, since charity, according to its very nature, causes peace; for love is *a unitive force*."[15]

According to Aquinas, then, the commands of justice may oblige men to give one another their due, in the sense of not harming one another. These commands do not, however, thereby positively enjoin charity; but, it is charity that unites human beings in a community. For this reason, one great tradition in the history of Western political thought teaches that mercy and charity are necessary to complete justice, or where necessary, set it aside . Thus Portia, in the *Merchant of Venice*, says "Earthly power doth then show likest God's when mercy seasons justice."

A moment's reflection on the precept "to give others their due" will prompt one to ask, What precisely is due or owed another human being? The adequate answer to this question reveals two other dimensions of justice, which the West, following Aristotle, has called "corrective justice" and "distributive justice." Corrective justice determines the just penalty for one who has committed a crime; and distributive justice has to do with the fair exchange of goods and the distribution of honors.

In his discussion of justice in the *Nicomachean Ethics*, Aristotle says that fairness in the exchange and distribution of goods or honors must be understood in terms of equality; and, similarly with the meting out of punishment. This means, however, that it is unjust for all to be treated equally without regard to condition or achievement. It is fair to

---

14 Thomas Aquinas, Summa Theologica, I-II, q. 90.

15 Ibid., q. 90.

give honors or rewards to those who deserve them; but it is also unfair to give the same honors and rewards to those who do not deserve them. That is, it is fair for awards and goods to be distributed according to merit, where merit may be based on condition or achievement.

Aristotle states that all human beings agree with this principle, "though they do not all specify the same sort of merit, but democrats identify it with the status of freeman, supporters of oligarchy with wealth or with noble birth, and supporters of aristocracy with excellence." That is, although all human beings agree that it is just for those of equal merit to get equal shares of good things, they do not agree upon the criterion of merit. For example, in an oligarchy, the criterion of merit is wealth or birth. It is equality with respect to wealth or birth which governs the fair distribution of goods and honors. The otherwise deserving poor man is not given an equal share in honors or political power. Similarly, in a democracy the criterion of merit is one's equality in freely participating in ruling and being ruled. Those who are equal in respect of being freemen are equally deserving of goods and honors. The naturally gifted or well-born get no more than anyone else, even though they may believe themselves to be more deserving on account of their superior talent or birth.

Because corrective and distributive justice are the principles which direct the fair exchange and distribution of goods, they are immediately relevant to any discussion of Adam Smith, whose system of natural liberty was conceived as a means of achieving the most equitable distribution of wealth, consistent with its maximization through the free efforts of individuals to improve their own material well-being. Indeed, Smith's great insight was that the system of free enterprise exploits man's natural acquisitiveness to achieve a general diffusion of wealth, precisely by encouraging the maximization of wealth. The radical critique of capitalism accuses it of creating, and even justifying, disparities of wealth, which are thought to violate the democratic principle of equality. It is here, therefore, where one must look to find Smith's answer to his critics.

When the transaction in question is an exchange of goods, or involves rewarding the expenditure of labor in the production of goods, we have then specifically to do with economic justice. Agreeing with one strand of the great tradition of Western political thought, Smith emphatically did not regard economic justice as something independent of considerations of political justice, which concerns itself with the status of human beings in a political community. He would have rejected the contemporary view, according to which economics is an autonomous discipline, proceeding independently of questions of political justice and morality. One must immediately add that Smith, like most political thinkers before the nineteenth century, also would reject the contemporary understanding of political science as a "value-free" discipline, which, as "scientific," limits itself to studying the distribution and use of power, while rejecting as unscientific the question of the just use of that power. Smith insists that the proper working of the system of natural liberty presupposes the existence of just government.

It is within this context that one must raise and answer the question of Smith's understanding of economic justice. According to Smith, *the unequal distribution of wealth is not as such unjust.* Neither does it necessarily conflict with the principle of democracy, which, to be sure, is equality, but equality emphatically understood as *equality of freedom.* Freedom, in turn, is understood by Smith to mean what we now call "equal opportunity." The system of natural liberty must allow each citizen to employ his capital in competition with any other citizen. Unequal distribution of wealth is inevitable in any society; but the inequities in the system of natural liberty will be less egregious than in other societies.

Moreover, any artificial effort by government to "correct" the unequal distribution of wealth will inevitably result in injustices greater than the inequities it set out to correct. Indeed, such an effort will itself violate the principle of justice according to which goods or rewards are to be distributed equally to equals: inferior effort or achievement will be rewarded equally with superior.[16] Human neediness, which previously had been regarded as the proper object of charity or

---

16 There exist critiques of capitalism which rely on empirical evidence allegedly showing that capitalism produces disparities of wealth, which it does not ameliorate but aggravates. These critiques then conclude that capitalism requires correction by some form of welfare state, or by socialism. *All such critiques which fail to show that their empirical data are taken from genuinely free market economies beg the question.* That is, it must first be shown that the disparities in question, if they in fact exist, resulted from policies congenial to free enterprise. For example, the United States has one of the highest costs of capital among the free market nations. Economic data on business failures, job growth, and so forth, which do not consider the deterrent effect of high capital costs, do not necessarily show the deficiencies of capitalism as such. The defenders of socialism often disparage appeals to facts which show the failure of socialist policies. They reply by saying that the facts show only that socialism hasn't worked, not that it won't work. "Pure" socialism has yet to be tried. Surely the defenders of capitalism deserve the same consideration.

benevolence,[17] will create both the presumption of injustice and the corresponding obligation upon government to correct it. In addition, the redistribution of wealth, through "transfers" and similar policies, will be a great disincentive to the industrious poor. Why should they labor to acquire wealth only to have it taken from them once they succeed? Policies of redistribution will thus reduce the annual economic output, resulting, to be sure, in equality, but an equality of penury. The equality envisioned by Smith, on the contrary, is an equality, if not of riches, then of the opportunity to acquire them. The compassion of the system of natural liberty lies, not in its proscription upon achievement, but in its firm insistence that equality of opportunity is no respecter of persons.

Accordingly, one may say that Smith's teaching on the system of natural liberty pertains essentially to the traditional questions concerning material wealth: what is wealth? what is economic justice, and how ought material wealth be pursued so as to conform to it? how ought wealth be distributed in a society? and so forth. However, Smith also accepts most of the premises of modern political philosophy, premises which contradict the teaching of both classical antiquity and the Bible at certain important points.[18]

Ancient writers like Plato believed that the best political society would be ruled by the wise, those who knew the human good insofar as it was attainable in and through political life. In the best society, selfishness would be overcome, or made to harmonize with dedication to the common good. As such, the best society was unlikely ever to exist, and one was accordingly obliged to turn one's attention to the political good attainable here and now. The best political society did not, for all that, cease to be *the* standard to which the political philosopher looked, and by which he took his bearings in reflecting upon the nature of political life.

Modern political thinkers, beginning with Machiavelli, were unwilling to live with the uncertainty that the best political society,

---

[17] See Smith, *WON*, 14: "Nobody but a beggar chooses to depend chiefly upon the benevolence of his fellow-citizens."

[18] We may summarize our earlier discussion of the modern premises as follows. Human passion is stronger than human reason in directing man to his proper end. Modernity disconnects reason from the good; the passions more surely guide man to his natural end than does reason. Reason is ancillary to the attainment of the ends set by the passions. One great division, therefore, between modern political philosophy and classical and biblical antiquity, is the modern concern with *certainty*.

understood in the ancient sense, would ever be realized. Let us desist, said Machiavelli, from our obsession with nobility and selfless dedication to the common good, and concentrate instead on the lower but more reliable human concerns for security, comfort and material well-being, and stability. It was in this spirit that Locke carried on his reflections upon human nature and the true origin of self-preservation in the nature of human consciousness.

As we saw in the discussion above, Locke teaches that the passion of self-preservation is rooted in the very being of the human person, understood essentially as self. Because to be a self is to be self-concerned, the fear of death and the resulting desire for self-preservation predominate over the other passions. Accordingly, collectivities of human selves arise, not because human nature is incomplete outside the political association and is thus drawn to political life, but because human beings are compelled by their neediness and exposed condition, to form communities, for their mutual self-preservation and protection of property. Human beings may be gregarious, but as selves, they are not naturally political. That is, human beings are not naturally drawn to live in a society united by a shared opinion of the good, or justice. Political society is necessary, because of human weakness and selfishness; it is, however, not desirable as something that essentially completes human nature.

Smith, as we have said, accepts many of these conclusions. Therefore, agreeing with other modern political thinkers, Smith does not teach that human virtue lies in the moderation of the passions by reason. This would be futile, or even counterproductive. Instead, the goal of political thought is to find the appropriate means to play the passions off against one another, to set up in the passions a system of "checks and balances," whereby certain desirable effects may be achieved, without the onerous and counter-productive imposition of duty.

In particular, the passion of sympathy, appears to be a sociable passion, one which involves our concern with the well-being or suffering of others. This passion will, says Smith, counteract, or even complement, the passion of self-interest, without requiring that self-interest transform itself into self-sacrifice.

Smith elaborates his moral teaching, based upon the assumption that self-interest and sympathy are original, fundamental human passions, in his book, *The Theory of Moral Sentiments*. Furthermore, Smith assumes this moral teaching when he presents his economic teaching, in *The Wealth of Nations*. Taken as a whole, Smith's philosophy elaborates a moral and economic teaching that gives scope to the acquisitive part of human nature, while mitigating the less attractive effects of free competition by encouraging sympathy.

What does Smith mean by "sympathy"? What is its function in his moral teaching? How does his teaching on sympathy affect his economic teaching? What, in other words, is the moral foundation of capitalism? In the course of answering this question, we must also raise and answer the question, "What is capitalism?" As we noted above, Smith never uses the word "capitalism," using instead the phrase "the system of natural liberty." Smith emphatically does, however, use the term "capital." We must therefore rephrase our initial question, and divide it into two parts: 1) What is the "system of natural liberty"; 2) What is "capital," and what is its connection to the "system of natural liberty"?

## IV

The phrase "system of natural liberty" appears in *The Wealth of Nations* in the context of Smith's critique of mercantilism, and other forms of artificially managed economies. By mercantilism, Smith meant a system of economy concerned principally with the "balance of trade," that is, with the net difference between a country's imports and exports. The guiding principle of mercantilism is always to maintain a "favorable" balance of trade: there should always be a trade surplus, never a trade deficit. All other things being equal, exports should always exceed imports. The normal way of encouraging a favorable balance of trade, therefore, is through the use of tariffs on imports.

Smith's occasionally vituperative criticisms of mercantilism are motivated mainly by what he regards as its fundamental error: like King Midas, mercantilism confuses money with wealth. Money is not wealth; rather, it is a means of acquiring wealth. On account of his confusion, the mercantilist believes that, if a country exports more than it imports—that is, if its sells to other countries more than it buys from them—then it is wealthier than those other countries. If country A sells two billion dollars' worth of goods to country B, but buys only one billion dollars' worth, then, according to the mercantilist, country A is wealthier than country B by one billion dollars. If money and real wealth were the same thing, then the mercantilist would be right; but they are not the same thing. In terms of real wealth, or the ability to satisfy the needs or desires of the consumer, country B is the wealthier.[19]

---

[19] To see that money and wealth are not the same, consider the condition of

The second great error of mercantilism is that it relies upon tariffs on imports to achieve a favorable balance of trade; but tariffs tend to favor, not the consumer but the producer. They give the producer a monopoly. Therefore, the producer may become wealthier, in the sense that he makes more money; but he, and all other consumers of his nation, are poorer in terms of real wealth. Money will increase, but the supply of goods available will decrease. All other things being equal, mercantilism must result in inflation and monopolies.

Smith concludes his discussion of mercantilism by stating that all systems of "encouragements" and restraints of trade slow the progress of society:

> It is thus that every system which endeavours, either, by extraordinary encouragements, to draw towards a particular species of industry a greater share of the capital of the society than what would *naturally* go to it; or, by extraordinary restraints, to force from a particular species of industry some share of the capital which would otherwise be employed in it; is in reality subversive of the great purpose which it means to promote. It retards, instead of accelerating, the progress of the society towards *real wealth* and greatness; and diminishes, instead of increasing, the real value of the annual produce of its land and labour. *All systems either of preference or of restraint, therefore, being thus completely taken away, the obvious and simple system of natural liberty establishes itself of its own accord. Every man, as long as he does not violate the laws of justice, is left perfectly free to pursue his own interest his own way, and to bring both his industry and capital into competition with those of any other man, or order of men.*[20] [emphasis added]

The system of natural liberty "establishes itself *of its own accord*" upon the elimination of "artificial" restraints and encouragements of trade. The contrast between "natural" and "artificial" indicates that the former term may be defined negatively as "that which happens of its own accord, without man's interference." Artificial things are man-made, natural things are not. Accordingly, the system of natural liberty is natural precisely because, absent any interference by governments—which are man-made things—it establishes itself of its own accord. The system of natural liberty will come to exist of its own accord, if everyone who desires to put his capital to work for the sake of increasing it, observing the laws of justice, is not otherwise interfered with in

---

the average citizen of the Soviet Union prior to its collapse. No matter how much money he has saved, there are no goods to buy. His accumulated savings thus represent only pent-up demand, not real wealth.

20 Adam Smith, *WON*, 650-651.

pursuing his own interest "in his own way." Thus, government and free markets differ as the artificial from the natural.

In particular, the system of natural liberty is natural in allowing all human beings to act as their instincts prompt them, as far as is compatible with "the security of the whole society (308)," without the meddling interference of human wisdom, which, Smith asserts, is incompetent to manage so vast an enterprise. Finally, we note that pursuing one's own interest in one's own way does not inherently conflict with the laws of justice. In fact, if justice means to mind your own business and not interfere with that of others, then capitalism and justice complement one another. Accordingly, the unequal distribution of wealth inevitably produced by the free pursuit of self-interest is not inherently unjust.

Indeed, as the above quote shows, Smith insists that the system of natural liberty presupposes the existence and observance of "laws of justice." The successful working of the system of liberal economics depends upon considerations of justice. In discussing another of the elements for which capitalism is famous, namely, the "division of labor," Smith writes, "It is the great multiplication of the productions of all the different arts, in consequence of the division of labour, which occasions, *in a well-governed society*, that universal opulence *which extends itself to the lowest rank of the people* (11)." [emphasis added] The diffusion of wealth resulting from the liberation of acquisitiveness and the division of labor presupposes a well-governed society. In such a society, evidently, the disparity between the wealth of the lowest and the highest ranks will not be as great as it is in a poorly governed society. The opulence "which extends itself to the lowest ranks of the people" in a well-governed society makes it likely that there will in fact be considerable mobility of individuals between the economic ranks of society.[21]

---

[21] Contra the assertion that income redistribution in the U.S. is both necessary and just, see "Income Dynamics," *Wall Street Journal*, 16 June 1992, 12, on the economic mobility of individuals in the US: "The usual [way of determining income distribution in the US] is to break down families or households into five groups of 20% each; the top, bottom and three middle quintiles. If the difference between top and bottom increases over a decade or so, incomes are becoming 'more unequal.' The unspoken assumption is that the same people inhabit the same quintiles in year one. This assumption is anything but accurate in a society as dynamic as America. With social mobility, people move up the quintile ladder, and down."

The Wall Street Journal then quotes from two studies, by the Treasury's

The general diffusion of wealth is made possible by the division of labor in a good society. The division of labor makes possible what previous political thinkers had regarded as a rarity, namely a large, affluent middle class. This simple discovery had potent implications for the American system of republican government, which was designed in part to avoid those ills which inevitably beset the ancient republics, by being of vast extent. The ancient republics were necessarily small, and characterized by great disparities of wealth, as well as the instability which these disparities inevitably bring about. The American republic, being based on the principle of representation, could comprehend a much greater territory and a much greater population than the ancient republics could. Thus, greater extent and population, coupled with a system of economy which creates and diffuses wealth, makes possible a large middle class, and lends stability to society.

What is the division of labor, and how does it contribute to the diffusion of wealth? The division of labor is that system of manufacture in which the various steps required to make something are distributed among various workers, instead of being assigned all to one worker.[22]

---

Office of Tax Analysis, and the liberal Urban Institute. According to the Urban Institute article, "When one follows individuals instead of statistical groups defined by income, one finds that, on average, the rich got a little richer and the poor got much richer." The Treasury study tracked the progress through the quintiles of 14,351 representative taxpayers, from 1979 to 1988. "In no quintile was turnover less than 33% during the decade. In the bottom three, at least 66% of the occupants changed quintiles, generally trading up. In fact, taxpayers were more likely to rise than fall by odds of nearly five to one, excluding people in the top quintile who had nowhere to go but down. Of those who started the decade in the bottom quintile, 65% moved up at least two quintiles during the decade. Indeed, more of these poorest taxpayers made it all the way to the top quintile than stayed in the bottom one. Treasury's Glenn Hubbard: "I suspect people's root fear is that there is no mobility. If that's their fear, it's misplaced." According to the authors of the Urban Institute report, Isabel Sawhill and Mark Condon, in 1977, the average family income in the bottom quintile was $15,853; in 1986, it was $27,998, an increase of 77%. The 1977 income in the top quintile was $92,531. It rose 5% to $97,140 in 1986. (all measured in 1991 dollars) This "may be surprising to the public, which has been led to believe that the poor were literally getting poorer over the last decade of two, and that the rich were skyrocketing. This is simply not true," according to Sawhill-Condon.

22 "The division of labour . . . so far as it can be introduced, occasions, in every art, a proportionable increase of the productive powers of labour." The great increase "of the quantity of work, which, in consequence of the division

The division of labor is essentially connected with the general diffusion of wealth in a society.[23] To illustrate this point, Smith gives the homely example of a wool coat, belonging to "the most common artificer or daylabourer in a civilized and thriving country." Behind the existence of this coat lies a vast system of manufacture and trade, from the shepherd to those who collect and prepare the wool, thence to the spinners and weavers, followed by the shipping and merchant trades. Moreover, there must be machine builders and ship builders, sailors and navigators, sail-makers and rope-makers, manufacturers of dye, and of tools of all sorts. To make tools there must be mines and blast furnaces, and all the many craftsmen and tradesmen necessary to support a smelting operation. In short, the daylabourer's coat is a mundane reminder of both the vast system of manufacture and trade necessary to produce it, as well as the great system of exchange required to put the coat into the daylabourer's possession.

If we then proceed to imagine all that is necessary actually to *supply* our worker with the rest of his necessities, of food, clothing, and shelter, that is:

> if we examine . . . all these things, and consider what a variety of labour is employed about each of them, we shall be sensible that without the assistance and cooperation of many thousands, the very meanest person in a civilized country could not be provided, even according to, what we very falsely imagine, the easy and simple manner in which he is commonly accommodated. Compared with the extravagant luxury of the great, his accommodation must no doubt appear extremely simple and easy; and yet it may be true, perhaps, that the accommodation of an European prince does not always so much exceed that of an industrious and frugal peasant, as the accommodation of the latter exceeds that of many an African king, the absolute master of the lives and liberties of ten thousand

---

of labour, the same number of people are capable of performing, is owing to three different circumstances; first, to the increase of dexterity in every particular workman; secondly, to the saving of the time which is commonly lost in passing from one species of work to another; and lastly, to the invention of a great number of machines which facilitate and abridge labour, and enable one man to do the work of many." Smith, *WON*, 11-12.

[23] "Every workman has a great quantity of his own work to dispose of beyond what he himself has occasion for; end every other workman being exactly in the same situation, he is enabled to exchange a great quantity of his own goods for a great quantity of theirs. He supplies them abundantly with what they have occasion for, and they accommodate him as amply with what he has occasion for, and a general plenty diffuses itself through all the different ranks of the society." Smith, *WON*.

naked savages (11-12).

Whence comes the division of labor? Not from human wisdom or foresight, says Smith. The "general opulence to which it gives occasion" was neither foreseen nor intended, but is the

> necessary, though very slow and gradual, consequence of a certain propensity in human nature which has in view no such extensive utility; the propensity to . . . exchange one thing for another . . . Nobody ever saw a dog make a fair and deliberate exchange of one bone for another with another dog. Nobody ever saw one animal by its gestures and natural cries signify to another, this is mine, that yours; I am willing to give this for that (13).

Unlike the other animals, man almost constantly requires the help of his congeners. As we saw in the example of the wool coat, "in civilized society [man] stands at all times in need of the co-operation and assistance of great multitudes." Why can he not rely upon the friendship and general humanity of others to move them to help him as required? In part, it is because life is short, and the possible scope of one's acquaintance and friendship is quite narrow. Moreover, given the predominance of self-interest, it is generally futile for a man to expect others to help him from "their benevolence only." He will do better, says Smith,

> if he can interest their self-love in his favour, and show them that it is for their own advantage to do for him what he requires of them . . . It is not from the benevolence of the butcher, the brewer, or the baker, that we expect our dinner, but from their regard to their own self-interest. We address ourselves, not to their humanity, but to their self-love, and never talk to them of our own necessities but of their advantages. Nobody but a beggar chooses to depend chiefly upon the benevolence of his fellow-citizens (13).

The division of labor arises from the natural human propensity to exchange one thing for another, in the following way. Due to the natural distribution of talents, some are good at making or procuring one thing, some another. Some are better at making bows and arrows, others are better at hunting. The one skilled in making bows discovers that he has a surplus, and can exchange his bows for meat, or other necessities. Others do likewise with their respective talents. There gradually emerges the realization that one can supply oneself and one's family with the necessaries of life more efficiently by devoting oneself exclusively to one particular species of business, than by being a jack of all trades:

[T]he *certainty* of being able to exchange all that surplus part of the produce of his own labour, which is over and above his own consumption, for
such parts of the produce of other men's labour as he may have occasion
for, encourages every man to apply himself to a particular occupation, and
to cultivate and bring to perfection whatever talent or genius he may possess . . . (15) [emphasis added]

We note that one must be reasonably *certain* of being able to make
a fair exchange of one's surplus for what one needs from another. Smith
thus partially indicates what he means when he insists that the division
of labor, in a well-governed society, conduces to the spread of opulence. Exchange is a form of contract. Contracts will be entered into
only if there is reasonable assurance that they will be complied with, or
enforced if necessary. One will therefore need things like government
and the rule of law, in order to be certain of being able to make a fair
exchange.

Finally, we note the egalitarian implication of the assertion that
"every man . . . is left perfectly free to pursue his own interest his own
way, and to bring both his industry and capital into competition *with
those of any other man, or order of men.*" In the system of economy
Smith has in mind, no one, regardless of order or rank, may expect to
be protected from the competition of others; and all have the right to
expect equal protection of the law in the enforcement of contractual
obligations.

We now see what capital is and how it first came into being. Capital
is a surplus of goods, an amount that exceeds what is necessary to provide for one's own needs and the needs of one's family. It comes into
existence as a result of the division of labor and the natural human
propensity to exchange one thing for another. Capital is accumulated
wealth; but it is unusable to its owner in its form as capital. It *must* be
exchanged, either for other goods, or for money, which is initially only
a medium of exchange, and thus represents pent up demand. One may
also exchange a portion of one's surplus stock, not simply for goods to
be consumed, but for goods to be employed in the further production
of goods. Capital is that stock of wealth which may thus be employed
in business, or exchange carried on for profit. Given the natural human
propensity to barter, stock will not sit idle; but, because one's real needs
are few and easily satisfied, the exchange of stock quickly and almost
naturally comes to be carried on for the sake of profit.

Goods employed in production are capital goods, as contrasted
with commodities, or goods that are to be used or consumed. Once the
division of labor has been introduced,

it is but a very small part of a man's wants which the produce of his own labour can supply. He supplies the far greater part of them by exchanging that surplus part of the produce of his own labour, which is over and above his own consumption, for such parts of the produce of other men's labour as he has occasion for. Every man thus lives by exchanging, or becomes in some measure a merchant, and the society itself grows to be what is properly a commercial society (22).

Exchange, however, is in the beginning inefficient. If the butcher wishes to purchase beer from the brewer, he has only meat to exchange for it; but if the brewer is already well-supplied with meat, he may be very glad to exchange his surplus of beer, but not for anything the butcher has to offer in return. Therefore, says Smith, in order to avoid

the inconveniency of such situations, every prudent man in every period of society, after the first establishment of the division of labour, must naturally have endeavoured to manage his affairs in such a manner, as to have at all times by him, besides the peculiar produce of his own industry, a certain quantity of some one commodity or other, such as he imagined few people would be likely to refuse in exchange for the produce of their industry (22).

Some one commodity, therefore, eventually is chosen to represent all exchangeable goods in terms of a common measure. This is the origin of money. Money, says Smith, has a double function. It is both the "instrument of commerce," as well as "the measure of value." We can obtain what we want with money more readily than by means of any other commodity: "The great affair, we always find is to get money. When that is obtained, there is no difficulty in making any subsequent purchase." As the common measure of all value, money is also that standard in terms of which we estimate the value of all other commodities, as well as the wealth, both of individuals and countries (398).

Once there is a medium of exchange, then no manufacturer of goods need limit his production to what he is certain he can exchange immediately for other consumable goods. He can accumulate stock for the purpose of exchange simply, and not merely for the purpose of obtaining the consumable goods he requires himself. Clearly he would have no interest in accumulating stock unless he intended to exchange it, and unless there existed a medium of exchange. Given these conditions, however, some of those who accumulate stock "will *naturally* employ it in setting to work industrious people, whom they will supply with materials and subsistence, in order to make a profit by the sale of their work, or by what their labour adds to the value of the materials (398)." [emphasis added] We note Smith's assertion that the accumulation of stock naturally leads some to employ the industrious for the sake of making a profit. Men naturally seek to employ their capital. Even if their motive for doing so is selfish, their employment of their capital cannot help but provide employment for other human beings as well.

What is profit and how does it arise? Moreover, what justifies the owner of capital stock in taking a portion of the sale price of a commodity for himself? Smith appears to believe that it is the labor of the workman that transforms materials into commodities. Labor is the sole source of the value of commodities. What right has the owner of stock to retain a portion of the sale price of a commodity for himself? Smith denies that profit may be regarded as a kind of wage, which the employer pays himself for supervising the labor of his employees:

> The profits of stock, it may perhaps be thought, are only a different name for the wages of a particular sort of labour, the labour of inspection and direction. They are, however, altogether different, are regulated by quite sufficient principles, and bear no proportion to the quantity, the hardship, or the ingenuity of this supposed labour of inspection and direction. They are regulated altogether by the value of the stock employed, and are greater or smaller in proportion to the extent of this stock (398).

Smith asserts that the basis for profit is that the accumulation of stock and the division of labor advance together; and, that the accumulation of stock enables the same quantity of labor to produce more:

> As the accumulation of stock must, in the nature of things, be previous to the division of labour, so labour can be more and more subdivided in proportion only as stock is previously more and more accumulated. The quantity of materials which the same number of people can work up, increases in a great proportion as labour comes to be more and more subdivided; and as the operations of each workman are gradually reduced to a greater degree of simplicity, a variety of machines come to be invented for facilitating and abridging those operations. As the division of labour advances, therefore, in order to give constant employment to an equal number of workmen, an equal stock of provisions, and a greater stock of materials and tools than what would have been necessary in a ruder state of things, must be accumulated beforehand . . . As the accumulation of stock is previously necessary for carrying on this great improvement in the productive powers of labour, so that accumulation naturally leads to this improvement (260).

It is therefore the "improvement in the productive powers of labour," resulting from the accumulation of capital, that enables the increase of both the quantity and efficiency of industry. More can be produced, and more can be produced in less time. Thus, the owner of capital who puts it to work is entitled to be compensated for having done so.

We may thus state more clearly the nature of the disagreement between Marx and Smith regarding profit. Marx believes profit to be unjust because it rests upon a system which transforms goods, or things intended to satisfy human needs through consumption, into commodities, things intended to be exchanged for the sake of profit. Profit satisfies no natural human need; or, stated in terms more congenial to Marx, profit is a sign of the alienation of human beings from one another.

Smith, by contrast, although he does not say that profit is unqualifiedly just, affirms that it is natural; and, the pursuit of profit, under the proper conditions, benefits society at large in compensation for whatever moral improprieties it may cause. While it is true that, in a purely rational economy, production would be solely directed to the satisfaction of human needs, Smith would nevertheless ask, What would motivate the producers to produce? Reason may teach that production should be for the sake of satisfying need; but why should I labor for the sake of satisfying the needs of others? Can one reasonably expect human beings to be motivated to produce by the exhortation "From each according to his abilities, to each according to his needs"? One may admire the nobility of the sentiment expressed by this dictum; but is it likely that one human being will be motivated to labor in the production of goods merely by a concern for the neediness of others?

By what right does the employer of capital lay claim to profit? The answer to this question, we recall, is based upon the principle that labor is the source both of value and the original title to property. Smith accepted this principle from Locke, who, as we saw above, taught that nature, in her unimproved state, is virtually worthless. It is man's labor that transforms nature into a state of utility; and it is thus man's labor which is the source of value, where "value" means "utility." Material goods have value precisely to the extent that they can be used to satisfy one's needs.

Unlike the other animals, however, man cannot be content with the bucolic life lived in accordance with the rhythms of natural needs and their satisfaction; and the source of this discontent is human consciousness itself, which, we recall, is essentially self-concerned. It is on account of man's natural restlessness and anxiety that unimproved nature is virtually useless to man. The inutility of nature is a reflection, not simply of the natural scarcity of those goods required to satisfy man's needs, but of man's limitless concern to acquire power upon power.

Man's natural anxiety over the future, expressed as *labor*, is the source both of *property* and the fundamental status of *property rights*. Labor is the source of ownership and the rights of ownership. What is it that naturally makes something *mine*? It is my labor. Being human, I have a natural right to preserve myself, and therefore a right to those things necessary for my preservation. It is my labor, however, which appropriates, out of the common store of natural goods, those things necessary for my preservation, and makes them mine; that is, labor transforms something from a common to a private good. Locke writes:

> Though the earth, and all inferior creatures be common to all men, yet every man has a property in his own person. This nobody has any right to but himself. The labor of his body, and the work of his hands, we may say, are properly his. Whatsoever then he removes out of the state that nature hath provided, and left it in, he hath mixed his labor with, and joined to it something that is his own, and thereby makes it his property. It being by him removed from the common state nature placed it in, it hath by this labor something annexed to it, that excludes the common right of other men.[24]

Labor then, according to both Locke and Smith, is the source of utility, and therefore of value: value, in its economic sense, means utility. The products of labor have value insofar as they are useful for the satisfaction of man's needs. Man, however, is not satisfied merely to labor for what he needs. What is necessary to satisfy man's needs is actually very little. The labor expended beyond what is necessary to satisfy man's needs is for the sake of exchange; but exchange can be carried on both to acquire those necessities which one cannot supply for oneself, as well as for the sake of profit through exchange.

There thus arose a two-fold distinction in classical economics, between use-value and exchange-value; but the critical point from Smith's perspective is that labor is the source of ownership. My labor transforms natural materials into useful things which, because of my labor, belong to me. They become my property on account of my labor. If I sell or exchange those goods, what I get in return belongs entirely to me. This observation immediately returns us to the question, What justifies profit? If what I make belongs solely to me, what can justify someone else in taking a part of the price of those goods?

To answer this question, consider again the example of the manu-

---

[24] Locke, 287-288.

facturer of bows and arrows. Suppose that the manufacturer decides that he could produce more bows if he could use the spinning machines belonging to the twine manufacturers. Then, the finished product is not entirely the result of his own labor and tools. The owner of the spinning machines thus has a right to share in the proceeds of the sale of the bows, even if he has no part in the labor of their manufacture. Why? Because the spinning machines are a *form* of labor. They came into existence on account of the labor of the twine manufacturer, who therefore acquires a right to a portion of the proceeds of the sale of the bows. Therefore, capital, understood as "congealed labor," produces value; and its employment entitles the owner of capital to a profit.

One must note that, in the foregoing example, human beings no longer labor merely for themselves, using only their own hands, or tools which they have made and therefore own. They now must use tools (or land) that belong to others. Thus, the others acquire the right to share in the product of the labor that employed their tools. Profit comes into being simultaneously with the accumulation of tools, or other means for producing goods, by some members of a society. Smith therefore disagrees with Marx, who maintained that profit results solely from the exploitation of the working class by the owner class who, says Marx, benefit from the "unpaid labor" of the workers.

Returning to our discussion of the system of natural liberty, we quote Smith's description of the duties of the sovereign in the system of natural liberty:

> The sovereign is completely discharged from a duty, in the attempting to perform which he must always be exposed to innumerable delusions, *and for the proper performance of which no human wisdom or knowledge could ever be sufficient; the duty of superintending the industry of private people, and of directing it towards the employments most suitable to the interest of the society.*

The invisible hand is greatly superior to any human wisdom when it comes to overseeing the "industry of private people." This is largely because it cannot be deluded, as can a human sovereign, by the very passions that drive human industry. The private pursuit of material interest more surely serves the interests of society, when it is left to go its own way, than when it is managed.

Smith continues:

> According to the system of natural liberty, the sovereign *has only three duties* to attend to: . . . first, the duty of protecting the society from the violence and invasion of other independent societies; secondly, the duty of protecting, as far as possible, every member of the society from the

injustice or oppression of every other member of it, or the duty of establishing an exact administration of justice; and, thirdly, the duty of erecting and maintaining certain public works and certain public institutions, which it can never be for the interest of any individual, or small number of individuals, to erect and maintain; because the profit could never repay the expence to any individual or small number of individuals, though it may frequently do much more than repay it to a great society.[25] [emphasis added]

Smith therefore teaches what appears to be a paradox about political economy. Law-abiding human beings, otherwise left to pursue their own self-interests, employing their capital as they see fit, promote the progress of a society "towards real wealth and greatness." The increase of a society's real wealth and greatness is the unintended consequence of the pursuit of private interest.

No "human wisdom" is competent to direct private interest towards those "employments most suitable to the interest of society"; and it would be folly for any society to allow one individual or group of individuals to decide how goods shall be distributed. For, being human themselves, those who decided would be no more likely to consult the public welfare than is anyone in business solely to make a profit. Whatever disparities of wealth are created by a system of free enterprise, they will not be as great as those that exist in managed economies.[26]

We note also in the above quotation, that the sovereign has only three duties, namely, national defense, the administration of domestic justice, and erecting and maintaining public works. We recall that Smith suggests that the government may take some pains to prevent the laboring poor from falling into those indolent and stupid habits to which, unfortunately, the progress of the division of labor renders them susceptible; but he does not positively enjoin this on the government as its duty. That is, he leaves open the question whether the government has a duty to provide for public education.

The first two duties, national defense and the administration of domestic justice, are both *negative*, in the sense that their principal object is to *protect*; that is, it appears that Smith would find the

---

[25] Smith, *WON*, 260.

[26] To convince oneself of the truth of Smith's view, one has only to compare the distribution of wealth in socialist economies and free market economies. Were the members of the privileged classes in the Soviet Union any less loath to be deprived of their wealth than the wealthy in America are to be taxed to "pay for" middle class tax cuts?

principle of limited government, as articulated by the Constitution and Declaration, congenial to his own views. The third duty, that of putting up and maintaining public works, devolves upon government by default: it can "never be for the interest of any individual or small number of individuals" to undertake this project. The assumption appears to be that, absent any compelling private interest, certain works become a matter for public policy.

Capitalism is often decried for its alleged capitulation to human greed; however, we see in the above quote that Smith, rather than giving in to greed, acknowledges certain limits to human wisdom. The negative reason for preferring "free enterprise" to a "managed" economy is that, however invidious the results of liberating human acquisitiveness, much worse would certainly ensue from attempting the artificial direction of private interest toward the greater interest of society.[27] This is impossible to human wisdom, however well-intended. Smith does not disparage the general welfare on behalf of private interest; rather, he insists that, under the proper circumstances, the unhindered pursuit of private interest conduces to the general wealth of a society more successfully than even the most benevolent efforts of the sovereign. Human wisdom and benevolence have their limits. The prudent and humane course is to acknowledge those limits.

What is impossible to men, however, is possible to the "invisible hand." This is Smith's famous metaphor, which evidently is intended to help us understand the mechanism whereby the system of natural liberty enables the diffusion of wealth. This phrase appears in both *The Wealth of Nations*, and *The Theory of Moral Sentiments*. We turn first to the former:

> The produce of industry is what it adds to the subject or materials upon which it is employed. In proportion as the value of this produce is great or small, so will likewise be the profits of the employer. But it is only for the

---

27 See Jonas Bernstein's review of *The Soviet Mafia: A Shocking Expose of Organized Crime in the USSR*, by Arkady Vaksberg, in *The American Spectator*, July 1992. Bernstein quotes Vaksberg: "In the final analysis all of [the members of the post-Stalinist Soviet oligarchy] from top to bottom are human beings with all the normal human qualities. All their dangerous and convoluted schemes to expand their power and increase their wealth are not the end but the means. The end they serve is the guaranteeing of a life of ease and maximum self-gratification, a life with nothing denied and every whim satisfied. To this end everything else is subordinated: operations, decisions, every move, no matter how these are 'dressed up' ideologically as being for the common good."

sake of profit that any man employs a capital in the support of industry; and he will always, therefore, endeavour to employ it in the support of that industry of which the produce is likely to be of the greatest value, or to exchange for the greatest quantity of money or other goods. But the annual revenue of every society is always precisely equal to the exchangeable value of the whole annual produce of its industry, or rather is precisely the same thing with that exchangeable value. As every individual, therefore, endeavours as much as he can both to employ his capital in the support of domestic industry, and so to direct that industry that its produce may be of the greatest value; every individual necessarily labours to render the annual revenue of the society as great as he can. *He generally, indeed, neither intends to promote the public interest, nor knows how much he is promoting it. By preferring the support of domestic to that of foreign industry, he intends only his own security; and by directing that industry in such a manner as its produce may be of the greatest value, he intends only his own gain, and he is in this, as in many other cases, led by an invisible hand to promote an end which was no part of his intention. Nor is it always the worse for society that it was no part of it.* By pursuing his own interest he frequently promotes that of the society more effectually than when he really intends to promote it. I have never known much good done by those who affected to trade for the public good. It is an affectation, and very few words need be employed in dissuading them from it.[28] [emphasis added]

The "invisible hand" appears in *The Theory of Moral Sentiments*, in a chapter devoted to discussing the pleasures, real or imagined, of wealth. Human beings do not, says Smith, envy the rich "so much on account of the superior ease or pleasure which they are supposed to enjoy, as of the numberless artificial and elegant contrivances for promoting this ease or pleasure." We do not "even imagine that they are really happier than other people: but [we imagine] that *they possess more means of happiness.*" [emphasis added]

It may happen that a wealthy man, when he has grown old, regards his wealth as giving no real satisfaction, nor pleasure and ease sufficient to repay him for having sacrificed his youth to the pursuit of gain. Whatever the wisdom of this view, we who observe what we imagine to be the pleasures of the rich soon forget this lesson: "We are then charmed with the beauty of that accommodation which reigns in the palaces and oeconomy of the great; and admire how every thing is adapted to promote their ease, to prevent their wants, to gratify their wishes, and to amuse and entertain their most frivolous desires." The rich and famous appear to us as beautiful human beings leading

---

[28] Smith, *WON*, 422-423.

beautiful lives.[29]

If, however,

> we consider *the real satisfaction* which all these things are capable of
> affording, by itself and separated from the beauty of that arrangement
> which is fitted to promote it, it will always appear in the highest degree
> contemptible and trifling. But we rarely view it in this abstract and philo-
> sophical light. We naturally confound it in our imagination with the
> order, the regular and harmonious movement of the system, the machine
> or oeconomy by means of which it is produced. The pleasures of wealth
> and greatness, when considered in this complex view, strike the imagina-
> tion as something grand and beautiful and noble, of which the attainment
> is well worth all the toil and anxiety which we are so apt to bestow upon
> it. [emphasis added]

In a word, Smith asserts that we confuse the *beauty* of the possessions of the wealthy with their real utility. Were we to reflect that the
great palaces of the rich shelter them from the elements no better than
the humble dwellings of the poor shelter *them*, we would be compelled
to wonder whether wealth is "well worth all the toil and anxiety" necessary to obtain it. For all the pleasure he derives from doing so, it is in
vain that the wealthy landlord surveys his fields, and imagines the
immensity of their produce; for, his stomach can hold no more than
that of the poor man's. Real wealth—and here Smith agrees with
Aristotle—is determined by the natural limits set to the satisfaction of
our desires. Wealth, being naturally for the sake of satisfying needs, is
naturally limited by the satiety of the needs it serves. Money, however,
is only a means to wealth, although it is often confused with wealth.
These are the teachings of reason and virtue; but, Smith evidently differs with Aristotle, both over the efficacy of reason and virtue in
producing the good political society, as well as the very meaning of the
goodness of that society.

The desire for acquiring money and the means of obtaining security
and comfort, is unlimited; but the desire for wealth is, although we
may not acknowledge it, naturally limited by the needs it satisfies. It is
a weakness of our nature, however, to be drawn to "the *beauty of that
arrangement* which is fitted to promote" the satisfaction of our needs,
rather than to a consideration of those qualities of things that give real
satisfaction. We come to desire, not the gratification that wealth brings,
but the means to gratification. Smith here appears to agree with Locke's
teaching, that human desire (or anxiety) is directed towards acquiring

---

[29] Smith, *TOMS,* 184ff.

144

the *means* of ensuring future pleasure, rather than the enjoyment of present pleasure.

Smith himself deprecates the common opinion according to which power and wealth, understood as the *means* to human happiness, are true means to human happiness. True happiness has little to do with those

> enormous and operose machines contrived to produce a few trifling conveniencies to the body, consisting of springs the most nice and delicate, which must be kept in order with the most anxious attention, and which in spite of all our care are ready every moment to burst into pieces, and to crush in their ruins their unfortunate possessor.[30]

Wealth and power are not germane to real human happiness:

> In what constitutes the real happiness of human life, [the poor and obscure] are in no respect inferior to those who would seem so much above them. In ease of the body and peace of mind, all the different ranks of life are nearly upon a level, and the beggar, who suns himself by the side of highway, possesses that security which kings are fighting for.[31]

Some readers of Smith may be surprised to discover his occasionally severe animadversions against wealth, especially in the seminal book by the author whose name is most associated with capitalism. For example, Smith added a chapter to a later edition of *The Theory of Moral Sentiments*, entitled "Of the corruption of our moral sentiments, which is occasioned by this disposition to admire the rich and great, and to despise or neglect persons of poor and mean condition." As we have asserted elsewhere, however, Smith stands within the tradition of Western political and economic thought, a tradition which includes, not only Hobbes and Locke, but Aristotle and the Bible, as well.

There are, of course, fundamental disagreements among the various authors in this tradition.[32] On the other hand, however great the disagreements between writers such as Aristotle and Adam Smith, they have substantially more in common with each other than either of them has with contemporary historicism or relativism. In the context of this discussion, the pertinent agreement between Smith and his classical predecessors concerns the nature and purpose of wealth, and the relation between acquiring and managing wealth to the art of making

---

[30] Ibid., IV, i.

[31] Ibid., IV, i.

[32] The Western tradition was likened to a battle between the ancient and modern thinkers, by Jonathan Swift, in his *Battle of the Books*.

money.

In his discussion of *oeconomia*, or the art of household management, Aristotle speaks of the origin of what we now call business, which, says Aristotle, grew out of the practice of exchange carried on between households and cities. Exchange may be either for other goods or for money. He says that expertise in exchange "arises in the first place from something that is according to nature—the fact that human beings have either more or fewer things than what is adequate." On account of this, goods were originally exchanged for goods, either among members of the same household, or among different households. This kind of exchange existed "in order to support natural self-sufficiency," and is not "contrary to nature." Business, that is, exchange carried on for money, arose from the former kind of exchange "reasonably enough. For as the assistance of foreigners became greater in importing what [the members of a single household or group of households] were in need of and exporting what was in surplus, the use of money was necessarily devised."

Aristotle thus asserts that money came into existence on account of foreign trade. That is, money is invented because trade came to be carried out between different political communities, each comprising households and small villages made up of households. Because political communities tend to differ from one another primarily by having different laws and customs, the word for money, *nomisma*, is related to the word for "law" or "custom," *nomos*. Business, understood as the art of exchange carried on for profit, or what Aristotle calls "commerce," thus came into existence.

Aristotle says that human beings tend to forget that money arose because people living together desired to be "self-sufficient": money exists as a means to self-sufficiency. His word for "self-sufficient" is *autarkeia*, which might be somewhat freely translated as "having a sufficiency in oneself for independent existence, to be strong enough on one's own to exist independently of help from others." Because households hadn't sufficient goods of various kinds and surpluses of others, they bartered and exchanged with other households, as did the political communities (which Aristotle calls the "cities") with one another. The resulting kind of expertise in exchange thus was not contrary to nature because it "existed in order to support natural self-sufficiency."

Later, however, business was carried on for the sake of making a profit, and:

> it is on this account that expertise in business is held, to be particularly connected with money, and to have as its task the ability to discern what

146

will provide a given amount [of it]; for it is held to be productive of wealth and goods. *Indeed, they often define wealth as a given amount of money, since this is what expertise in business or commerce is connected with.* At other times, however, money seems to be something nonsensical and [to exist] altogether by law, and in no way by nature, because when changed by its users [i.e., when the currency is changed] it is worth nothing and is not useful with a view to any of the necessary things; and it will often happen that one who is wealthy in money will go in want of necessary sustenance. Yet it would be absurd if wealth were something one could have in abundance and die of starvation—like Midas in the fable, when everything set before him turned into gold on account of the greediness of his prayer.[emphasis added] [33]

Therefore, Aristotle concludes, there are two kinds of expertise in acquiring or using wealth: household management, which is according to our natural desire for self-sufficiency; and commercial expertise aimed at making a profit, which is contrary to nature *when pursued as an end in itself.* The wealth derived from the latter is indeed without limit. You can never have too much money; but the example of King Midas vividly reminds us that money in itself is not true wealth. We tend to think that the acquisition of wealth is limitless, because we forget that money is essentially an instrument; and any instrument is naturally limited by the end it serves. Thus, the art of making money is essentially subordinate to the art of household management, the art which uses the money acquired, to purchase goods of an amount and kind necessary for the self-sufficiency of the members of the household. Therefore, the acquisition of true wealth is limited by the natural human needs and desires.

Aristotle concludes his analysis of wealth-getting by saying that some people mistakenly believe that the end of household management is to "preserve or increase without limit their property or money." Why do people make this mistake?:

The cause of this state is that they are serious [*spoudadzein*] about living, but not about living well; and since that desire of theirs is without limit, they also desire what is productive of unlimited things. Even those who aim at living well seek what conduces to bodily gratifications, and since this too appears to be available in and through possessions, their pursuits are wholly connected with business, and this is why the other kind of business expertise [i.e., the one aimed at making money] has arisen. For as gratification consists in excess, they seek the sort that is productive of the excess characteristic of gratification; and if they are unable to supply it

---

[33] Aristotle, *Politics*, 1257b5ff.

through expertise in business, they attempt this in some other fashion, using each sort of capacity in a way not according to nature. For it belongs to courage to produce not goods but confidence; nor does this belong to military or medical expertise, but it belongs to the former to produce victory, to the latter, health. But all of these they make forms of expertise in business, as if this were the end and everything else had to march toward it.[34]

Therefore, it belongs to the expert in household management to make use of money, but not to increase it without limit. The art of making money is essentially subordinate to the art of using it well, for the purpose of contributing to the good life of the members of the household.

It should be pointed out that the Greek word *spoudadzein*, translated above as "to be serious about," has the connotation "to be anxious or concerned about," or "to be busy, eager, or zealous about." Aristotle's point is that the concern for living for its own sake includes an element of anxiety, which may distract one from the ends that define the good life for a human being.

There is, therefore, a direct connection between the unlimited desire for life simply, and the unlimited desire for money, which is not genuine wealth, but the means to genuine wealth. Smith's discussion of the natural human tendency to confuse the comfort wealth brings with the means for attaining that comfort is solidly in the tradition originated by Aristotle. What distinguishes Smith from the classical tradition is that he re-thought the relation between human desire and wealth, and came to a conclusion which differed from that of Aristotle.

For this reason, in the passage quoted above, Smith does not lament what might be called our natural tendency to confuse luxury with utility. Indeed, he continues by observing that

it is well that nature imposes on us in this manner. It is this deception which rouses and keeps in continual motion the industry of mankind. It is this which first prompted them to cultivate the ground, to build houses, to found cities and commonwealths, and to invent and improve all the sciences and arts, which ennoble and embellish human life; which have entirely changed the whole face of the globe, have turned the rude forests of nature into agreeable and fertile plains, and made the trackless and barren ocean a new fund of subsistence, and the great high road of communication to the different nations of the earth. The earth by those labours of mankind has been obliged to redouble her natural fertility, and to maintain a greater multitude of inhabitants.

---

34 Ibid., 1258a1-20.

Thus, "this deception" is the source of those great exertions which produce not only the whole system of human economy, but, indeed, civilization itself.

One is therefore moved to reflect that much of human civilization aims far beyond the simple satisfaction of our natural needs. In regard to the latter, all human beings are indeed equal. The rich man can consume no more than the poor:

> The rest he is obliged to distribute among those, who prepare, in the nicest manner, that little which he himself makes use of, among those who provide and keep in order all the different baubles and trinkets, which are employed in the economy of greatness; all of whom thus derive from his luxury and caprice, that share of the necessaries of life, which they would in vain have expected from his humanity or his justice . . . [The rich] consume little more than the poor, and in spite of their natural selfishness and rapacity, though they mean only their own conveniency, though the sole end which they propose from the labours of all the thousands whom they employ, be the gratification of their own vain and insatiable desires, they divide with the poor the produce of all their improvements. *They are led by an invisible hand to make nearly the same distribution of the necessaries of life, which would have been made, had the earth been divided into equal portions among all its inhabitants, and thus without intending it, without knowing it, advance the interest of society, and afford means to the multiplication of the species.* When Providence divided the earth among the few lordly masters, it neither forgot nor abandoned those who seemed to have been left out in the participation. These last too enjoy their share of all that it produces. In what constitutes the real happiness of human life, they are in no respect inferior to those who would seem so much above them. [emphasis added]

Smith makes the same point in *The Wealth of Nations*: "The rich man consumes no more food than his poor neighbour . . . The desire of food is limited in every man by the narrow capacity of the human stomach; but the desire of the conveniencies and ornaments . . . seems to have no limit or certain boundary."[35] Again, we are reminded of Aristotle's distinction between genuine wealth, which is limited by the requirements of natural satisfaction, and the means of acquiring real wealth, or money, for which no natural limit exists.

Aristotle teaches the necessity of accommodating, to a certain extent, the natural human desire for gain. He also teaches, however, that the statesman ought positively to inculcate in the citizens those virtues necessary to correct or restrain the unlimited desire for wealth, a

---

[35] Smith, *WON,* 423.

desire which turns men's thoughts from the common good to concern for their own material gain. Such a society would, admittedly, be characterized by a degree of austerity which runs counter to democratic tastes; but it would compensate for this by producing citizens dedicated to the common good, who display the virtues of generosity and philanthropy which perfect the common good, and would partially overcome the division between private and public interest.

Through the image of the invisible hand, however, Smith shows how liberating the pursuit of wealth, in a society characterized by good laws and just principles of government, can lead to the reconciliation of the public welfare and private interest. Such a society would, moreover, also be characterized by a general affluence impossible to the ancient republics. Thus, if the rare virtues of liberality and philanthropy upon which the ancient republics depended, are less frequent in the affluent society, they are also less necessary.

There are certain moral irregularities in such a system, to be sure; but, given the limits set to human wisdom by the predominance of self-interest, these irregularities are immeasurably less than any which would exist in managed economies. Moreover, the general diffusion of wealth made possible in such a society offsets those irregularities, by enabling the greater part of the people to live a comfortable, secure life, pursuing their private interests, to be sure, but along the way contributing to the economic well-being of the whole society. Moreover, if every man has the same opportunity as every other to acquire wealth, there will be less occasion for dissatisfaction and envy.

## V

We turn now to what may be called Smith's own critique of the system of natural liberty. Smith discusses the moral irregularities of capitalism in a manner that is remarkable both for its candor and for the harshness of its criticisms of the less attractive elements of capitalist economies. Indeed, one may say that Smith was the most profound of the critics of capitalism. He anticipated most of the principal criticisms of Marx and other modern critics; but he continued to regard capitalism as superior to the other forms of economy available to a free society, and was therefore prepared to accept its shortcomings. No other system better suited the strengths and weaknesses of human nature.[36]

---

[36] The following analysis is indebted to the excellent presentation by Joseph Cropsey in "Adam Smith," *History of Political Philosophy*, Third Edition, ed.

First, although the division of labor augments the productive power of a society, and thus makes it prosper, this is not achieved without certain harmful consequences for its laborers. The division of labor becoming ever more refined, each laborer's task becomes commensurably narrower:

> The man whose whole life is spent in performing a few simple operations . . . has no occasion to exert his understanding, or to exercise his invention in finding out expedients for removing difficulties which never occur. He naturally loses, therefore, the habit of such exertion, and generally becomes as stupid and ignorant as it is possible for a human creature to become.[37]

This obviously has certain undesirable consequences for the laborer's capacity for citizenship: "Of the great and extensive interests of his country he is altogether incapable of judging; and unless very particular pains have been taken to render him otherwise, he is equally incapable of defending his country in war." Furthermore, "[h]is dexterity at his own particular trade seems, in this manner, to be acquired at the expence of his intellectual, social, and martial virtues. But *in every improved and civilized society* this is the state into which the labouring poor, that is, the great body of the people, must necessarily fall, unless government takes some pains to prevent it." [emphasis added] Accordingly, Smith concludes that "the education of the common people requires, perhaps, in a civilized society, the attention of the public more than that of people of some rank and fortune." Some form of public education, at least in the rudiments of reading, writing, and arithmetic, is therefore necessary to mitigate the inevitable narrowing of the human person that results from the division of labor (734-737). Obviously, public education will be even more necessary to a representative republic like the United States, where the intelligent participation of its citizens is necessary for good government.

Second, "stock that is employed for the sake of profit," that is, capital, "puts in motion the greater part of the useful labour of every society. The plans and projects of the employers of stock regulate and direct all the most important operations of labour, and profit is the end proposed by all those plans and projects." Smith asserts that the interests of the employers of stock, namely the merchants and manufacturers, thus tend to predominate over other interests in a free economy. Their interest, however,

---

Strauss and Cropsey, (Chicago: University of Chicago Press, 1987).
[37] Smith, *WON,* 734.

is always in some respects different from, and even opposite to, that of the public. To widen the market and to narrow the competition" is always their aim. While the public interest may frequently be served by widening the market, narrowing the competition "must always be against it, and can serve only to enable [the owners of capital], by raising their profits above what they naturally would be, to levy, for their own benefit, an absurd tax upon the rest of their fellow-citizens (249-250).

Any proposal regarding the regulation of commerce from this class ought always to be regarded with suspicion, for it "comes from an order of men, whose interest is never exactly the same with that of the public, who have generally an interest to deceive and even to oppress the public . . ." Indeed, when the interests of the capitalists prevail in foreign trade, that is, when one trade is given preferment through favorable legislation, war often results. Restraints on foreign trade are always urged by that class of trader whose interests will best be served by the resulting elimination of cheaper labor or competition from better products; but the members of that trade always pretend that their recommendations will serve the public interest.

The reverse, however, is true. Being deceived by the

> sneaking arts of underling tradesmen . . . nations have been taught that their interest consisted in beggaring all their neighbours. Each nation has been made to look with an invidious eye upon the prosperity of all the nations with which it trades, and to consider their gain as its loss. *Commerce, which ought naturally to be, among nations, as among individuals, a bond of union and friendship*, has become the fertile source of discord and animosity. *The capricious ambition of kings and ministers has not, during the present and the preceding century been more fatal to the repose of Europe, than the impertinent jealousy of merchants and manufacturers*. The violence and injustice of the rulers of mankind is an ancient evil, for which, I am afraid, the nature of human affairs can scarce admit of remedy. But the mean rapacity, the monopolizing spirit of merchants and manufacturers, who neither are, nor ought to be, the rulers of mankind, though it cannot perhaps be corrected, may very easily be prevented from disturbing the tranquillity of any body but themselves (460).[38] [emphasis added]

---

[38] It is instructive to compare Smith's reference to commerce as a "bond of union and friendship," with Aristotle's discussion of the kinds of friendship, in the *Nicomachean Ethics*. There, he says that friends have "all things in common," and distinguishes among the kinds of friendship, depending upon the kind of things shared. The kinds are three in number: pleasure, utility, and intellectual interests, or, what Aristotle calls "philosophy." The friendship

One may search at length in the writings of Karl Marx and seldom find a more severe criticism of the selfishness of "the employers of capital"; but we again note Smith's insistence upon the permanent limitations of human nature. Contrary to the teaching of certain dogmatic enthusiasts of *laissez-faire* who came after him, Smith insists that it is the duty of government to do what is necessary to encourage the productive tendencies of capitalists, while preventing them from "disturbing the tranquillity of any body but themselves."

Finally we note that Smith, although he may be regarded as having taught a labor theory of value, qualified his teaching in some important ways. We may state these qualifications in the following manner. Whence comes the exchangeable value of goods? Undoubtedly from the labor that transformed materials into commodities; but, as we noted above, the accumulation of capital results in a manifold increase in "the productive powers of labour," and thus makes profit a legitimate part of the price of goods. Therefore, not all value comes from labor, unless one is willing to regard capital as itself as a form of labor. Another part of the price of goods is, naturally enough, the wages of the laborer. There is a third component, however, namely rent for the use of land. Those who own land, although they do not labor in the production of goods, nevertheless receive a portion of their price. Smith says of landlords that "[a]s soon as the land of any country has all become private property, the landlords, like all other men, love to reap where they never sowed, and demand a rent even for its natural produce (49)." The advantages of this evident infringement upon value-producing labor, Smith argues, outweigh its injustices.

Indeed, this must be affirmed about Smith's view of the other irregularities of capitalism discussed in the preceding remarks; but, as we have said elsewhere, Smith is a moralist who does not moralize. He thus exhibits the classical virtue of prudence, which may be defined as the disposition to accommodate oneself to the limits set by given con-

---

engendered by commerce falls into the class of friendship based on utility. Friends of this sort are useful to one another. Admittedly, this is not the highest or noblest kind of friendship; but it *is* a kind of friendship. Indeed, with respect to friendship among nations, utility may be the highest kind practicable. The only higher kind of friendship, according to Aristotle, is that between like minds, who love the truth, and desire to spend their time either in contemplation, or in conversation with others similarly inclined. As such, this kind of friendship is available only to individual human beings, not to nations. Therefore, commerce is not to be despised, because it is a source of comity and peace among nations.

ditions, without compromising on principles or ends. Prudence, therefore, presupposes the existence of certain unavoidable givens, including first and foremost, human nature.

Prudence is distinguished from both cynicism and utopianism by the same thing, namely a view of the potential of human nature for both good *and* evil. If human beings are fundamentally motivated by self-interest, it does no good to cluck one's tongue and wish that it were otherwise; and Smith had very little use for those who would reform mankind, or undertake to impose upon their fellow human beings ambitious projects in social engineering. Neither ought one despair of the possibility of the amelioration of the human condition, and for precisely the same reason: the potential of human nature is for both good and evil.[39]

VI

We turn finally to Smith's teaching concerning man's natural sociability exhibited in the passion of sympathy, or compassion. Through the mechanism of this passion, Smith evolves a morality that is humane in its accommodation to the limits of human nature, yet uncompromising in its support for what we may call the morality of decent common sense.

*The Theory of Moral Sentiments* was Adam Smith's first book. It was published in 1759 while he occupied the Chair of Moral Philosophy at the University of Glasgow. The first edition of *Wealth of Nations* was published in March, 1776. Both books appear to have emerged from lectures on moral philosophy he gave at the University of Glasgow.

In *The Theory of Moral Sentiments*, Smith raises the following question: What is moral virtue, and why ought one choose to be virtuous? In the *Wealth of Nations*, Smith asks a different, and apparently unrelated question: What are the nature and origins of wealth, and how ought a nation conduct its economic policy so as to become as prosperous as possible? Because there is no evident good reason to believe that Smith substantially revised the teaching on human nature and morality which he presents in *The Theory of Moral Sentiments* during the interim between its publication and the first appearance of the *Wealth of*

---

39 We mark here another difference between Smith's system of natural liberty and Marxist socialism. Marx had no use for prudence, precisely because he denied the existence of permanent natural limitations to political life. His rejection of prudence accounts in part for the occasionally intemperate character of Marx's rhetoric.

*Nations*, one must assume that Smith believed that an economy based upon the system of natural liberty was not incompatible with the system of morality he evolved from the principle of sympathy.[40]

As Smith asserts at the beginning of *The Theory of Moral Sentiments*, "sympathy," in its literal acceptation of "feeling with another," is that sociable passion upon which moral life is founded. Sympathy may be called a sociable passion because it essentially involves our own feelings with the feelings of others, and thus may act as a counterpoise to self-interest.

Smith states it as a fact needing no corroboration beyond one's own observations, both of oneself and of one's fellow human beings, that human beings spontaneously sympathize with the passions of others. Sympathy is accomplished through the imagination. We do not *literally* feel the joy or terror of another human being; but, through our imagination, we do partially experience the other person's passion in and for ourselves.

Smith adds that, precisely because we are at some remove from the one actually suffering terror, to that extent we become disinterested spectators of that suffering. The disinterested, or "universal" spectator is a construction of Smith's, which, he says, is *the* standard of our bestowing approbation and disapprobation, merit and demerit. If we, as the disinterested spectator, beholding the suffering of another, and, knowing what caused it, are nevertheless able to feel the sufferer's pain to the same degree that the sufferer feels it, then we may be said to sympathize with the sufferer. We experience the *feeling* of approbation. We would not experience this feeling if, for example, we, as disinterested spectator, felt that the suffering of the other were disproportionate to its cause.

Smith thus immediately connects the question "What is virtue?" with the question "What deserves our moral approval or disapproval?" Approbation and disapprobation are bestowed upon actions, says Smith, according to whether we are able to sympathize with the passion which motivated the action. In bestowing our approbation and disapprobation upon an action, we consider whether the action corresponds to the passion which motivates it. For example, indignation is the appropriate passion in one whose family has been slandered; but to respond to slander by reciprocating it would not deserve our moral approval. We can sympathize with the passion that motivated the action; but we cannot sympathize with the resulting action, regarding it

---

[40] In this summary of Smith's moral teaching, I have relied extensively on Joseph Cropsey's excellent discussion in "Adam Smith," already cited above.

as exceeding the bounds of propriety. Similarly, we would disapprove of one who felt no indignation at having been slandered, regarding such a person as lacking in spirit.

As this example shows, the passion from which an action proceeds may be considered in two ways, in relation to the cause which excites it, or relative to the end which it proposes or the effect it tends to produce. Insofar as the sentiment is proportioned to its cause, it has propriety or impropriety. For example, neither spiritless passivity nor blind fury would be considered the proper passion on the part of the one slandered; rather, we would sympathize with the passion of righteous (*not* self-righteous) indignation.

Similarly, in bestowing merit or demerit, reward or punishment upon an action, we consider the proportion of the passion to the action which it causes. That is, we consider, writes Smith, "the nature of the effects which the affection aims at, or tends to produce." Its "beneficial or hurtful nature" is the source of its merit or demerit, of being worthy of reward or punishment. Smith writes:

> . . . that action must appear to deserve reward, which appears to be the proper and approved object of that sentiment, which most immediately and directly prompts us to reward, or do good to another. And in the same manner, that action must appear to deserve punishment, which appears to be the proper and approved object of that sentiment which most immediately and directly prompts us to punish, or to inflict evil upon another. The sentiment which most immediately and directly prompts us to reward, is gratitude; that which most immediately and directly prompts us to punish, is resentment. To us, therefore, that action must appear to deserve reward, which appears to be the proper and approved object of gratitude; as, on the other hand, that action must appear to deserve punishment, which appears to be the proper and approved object of resentment.[41]

Therefore, if a man who had been slandered were to respond with a vigorous and spirited defense of his family, then the disinterested observer could sympathize with the feeling of gratitude aroused in the members of his family who benefited from his defense, and would accordingly judge his action meritorious. If we are able to feel sympathy for the gratitude aroused in the one who is the object of an action, then we regard that action as meritorious. In short, "if the actual or supposed impartial spectator should sympathize with the passion both of the agent (propriety) and of the patient (merit), then the agent's act

---

41 Smith, *TOMS*, 67-68.

may be pronounced virtuous on the basis of the spectator's feeling of approbation."[42]

Consider any action, Smith says, which we would put into the class of things worthy of approbation or disapprobation. There will be both an agent and a patient. If an impartial observer of the action sympathizes with the agent, that is, feels in himself to the same degree the passion that moved the agent, then the observer approves, or experiences the sentiment of approbation. In this consists the propriety of the action. Propriety, however, is not the only ground of virtue. If the impartial spectator, informed of the relevant circumstances, also sympathizes with the sentiment of gratitude of the patient, the action is also said to be meritorious.

Smith therefore demonstrates that morality is grounded upon two non-rational capacities, the passion of sympathy and the faculty of the imagination.[43] Accordingly, Smith believed he had based morality upon the passions alone, a fact indicated by the title of his book, *The Theory of Moral Sentiments*. That is, morality, in Smith's view, is based on the sentiments, and not upon reason.

This does not mean that Smith disdained either morality or reason. On the contrary, the moral teaching of *The Theory of Moral Sentiments* is rather strict. Rather, Smith shows how morality may be deduced from the passions and the imagination alone, without the necessity of imposing rationally deduced obligations upon mankind. Given the inherently self-regarding nature of the other fundamental human passion, self-interest, such obligations could only be regarded as onerous, and would inevitably be sacrificed to man's more selfish concerns whenever duty and self-interest came into conflict.

It is important to note that, in Smith's teaching, sympathy cannot be separated from the imagination. Sympathy and imagination combine to form man's natural gregariousness. Through the mechanism of these two capacities, each human being is naturally led to transcend his own self-concern by sympathetically imagining the point of view of another human being. The natural human ability to participate in the feelings of another indicates Smith's answer to the question, What motivates human beings to choose moral virtue, where virtue means to

---

[42] Cropsey, "Adam Smith," 638.

[43] In so doing, Smith disagreed with his teacher David Hume, who believed that all moral judgments were based on utility. That is, according to Hume, we judge those things morally good which we deem to be useful. Smith did not reduce all approbation or disapprobation to utility, because utility is not something sensed or felt, but is recognized only by a calculation of reason.

be worthy of approbation? Man by his nature desires the approbation and love of his fellow human beings: "the chief part of human happiness arises from the consciousness of being loved."[44]

This is Smith's correction of Hobbes' teaching that human life is the "war of all against all." According to Hobbes, not only is man not naturally sociable, he is naturally hostile too, or at least suspicious of, his fellow man. Indeed, Smith mollifies even the harsher aspects of Locke's dictum that we have a natural *duty* to preserve the rest of mankind when our own preservation does not conflict with it. By calling it a duty, Locke indicated his opinion that any conflict between our natural desire and consequent right to preserve ourselves, and our duty to the rest of mankind, would always be resolved in favor of self-interest. Humankind appears compelled to be sociable in Locke's teaching, principally by the combination of self-interest and man's awareness of his naked and unprotected state outside civil society. We need others to help us protect ourselves and our property. Any additional positive obligation to others, or any interest in promoting their happiness, must arise from and be subordinate to the principle of self-preservation.

By contrast, Smith teaches that human nature combines imagination, sympathy, and the need for the love and approbation of others, thus making man naturally sociable. Smith is thus justified in referring both to man's natural sociability and to the *natural* character of the moral law. That is, the moral law is neither conventional, nor imposed upon man's nature from without, in potential conflict with his natural inclinations. Moreover, when Smith refers to "the natural principles of right and wrong," by "right" he does not mean merely what benefits or does not harm the *agent*. As we have seen, judgments of morality inherently involve our sympathetic involvement with the feelings of the recipient of the action as well. Morality is, according to Smith, based upon our natural concern for the good of others, expressed as our natural gregariousness.

The principle of gregariousness connects the teaching of *The Theory of Moral Sentiments* with that of the *Wealth of Nations*, and incidentally helps to explain certain pacific tendencies of commercial republics. Human beings are immediately connected with one another by sentiment or feeling; but they are connected with their fellow citizens by the less immediate considerations of utility. That is, the bond between men as men is naturally stronger than the bond between men as citizens, a bond which is based, as we saw, partly on calculation,

---

44 Smith, *TOMS*, 40.

and considerations of utility. Commercial republics, being bound to one another by their common interests and less by considerations of justice, more readily overcome the less attractive aspects of "nationalism" than do non-commercial republics. Thus, the system of natural liberty tends toward the overcoming of those interests that divide the nations from one another. Capitalism inherently tends toward "internationalism."[45]

This means that the perfection of human nature may conflict with those considerations of justice that are essential to the existence of any political community. On the one hand, "to feel much for others and little for ourselves, . . . to restrain our selfish, and to indulge our benevolent affections, constitutes the *perfection of human nature*; and can alone produce among *mankind* that harmony of sentiments and passions in which consists their whole grace and propriety."[46] On the other hand, as Smith says in the *Wealth of Nations*, one of the principal duties of the sovereign is to "[protect], as far as possible, every member of the society from the injustice or oppression of every other member of it, or [to establish] an exact administration of justice . . ."[47]

That is, justice appears, as Smith says in *The Theory of Moral Sentiments*, as "but a *negative* virtue, and only hinders us from hurting our neighbour. The man who barely abstains from violating either the person, or the estate, or the reputation of his neighbours, has surely very little positive merit." Justice requires one to do "every thing which [one's] equals can with propriety force him to do, or which they can punish him for not doing." The "safeguard of justice" is resentment, which "prompts us to beat off the mischief which is attempted to be done to us, and to retaliate that which is already done; that the offender may be made to repent of his injustice, and that others, through fear of the like punishment, may be terrified from being guilty of the like offence."

Justice, Smith asserts, being based upon the feeling of resentment, is perforce based upon an unsociable passion. We may observe the precepts of justice by merely leaving others alone. Therefore, says Smith, "[t]hough the breach of justice . . .exposes to punishment, the observance of the rules of that virtue seems scarce to deserve any reward." "There is," he continues, "a propriety in the practice of justice, and it

---

[45] This is illustrated by such phenomena as the trade agreements now being negotiated among the European nations, or between the United States, Canada, and Mexico.
[46] Smith, *TOMS*, 24.
[47] Smith, *WON*, 651.

merits, upon that account, all the approbation which is due to propriety. But as it does no real positive good, it is entitled to very little gratitude . . .We may often fulfil all the rules of justice by sitting still and doing nothing."[48]

While it is true, says Smith, that the state is necessary for our protection, it is also true that "the love of our own nation often disposes us to view, with the most malignant jealousy and envy, the prosperity and aggrandizement of any other neighbouring nation." "The love of our country," he continues, "seems not to be derived from the love of mankind. The former sentiment is altogether independent of the latter, and seems sometimes even to dispose us to act inconsistently with it . . . We do not love our country merely as a part of the great society of mankind: we love it for its own sake, and independently of any such consideration."[49]

Justice is, to be sure, indispensable to both the preservation and well-being of political society; but it rests upon the unsociable passion of resentment, and the attachment to one's own country and its conception of justice is sometimes at odds with the natural human affection for mankind. Commerce, on the other hand, while it intends to procure wealth for individual human beings, has certain irenic tendencies. Commercial nations tend not to go to war with one another. Therefore, the desire for material gain, under the right circumstances, can lead to the comity of nations better than the appeal to such principles as the "international brotherhood of man."

We may thus conclude that Smith understands morality, which is naturally concerned with the well-being of others, to be connected with a system of economics which, aiming at the accumulation of as much wealth as possible, aims primarily at preservation. This connection is made possible by the two passions of self-interest and sympathy. Accordingly, as a serious, sustained, and intelligent effort to overcome the division between self-interest and the common good, Smith's teaching recommends itself to all people everywhere of good will. As Joseph Cropsey writes, Smith teaches that man is

> by nature altruistic and egoistic—a species-member moved by love of self and fellow feeling with others . . .When it is borne in mind that Smith's teaching aims at the articulation of morality and preservation, and that the practical fruits of his doctrine are intended to be gathered by emancipating men, under mild government, to seek their happiness freely

---

[48] Smith, *TOMS*, 78ff.
[49] Ibid., 227ff.

according to their individual desires, the accomplishment as a whole commands great respect. The reconciliation of the private good and the common good by the medium not of coercion but of freedom, on a basis of moral duty, had perhaps never been seen before.[50]

---

[50] Cropsey, "Adam Smith," 642.

# CHAPTER FIVE

## *Critiques*

### I

In this chapter, we undertake to defend America's system of democratic capitalism against one of the criticisms most commonly made against it, namely, that capitalism inevitably produces economic injustice. This charge is aimed at the *principles* of the American system, and is motivated by the desire, not to reform, but to transform that system. The American system is said by its radical critics to be economically unjust, not merely in deed, but in principle.

American capitalism is alleged to be economically unjust because it causes or encourages, or is otherwise complacent about the unequal distribution of wealth. Under capitalism, we are told, the rich get richer than they should be, usually at the expense of the poor, while the poor inevitably become destitute. This disparity is thought to be unjust because we are a democratic society, and are thus committed to egalitarian principles which deprecate the unequal distribution of wealth. Therefore, justice requires us to ignore or qualify certain parts of the Constitution, for example the "takings clause," heretofore believed to protect property rights, in order to distribute wealth more equitably.

This criticism rests upon a distortion, in some cases intentional, of the true intent and language of the Constitution. Our purpose in this chapter is to correct that distortion.

While this book was being written, the world was witnessing events in Eastern Europe and what had formerly been the Soviet Union, which had previously seemed like impossible dreams: the dissolution of the Soviet Union, the collapse of the communist regimes in many of its client states, and the universal repudiation of the political and economic principles on which it stood. Yet, despite the historic collapse of socialism, and the spread capitalism and democracy, it is still necessary to ask: Has socialism failed? Has capitalism triumphed?

It is remarkable that the almost universal collapse of socialist regimes came about without what had been thought to be inevitable, namely, a military confrontation between East and West. The implacable enmity between the free West and the totalitarian East was

162

resolved, not by the triumph of the West's military strength, but of its political principles.[1] In the light of those principles, the failure of communism and the totalitarian Soviet regime to provide even a minimally decent standard of living for its citizens, was plain to all who had eyes to see. Stripped of its military power, the Soviet Union was revealed to be merely another Third World nation.

Communism collapsed because of its own inadequacies; but it also collapsed because whole peoples living under communist rule believed that the West offered something better, namely, a life of political and economic liberty, protected by a government whose right to rule is based upon and limited by the consent of the governed. The failure of communism has thus both a negative and a positive significance: communism failed both because of its own weaknesses, not to mention its unparalleled cruelty, and because of the evident superiority of the principles of democratic capitalism.

We are compelled, however, for reasons already discussed, to return to our initial question. In what respect, if at all, can democratic capitalism be said to have triumphed? The simple answer is that most people seem to have decided that capitalism is preferable to communism. It is preferable to communism because it is vastly more efficient in enabling the "allocation of scarce resources." It has shown itself superior to any known system of government ownership of the means of production, in creating wealth and raising the standard of material well being of a people. Capitalism has not, despite Marx's baleful predictions to the contrary, resulted in massive and irreducible unemployment, the "pauperization of the bourgeoisie," or the reduction of the proletariat to a condition of utter poverty. It has not produced an "accumulation of misery, corresponding with an accumulation of capital." It has not culminated in the great uprising of the working class, predicted by Marx. Indeed, the great irony of history is that it is communism, not capitalism, which has suffered all these, and worse.

Whereas Marx looked forward confidently to the demise of capitalism, destroyed by its own internal contradictions, and the consequent elimination of class warfare, in fact it was the communist regimes which invariably erected rigid systems of class privilege. That is, communism resulted in the creation of certain reactionary,

---

[1] To be sure, the West did not neglect to support its principles by military might. The success with which the West exploited the technological superiority of its military weapons over the Soviet Union was itself a signal instance of the superiority of capitalist to communist economies.

privileged classes, which staunchly resisted every attempt to "reform" communism.[2]

Attempts by socialist governments to control the accumulation of wealth, except, of course, the wealth of the members of the privileged classes, also led to the growth of black markets and the corruption that invariably accompanies them. Socialism destroyed the economic ambition of a people, and replaced it with apathy, cynicism and despair. The radical Left charges that free markets are indifferent to the fates of individual human beings; but *genuinely* free markets do not, as does socialism, distribute goods and power merely in accordance with the interests of a political elite, thus rendering individual ambition futile.

These facts appear to be uncontested by the great majority of those who have actually lived under communist regimes. There exists, however, particularly in the United States, a certain lingering fondness for socialism, or, at least, for the moral ideal it professes. One sees this especially in certain departments of our universities and colleges, or, in general, among the intellectuals of this country.

May we not simply dismiss this as the melancholy of disgruntled romantics and utopian dreamers? Or, perhaps the widespread enthusiasm for socialism, found so often in academic institutions, is the product of resentment over the fact that academics are, for the most part, not as wealthy or influential in American society as are, say, investment bankers and presidents of corporations. Perhaps the enchantment of the intellectual Left with socialism is only a form of sublimation, an attempt to give the color of moral respectability to envy; but, whatever may be the psychological cause for their loyalty to socialism and loathing for capitalism, are not the intellectual Left's criticisms overwhelmed by the mass of contrary factual evidence?

The intellectual Left's loyalty to socialism is not new. Accordingly, one may say that its current refusal to abandon socialism's moral ideals

---

2 Enthusiasts for socialism will, perhaps, argue that the intransigence of the privileged classes in the Soviet Union was precisely one compelling reason for the West to support the efforts of Mikhail Gorbachev to reform the communist system. This rejoinder begs the decisive questions, namely, whether communism, according to its own self-understanding, is amenable to reform; and, whether communism does not inevitably result in the erection of a system of rigid class privilege for a few, accompanied by deprivation for many. In a totalitarian regime, what will compel the *nomenklatura* to be accountable to the people, in return for the privileges they enjoy? And, in the absence of any system of accountability, why would any member of the privileged classes voluntarily give up his privileges?

is merely a continuation of that loyalty. Writing in *Commentary*, Owen Harries gives a history of the intellectual Left's defense of socialism, as well as its prediction of the imminent collapse of democracy and capitalism. Harries notes that, between 1975 and 1990, "[e]ven as the death knell of democracy was being sounded by intellectuals, it was rapidly gaining ground in Europe, Latin America, and Asia . . . [O]ver 30 countries abandoned authoritarian regimes in favor of democratic ones."[3] Despite this evidence, there continued to prevail among intellectuals "pessimism, and in some cases hostility, toward both capitalism and democracy . . . which persisted even in the later stages of the cold war."

Harries also makes the following observation:

> The cold war ended with a smashing victory for what we have come to think of naturally as the democratic-capitalist ideology and system, and the prestige of both ideology and system is now at an all-time high. Nothing would have seemed less likely to most intellectuals when the cold war began, or for a long time after that. *Indeed, in the 1940s the compatibility and interdependence of democracy and capitalism, so readily assumed today, were not generally, accepted. On the contrary, they were widely considered to be at odds with each other, with capitalism working to destroy the equality and sense of community that were deemed conditions of genuine democracy, and democracy requiring a 'fairness' and social justice that frustrated the reward system necessary to drive capitalism.* So George Orwell would write in the preface to his allegorical novel *Animal Farm*, as if he were merely pointing to the obvious: 'Yet one must remember that *England is not completely democratic. It is also a capitalist country with great class privileges . . .*'" [emphasis added] [4]

Intellectual honesty will compel us to admit that the alleged moral deficiencies of capitalism are not refuted simply by an appeal to the fact of the demise of communism; and the facts also show that the Left's moral aversion, if not hatred, for capitalism has not been mollified by the epochal collapse of communism. No matter how incontestably capitalism may have shown itself to be the superior of communism in respect to efficiency and creation of wealth, one cannot conclude from the preference for capitalism that it is morally superior to communism.

On the other hand, one must wonder whether the mass movement away from communism toward capitalism and democracy can be satisfactorily explained only in terms of a desire to improve the material

---

[3] Owen Harries, "The Cold War and the Intellectuals," *Commentary*, October 1991.
[4] Ibid., 13-14.

conditions of one's life, or to distribute political power more equitably. Apart from a conception of the good life for human beings, wealth and power rapidly loose their luster. Accordingly, one must consider the possibility that contemporary political science and economics are incapable of doing full justice to the phenomena.

Contemporary political science and economics regard themselves as independent disciplines. They assume that political phenomena may be adequately understood apart from economic considerations, and similarly for the economic phenomena. Furthermore, political science and economics, being sciences, are thus "value-free." They may describe their respective phenomena, but they may not evaluate them. They may not take sides. They may not, as sciences, conclude that one political regime or form of economy is morally superior to another. They may not, therefore, assume the point of view of those who actually live and act under certain political and economic conditions, for these people manifestly do act, not only in their own self-interest, but with a regard to considerations of justice, freedom, and the like, that is, with regard to issues of good and bad. If, however, the actors in the political phenomena *are* motivated by moral considerations, then no account of the phenomena which dismisses those considerations can be "objective."

We must therefore qualify our initial observation. While it is true that the massive rejection of communism in favor of democratic capitalism does not by itself demonstrate the moral superiority of the latter, it is also true that contemporary political science and economics, and intellectuals generally, insofar as they agree with the assumption that science must be "value-free," are prohibited from taking seriously the moral considerations of those who have rejected communism. A more humane and genuinely empirical political science would not ignore the opinions of these people, but would take them seriously, in order to see whether the belief in the moral superiority of democratic capitalism can be vindicated rationally.[5]

The quarrel between capitalism and communism is essentially a quarrel about morality, which is to say that it is ultimately a quarrel about the ends appropriate to human nature, or the good life for man. While the cold war was still being waged, Isaiah Berlin wrote that it was a war "fought between two civilizations and two systems of ideas which return different and conflicting answers to what has long been the central question of politics-the question of obedience and coercion."[6]

---

5 For example, such a science would take seriously the fact of Lech Walesa's admiration, not for Mikhail Gorbachev, but for Ronald Reagan.
6 Harries, "The Cold War," 13-14.

One must qualify Berlin's statement in order to make intelligible the righteous intensity with which the cold war was fought. The "central question of politics" is not primarily the "question of obedience and coercion." That is, the central issue of politics is not the distribution of power simply. It is, rather, the question of the just use of power. It is, in a word, not an issue that "has long been the central question of politics." It is, in fact, *the* central question of politics. It is the question of the just or good society. Accordingly, the only adequate explanation for the Left's refusal to admit the triumph of capitalism is that, despite its rejection of independently existing moral standards, it affirms the moral superiority of socialism to capitalism.

Consider, for example, that the 1980s, by many reasonable measures a most prosperous and peaceful decade, have come to be known widely as "The Decade of Greed." Popular culture, for example, has consistently portrayed Wall Street financiers, who stood as symbols of America's prosperity in the 1980s, as ruthless and selfish. It must be admitted that this portrait has some basis in fact. Wall Street arbitrageur Ivan Boesky announced that "Greed is good" to cheering audiences, and then himself became the first of many financiers to be implicated in scandal. Tom Wolfe's *Bonfire of the Vanities* described the breathtaking arrogance of young men in their late twenties and early thirties, who made unimaginably huge sums of money in complex transactions that eluded the understanding of most ordinary Americans.

Moreover, some have doubted whether the 80s were in fact as prosperous as others have said. While Wall Street flourished, the American dollar struggled against foreign currencies, and the budget and trade deficits grew to unprecedented size. American competitiveness suffered, and foreign investors rapidly bought up America's assets. America's ability to raise capital seemed to receive just the boost it needed, in the form of junk bonds, only to have them become just another symbol of the unscrupulous behavior that seems to flourish in unregulated economies. In the Southwest and Northeast, the banking system collapsed under the weight of too many bad real estate loans. America's standard of living was alleged to have declined, under the burdens of increased debt, tax disincentives on investment, and rising inflation. The emergence of the "underclass" was said to be a symptom of the widening disparity between the rich and poor, caused by the policies of "supply-side economics," which is, after all, just a fancy name for capitalism.

Many believed that these events were the signs of our decline, the inevitable results of a system which, as Marx taught, carried within itself the seed of its own destruction. The alleged growth of economic disparity in America was widely decried as a sign of a system that is inherently unjust and lacking in compassion for the poor, and thus doomed to fail. Many Americans might have agreed with Michael Walzer, that the great disparities in wealth in this country enable those who have "money . . . to purchase every other sort of social good."[7] Would it not, therefore, be more just to promote economic equality through a radical redistribution of wealth?

According to the critique by the radical Left, great wealth enables its possessors to gain inordinate political power, thus contravening what the Left regards as the egalitarian promise of the Declaration of Independence. What socialists desire, according to Walzer, is "the abolition of the power of money outside its sphere." Socialists want "a society in which wealth is no longer convertible into social goods with which it has no intrinsic connection."[8] We are compelled to wonder whether justice does indeed require a radical redistribution of wealth. Do our egalitarian principles mandate the effort to achieve greater economic equality, in the sense of greater parity of ownership, rather than the great inequalities of wealth which seem inevitably to result from an unregulated economy?

On the other hand, one must wonder whether "what socialists want" is desirable, or even possible.[9] If by "social goods" one means those goods which promote the common welfare as contrasted with the private well-being of individuals, then capitalism appears to be superior to socialism. The wealth created by the system of free markets becomes diffused throughout society in countless ways; through the creation of jobs and economic opportunity, through private philanthropy and charity, through corporate support for education and medical research, and so forth.

If, however, by "social goods" one means "political influence," or even "power," then the socialists appear to want a society where money cannot buy political influence. A moment's reflection on the history of

---

7 Michael Walzer, *Radical Principles* (New York: Basic Books, 1980), 240, quoted in Stephen Miller, "The Constitution and the Spirit of Commerce," in *How Capitalistic Is The Constitution?* (Washington: American Enterprise Institute, 1982), 165.

8 Miller, *Constitution*, 165.

9 There is, of course, also the consideration that the great majority of Americans may not want socialism.

political institutions suggests that this is a desire impossible to fulfill. One may agree that justice requires that some effort be made to reduce the political influence of wealth; but here, as is often the case, the question concerns means, not ends. Or, to put the point more accurately, the question concerns those means compatible with the ends. Is it better to reduce the political influence of wealth through the imposition of policies of redistribution; or, is it better to neutralize the political influence of the wealthy few, by securing to each citizen the opportunity to acquire wealth? There is the further consideration that, as Aristotle saw, in regard to the political power of wealth, the middle class taken as a whole may wield more power than the rich; and, capitalist societies tend to create large middle classes. Therefore, the encouragement of free enterprise may counteract the inordinate political power of the wealthy few.

Of course, the socialists will reply that what they desire is a more just society, and that justice in a democratic society *requires* the re-distribution of wealth. In preceding chapters, we have argued that the political thinkers, both ancient and modern, who were the intellectual architects of the American system, agreed that democratic societies tend to be preoccupied with the acquisition of material wealth, and that it is imprudent simply to oppose this tendency.

The modern thinkers disagreed with the ancient thinkers concerning the best way to accommodate this tendency. To put this disagreement simply, the ancients taught that the prudent ruler will attempt to moderate the democratic passion for acquiring wealth, through the inculcation of the virtues of temperance, generosity, and civic-mindedness. This effort intends to produce citizens who are virtuous, as well as to mitigate the vulnerability of democracies to demagoguery and faction.

The moderns replied that a democracy, thus understood, must always remains small, and therefore weak. Moreover, the importunity of self-interest will always tend to undermine the effort to inculcate public virtue. The discovery of the principles of representative government, however, enabled the establishment of a large republic. The protection of property rights and freedom of association in such a republic cause factions to proliferate; but the great extent of the republic will ensure that there are many factions, with the result that no one faction is likely to become powerful enough to prevail over the others. Interest can thus be played off against interest.

Moreover, the modern thinkers taught that by liberating the acquisitive passion, wealth will be, not merely distributed, but *created*, with the result that a relatively affluent and politically stable middle class can exist. If the ancient republics were too often characterized by a sharp division between the wealthy few and the many poor, the modern affluent democratic state would be predominantly middle class. In such a society, justice, understood essentially as equality of opportunity, coupled with certain rewards for achievement, would generally prevail. The resulting social and economic mobility would, it was believed, provide an outlet for the restless, acquisitive, and ambitious dimensions of human nature. Given these facts of human nature, the moderns believed that this conception of justice and the society based upon it, were the most humane for which one might reasonably hope.

Thus it is that the true nature of the Left's critique of the American system comes to be seen for what it is. The Left's critique is not ameliorative, but *radical*. Unlike, for example, the civil rights movement of the 1960s, which was able to capture the conscience of Americans by appealing to the very principles upon which the United States claims to stand, the Left has attempted, in criticizing American liberal democracy, to transform America's self-understanding and vision for the future. The Left has attempted to persuade the American people that it understands America's true purpose better than they do. Accordingly, the Left wishes to replace the conception of justice which one finds articulated in the Declaration and Constitution, a conception which acknowledges the inherent imperfectibility of man, with one that seeks to achieve equality of result, even at the price of politicizing what were previously thought to be the essentially private dimensions of human life.

Thus, partly as a result of the intransigent character of the Left's critique, many Americans continue to believe that socialism is a more just and compassionate system than capitalism, despite its evident and massive failures abroad, and despite the harmful consequences of radical egalitarianism for the quality of American life. They appear to hope that a reformed and chastened socialism, having learned from the mistakes of the past, may still be possible. Perhaps the economic failures of socialism are merely accidental, as is the fact that socialist governments have been, almost without exception, the most totalitarian and murderous in human history.[10]

Let us, therefore, ignore the Marxist criterion of appealing to historical conditions, which is to say, let us ignore the evidence of history,

---

10 There are, for example, still some socialists who continue to deny that there is any intrinsic connection between true communism and Stalinism.

and ask: may we not be obliged by a concern for moral decency to wonder whether it is possible to construct a socialist government that would, on the one hand, allow and protect political freedom, while eliminating economic disparity? Would not such a political and economic system accord better with the democratic principles set forth in our Declaration of Independence and Constitution? Perhaps our own principles, not to mention justice itself, inevitably commit us to democratic socialism. Is it not true that "the present distribution of wealth makes no moral sense?"[11]

Perhaps it would make better moral sense for wealth to be distributed according to the inherent worth of persons as such, each of whom has been, in the words of the Declaration of Independence, "created equal," equally endowed with certain inalienable rights. Perhaps we are compelled to wonder whether justice itself commends to us the combination of political freedom and economic equality, as the only fair polity.

## II

It is especially clear that the Left's critique of capitalism was not mollified by the apparently spectacular success of America's capitalistic economy during the Reagan years. Indeed, it seems that this very success intensified the Left's conviction of the moral depravity of capitalism: the more capitalism succeeded, the more assiduously did the Left search for ways to discredit it. Consider the following passage from an article by Robert Lekachman, written at the beginning of the Reagan years:

> Political parties on the right are peopled mainly by the affluent and those who hope to join them. Socialists and social-democratic parties, on the other hand, traditionally have drawn their recruits from men and women who attach their own aspirations to the improved fortunes of the group of which they are a part. Thus, as awareness spreads that the prospects for individual riches have drastically diminished, the times are likely to become receptive at last to the emergence of a credible Left. Because without hope, life is intolerable, I choose to assume that after the conservative interlude represented by the Reagan administration, American politics will gradually polarize around credible conservative and radical alternatives. To be an optimist in 1981 or 1982, an American must cultivate the capacity to look beyond 1984 and see visions of a society quite different from Orwell's nightmare . . . [I]t is worth mentioning that conventional economics has been discredited by the test of its own market. A

---

[11] Miller, *Constitution,* 165.

thinner-skinned set of professional practitioners would have been shamed into silence long since by errors of diagnosis and prophecy so numerous and glaring. Notoriously, standard economics, whether Keynsian or monetarist, has groped uncertainly with inflation, unemployment, and international economic relations. *Its newest offspring, the supply-side theology, scarcely warrants discussion; it is a wager placed with religious fervor on the capacity of human avarice to revitalize declining industries, renew historical rates of growth, and, ultimately, improve general living standards.* Like any other strongly held faith, supply-side economics persist [sic] in spite of both the absence of evidence for it and the presence of evidence against it. Among a growing number of economists, many of them young, a revival of Marxist and institutionalist approaches holds some promise of intellectual progress.[12] [emphasis added]

Lekachman thus appears to regard "supply-side" economics as the "off-spring" of something he calls "standard economics, whether Keynsian or monetarist." That is, he does not take seriously the possibility that "Reaganomics" was, relative to prevailing economic views, radical in its challenge to the assumptions of what Lekachman lumps together under the heading "standard economics." Perhaps standard economics had, imperceptibly, come to be dominated by a distrust of the free market. The radical character of Reaganomics lay therefore in its return to the principles of free enterprise.

Lekachman therefore fails to consider the simpler possibility, namely, that "supply-side" economics is really just another, perhaps slightly misleading name, for Adam Smith's version of entrepreneurism and free market economies. At any rate, Lekachman, unlike Smith, is evidently unwilling to live with revitalized industries, renewed rates of growth, and improved living standards, unless these things result from morally pure intentions. Thus, any empirical evidence to the contrary notwithstanding, Lekachman shows that he is in principle disinclined to attribute any desirable qualities to capitalism in its classic form. At any rate, Lekachman appears to prefer systems of economics that "hold some promise of intellectual progress," to those systems that, despite certain moral irregularities, produce wealth.

Moreover, although he does not share with his reader the empirical evidence that, in his view, allows him to dismiss supply-side economics, it seems likely that Lekachman would agree with those who came to conclude, despite massive evidence to the contrary, that "the Reagan years" were both morally and economically catastrophic. The substance

---

12 Robert Lekachman, "Capitalism or Democracy," in *How Capitalistic Is the Constitution?* (Washington: American Enterprise Institute, 1982), 140-141.

of the Left's critique of capitalism, as articulated by Lekachman, is essentially the same now as it was when Lekachman wrote the article from which we have quoted; and, to judge by the extent to which the Left is willing to revise the history of the Reagan administration, the passion which animates that critique has, if anything, grown in intensity.

For example, the phrase "the Reagan deficit" is now regularly used, even by those who ought to know better, to indicate the alleged fact that the budget deficit grew in the Eighties *because* of the Reagan tax cuts. These cuts, so the revisionists have argued, were cynically intended to lower taxes on the rich, raise taxes on the middle class, and actually *create* deficits, in order to compel a reduction in social spending.[13]

Anyone who has ever had a civics course, or has actually read the Constitution of the United States, knows that, according to Article I, sections 7 and 8, it is the Congress, not the Executive branch, which has sole authority to originate bills for raising revenue, or for allocating funds for expenditures. The President has no direct authority over taxing and spending, and thus cannot be directly or solely responsible for a budget deficit. It is, therefore, *prima facie* impossible to speak meaningfully about "the Reagan deficit," or any other president's deficit, as though the President himself were responsible for creating it.

Neither does the historical evidence support this view. Norman Ture, Undersecretary of the Treasury for Tax and Economic Affairs in 1981-82, gave an account of the history of Reagan's economic policies, in which he said:

> . . . [F]ollowing ERTA, every tax bill proposed or supported by the Administration was a revenue raiser. It is impossible to reconcile this record of tax increases with the inane notion that the Reagan Administration's objective was to enlarge budget deficits. The key to the deficits is the role of the Congress in budget making. Most of the budgets that President Reagan sent to Congress after 1981 were either rejected out of hand or very materially altered (35ff.).

---

[13] See Norman Ture, "To Cut and to Please," *National Review* 31 August 1992, 35ff. Ture quotes U. S. Representative Donald J. Pease (D., Ohio), speaking on 11 June 1992, who said: "Let us look at the big deficits we have and try to find out what caused them . . . Fundamentally, our $4-trillion deficit or debt is caused by loss of revenue. The $4-trillion debt is caused by the 1981 tax cut and misguided supply-side economics."

Moreover, regarding Reagan's alleged complicity in a plot to favor the rich, Ture writes:

According to the mythmakers, in addition to starving social spending, the Reagan policies were intended to favor the rich at the expense of the poor. As Governor [of Arkansas, Bill] Clinton's *Putting People First: A National Economic Strategy for America* (June 20, 1992) stated it: "For twelve years, the driving idea behind American economic policy has been cutting taxes on the richest individuals and corporations . . ." The Governor has a fragile grasp of history, even that of the recent past. For one thing, during the Reagan Administration, only one tax bill, ERTA, reduced taxes for upper-income individuals and corporations. The central objective of the initial Reagan program, of which ERTA was a critically important part, was to reorient national economic policy. Instead of focusing on income redistribution and aggregate demand management of the economy, the Reagan policy aimed at reducing the Federal Government's intrusion into the nation's economic life. It sought to provide a policy climate in which individuals' incentives to pursue their own economic progress would not be frustrated by government tax, spending, regulatory, and monetary policies. ERTA's role in this economic strategy was to reduce the disincentives of high and steeply progressive individual tax and the biases they exerted against working, saving, and investing . . . (35ff.)

In short, what Reagan proposed was that we encourage entrepreneurial capitalism. The remarkable rise during the 1980s, in rates of job growth, as well as those for budget receipts as a per cent of GNP, appear to vindicate his proposal;[14] but, the intensity with which Reagan's opponents sought (and still seek) to discredit his policies

---

[14] In the same article, Ture reminds the reader of the "several substantial tax *increases* from 1982 through 1989," and argues that whether these "contributed to rather than retarded this growth in revenue [from 18.1% of GNP in 1983 to 18.9% of GNP in 1990] is, at the least, debatable. Unless one believes, however, that tax increases necessarily lose revenue (a not entirely implausible proposition), there is no basis in fact for insisting that tax-policy developments were responsible for the budget deficits of the Reagan years." Ture goes on to show that the Gramm-Rudman-Hollings deficit reductions did in fact slow the growth of federal outlays from fiscal 1985 through fiscal 1989; but, despite this, "with the single exception of fiscal 1984, actual outlays, in each of the fiscal years 1981-89 exceeded the Reagan budget requests, by as much as $50 billion in fiscal 1989." Accordingly, Ture concludes, "Spending excesses, not excessive tax cuts, account for the sorry budget deficit record of the past decade." It must also be noted that Reagan did not cut taxes, but *tax rates*. Although tax rates declined, tax revenues increased during the Reagan presidency.

forces one to conclude that they are driven, not simply by hatred of Ronald Reagan, but also by a deep contempt for capitalism. It thus seems reasonable to conclude that the radical critics of capitalism, such as Lekachman, have succeeded in their efforts to make Americans ashamed of their economic system.

In fairness to Lekachman, it must be said that he does not claim to be a spokesman for the Left. It is also fair to say, however, that Lekachman's strong faith in the moral superiority of socialism to capitalism is typical of the Left, as is his hope that somehow, somewhere, the truly decent character of socialism will eventually become evident to all, and that humankind will at last come to its senses. One must nevertheless wonder whether the Left's critique is not driven by what Lekachman himself calls the "religious fervor" of a "strongly held faith." It would be difficult to find a religious faith so resolutely blind to facts as the Left's indestructible faith in socialism.

In the passage quoted above, Lekachman asserts, without evidence or argument, that right-wing political parties are made up of the wealthy and those who desire to become wealthy. Socialists, on the other hand, do not desire to become wealthy; rather, they are evidently moved solely by their desire to promote the well-being of the community to which they belong. We say "evidently," because Lekachman does not use the word "community." Instead, he says that socialists identify their interests with those of the "group" to which they belong. To identify one's interests with those of the group to which one belongs is not necessarily to subordinate one's interest to the common good. It may only be to align oneself with a particular faction. Furthermore, a faction may be defined as a collection of individuals united by a common interest. This interest may or may not be inimical to the public welfare. It is thus not self-evident that identifying one's aspirations with those of the group to which one belongs is to be admired as a form of altruism. Group interests are not necessarily the same as the good of the community, or the public welfare. It is characteristic of the radical Left to be more concerned with class interests than with the public good. Indeed, the Left typically analyzes political phenomena in terms of class interests, thus suggesting that the class is the fundamental unit of political life. To speak meaningfully of the public welfare, on the other hand, one must take the individual citizen as fundamental, and consider whether there exists some good in which all citizens as such may share.

However this may be, it is evidently this difference of aspiration between the Right and the Left which, according to Lekachman, allows the Left to claim the moral high ground. We recall Marx's famous formula, "From each according to his ability, to each according to his need." The alleged moral superiority of socialism to capitalism consists in this: whereas capitalism promotes selfishness, socialism appeals to a nobler passion, the desire for selfless dedication to the common good. Capitalism is allegedly dedicated to encouraging the employment of human ability in the interest of selfishness, while simultaneously distorting the natural human needs, in order to foster unnatural "demands" for the goods it produces. Furthermore, because capitalism requires unlimited economic growth, it must continue to distort true human needs and further alienate man from himself. Socialism, however, is dedicated to the altruistic employment of one's abilities in the service of the rational satisfaction of the natural needs of others.

Despite the foregoing, one is forced to wonder whether socialism can articulate and promote the common good, or public welfare, better than democratic capitalism. It must be remembered that, according to Marx, the just society will be achieved only after class divisions have been overcome. That is, Marx conceives political unity negatively, in terms of the elimination of conflict, or of the causes of conflict, which causes are said by Marx to be fundamentally economic.

Marx argues that this elimination of conflict is achieved through the dialectical motion of history. The opposition of class interests is accordingly reinterpreted in the light of the dialectic of history, and the conclusion is drawn that this opposition *must* itself be overcome, not by compromise or mutual accommodation, but by revolutionary action. Such action must be undertaken for the simple reason that it is necessary to destroy the conflicting classes, in order to eliminate their conflicting interests. This necessity derives from the dialectic of history. Thus, Marxism necessarily culminates in a program of revolutionary action directed at the elimination of certain classes.[15]

Democratic capitalism, on the other hand, holds that, under the proper conditions, political unity and a concern for the public good can consist with factional disputes, and that the healthy competition of free markets is not the same thing as class conflict, or the oppression of one class by another. Capitalism is based on the view that some conflicts of interest are ineradicable, or that the causes of such conflicts are rooted

---

[15] It is in this light that one must view, for example, Stalin's "dekulakization and collectivization" policies during the period 1929-1933, when millions of Soviet peasants were killed, or deported to the Arctic. See Robert Conquest's powerful account of this period, in his *The Harvest of Sorrow* (New York: Oxford University Press, 1986).

in human nature. Moreover, democratic capitalism, adhering to the principle of the consent of the governed, resolutely insists on the distinction between the public and private spheres. It does not try to "politicize" everything; nor, does it try to explain all of human life in economic terms. Thus, whereas democratic capitalism insists upon distinguishing "state" from "society," Marxism insists that everything is political. There can be no separation of state from society. According to its principles, the Communist state must absorb society, in order to ensure the eradication from it of all activities and institutions which tend to alienate human beings from one another, the most egregious of these being free markets and commerce.

Lekachman, in order not to be forced into despair, "chooses to assume" that the nobler cause of socialism will gain credibility as Americans come to realize that the prospects for acquiring wealth are diminishing. Thus, Americans will perforce emerge from "the conservative interlude" of the Reagan years, and will repudiate the alleged appeal of "supply-side" economics to human avarice. American political life in the future will be characterized by the contrast between "credible conservative and radical alternatives." Supply-side "theology" will have no place among these alternatives. Indeed, it scarcely warrants discussion, not because of any theoretical incoherence of its own, or because of any empirical disconfirmation, but because it allegedly celebrates the dark side of human nature. Accordingly, Lekachman dismisses it without argument or appeal to fact.

Thus, the "root cause" of Lekachman's aversion to Reaganomics indeed appears to be a form of optimism, but an optimism of a peculiar kind. The old optimism held that the actual world, warts and all, is still the best of all possible worlds: ultimately, good will prevail over evil in the universe. Thus, one may say that, in this sense, Adam Smith and Ronald Reagan are optimists. They both believe that, if human beings are allowed to employ their capital where they will, they, along with most of the rest of society, will benefit more than they will be harmed, human avarice notwithstanding.

The new optimism, by contrast, refuses to accept a world with warts and avarice. The new commandment of the new optimists is: let there be no warts. Instead, let there be "institutionalist approaches" to economics, to ensure that economic well-being, understood as the equal distribution of wealth, results only from good intentions.

Therefore, despite the fact that, during the 1980s, supply-side economics did indeed enjoy great success in revitalizing declining industries, renewing historical rates of growth, and, ultimately, improving general living standards, one must conclude that Lekachman, and those who agree with him, have not been dissuaded from their loathing for free enterprise.

### III

On the morning of August 19, 1991, Americans awoke to the news that Mikhail Gorbachev had been deposed as President of the Soviet Union. Ruling instead was a group of Soviet "hardliners" opposed to Gorbachev's attempts to reform the Soviet economy. Within forty-eight hours, however, the coup had begun to collapse. One week later, the Communist Party and the Soviet Union appeared to be headed for the historical oblivion to which Marx had consigned capitalism. The Union's constituent republics began to declare their independence, and various former Soviet leaders publicly repudiated communism.

These events were celebrated in a *Wall Street Journal* editorial entitled "Those Who Served":

> The Communist Party of the Soviet Union collapsed this weekend with breathtaking suddenness. But the enemies of communism have been grinding away at its foundations for nearly a century . . . The fury that greeted the Western critics of communism can scarcely be imagined in today's world, but during the 1930s, 40s and 50s, conservative philosophers as well as liberals in the classic tradition systematically dismantled Marxist logic . . . [Among these critics] was the celebrated historian Arthur Schlesinger, an emblem of liberal anti-communism. Mr. Schlesinger was also an officer in the Congress for Cultural Freedom, along with [Sidney] Hook, James Burnham, Irving Kristol, Ignazio Silone and others. The organization once and for all destroyed communism as a force in Western intellectual life . . . George Meany, leader of the AFL-CIO was a stalwart enemy of totalitarianism, siding with free workers against what professed to be a working class ideology. George Orwell, who had devastated Soviet-style rhetoric in "1984," once wrote, "We have now sunk to a depth at which the re-statement of the obvious is the first duty of intelligent men." After the New Left inroads of the late 60s and the detente of the 1970s, the West had reached a similar state of high folly, in which Gerald Ford would not meet with Aleksandr Solzhenitsyn for fear of upsetting the Soviets, and Jimmy Carter warned of an "inordinate fear of communism."

On the same morning that the above editorial appeared, while even some Soviet politicians were themselves publicly describing the Soviet Union in terms that recalled Ronald Reagan's "evil empire" speech, Anthony Lewis, a New York Times columnist, was unfavorably comparing the Reagan and Bush Administrations to those Soviet leaders who had *opposed* the coup, most of whom had for years been loyal Communists. Lewis charged that Reagan and Bush had violated the United States Constitution in their zealous pursuit of anti-communist aims.

One might plausibly reply by pointing out that the zealous pursuit of anti-communist goals accords fully with the Preamble of the Constitution, which lists several desiderata, including promoting the "general welfare." Given the mortal enmity, said by Marx himself, as well as his students, to exist between capitalism and communism, it seems reasonable to conclude that pursuing anti-communist aims does indeed promote the general welfare of the United States.

It is instructive to recall that the Lekachman article discussed above was entitled "Capitalism *or* Democracy," (emphasis added), and began as follows:

> The Constitution and the Bill of Rights make two promises to Americans that have frequently clashed in the course of our national history. *In recent years, their inherent incompatibility has become glaringly apparent.* One commitment is to political equality, *an implication that any individual's vote, effect upon his neighbors, and influence upon his elected representatives is approximately as important as another's.* The second is an open invitation to all comers to enrich themselves by their own efforts. [emphasis added]

Democracy and capitalism are said to contradict one another because those who acquire great wealth are able to wield more political influence than those who do not. The "or" in the title of Lekachman's essay is thus exclusive in sense. We may have capitalism or democracy, but not both. Lekachman evidently believes, then, that Marx was right: political interests merely reflect economic interests. Thus democratic capitalism is an inherently contradictory system.

From these and other examples, it is evident that, even though socialism as an economic theory has been thoroughly discredited by the test of history, it retains its power as a moral ideal. In particular, the assertion that socialism is morally superior to capitalism remains credible to many Americans, the great majority of whom have never lived under a socialist regime. By contrast, the great majority of those living in countries long ruled by socialist regimes have firmly rejected socialism, on the grounds of both economic efficiency and moral decency.

Writing in the *Wall Street Journal*, Lindley H. Clark observed:

> Socialism, as a system for running a country, has been badly battered . . . [b]ut socialism always was more than a scheme for economic management; it was a plan for the moral ordering of people's lives. The ultimate aim of socialism . . . hasn't been fully successful anywhere for more than

brief periods . . . But Michael Keran, chief economist of Prudential Insurance Co., points out that a number of socialist ideas about morality are still alive and well, not only in the Soviet Union but also in the U. S. and other Western nations. There's a widespread feeling, for instance, *that income inequality is somehow bad . . . As Mr. Keran says, it's not as though capitalism had no morality of its own to offer and so had to settle for socialist notions.* "The economic theory of capitalism," he says, "is that capital *and* labor [instead of labor alone, as Marx taught; emphasis added] both contribute to the production of goods and services. Voluntary exchange in the marketplace sets the value of both capital and labor . . . Income inequality is not exploitation but rather reflects the relative value to society of individual skills." *The focus of unalloyed capitalism is equality of opportunity, not equality of income.*[16] [emphases added]

Socialism must thus be understood as primarily a moral, and not merely an economic, system.

Despite the many failures of socialism to prove otherwise, the view that disparity of income is unjust is still accepted by many. Capitalism is thus thought to be amoral, and to require reform by the importation of socialist principles. Capital's contribution to the value of goods and services is deprecated on the grounds of the Marxist teaching that labor is the only source of value. As one writer has pointed out, however, Marx does not demonstrate his assertion that labor alone is the source of value, but appears to accept it as self-evident.[17]

---

16 Lindley H. Clark, "We Have Met the Socialists, and They Are Us," *Wall Street Journal*, 17 September 1991. During the week this editorial appeared, Senator Tom Harkin of Iowa announced his candidacy for Democratic nominee for the 1992 presidential election. In making his announcement, Senator Harkin criticized "supply-side" economics, which belonged, he said, on the "trash heap of history," along with communism. Another *Wall Street Journal* editorial observed that "[t]his must mean [Senator Harkin] plans to stay away from the former communists in Europe now trying to implement a supply-side program. It's an irony of the age that Mr. Harkin's economic message has more adherents now in Iowa City than in Moscow, or even Stockholm."

17 Joseph Cropsey, "Karl Marx," in *History of Political Philosophy*, Third Edition, ed. Strauss and Cropsey, (Chicago: University of Chicago Press, 1987), 817. See Karl Marx, *Capital*, vol. 1, 44ff.: "Productive activity, if we leave out of sight its special form, viz., the useful character of the labor, is nothing but the expenditure of human labor-power . . . which remains the same under all its modifications . . . [T]he value of a commodity represents human labor in the abstract, the expenditure of human labor in general . . . While, therefore, with reference to use-value, the labor contained

Marx asserts that labor is the only source of value in the course of asking how it is that goods which differ qualitatively, that is, goods which have different uses, such as shirts and shoes, may nevertheless be *exchanged.* How can they be assigned value relative to one another, as well as to other equally distinct goods? In other words, how can you trade shirts for shoes, if there is no common measure of their worth? Traditional political economy had distinguished "use value" from "exchange value," in order to answer this question. Understood as having qualitatively different uses, shirts and shoes are incommensurable; but, understood as goods manufactured for the purpose of exchange, they are commensurable. Their exchange-values may be compared in terms of money, the "medium" of exchange; and, their relative values are established by the marketplace.

Why does Marx reject the category of exchange-value in order to solve the problem of the mensurability of goods? It is because he believes that exchange is not a permanent economic institution, but is rather a transitory phenomenon, which will pass away when capitalism passes away. According to Marx, classical economics failed to notice the transitory character of exchange, because classical economics was itself a phenomenon of a particular historical epoch.[18] In his critique of classical economics, Marx thus replaced the dichotomy of classical economics, exchange-value/use-value, with use-value/value. It is their value, pure and simple, which is the ground of the exchangeability of goods.

Therefore, Marx concludes that the source of the comparability of goods, or of their value as goods, must be *labor;* but labor comes to sight initially as itself being divided into qualitatively distinct kinds. The labor of making shoes is qualitatively distinct from the labor of

---

in a commodity counts only qualitatively, with reference to value it counts only quantitatively, and must first be reduced to human labor pure and simple . . . Since the magnitude of the value of a commodity represents only the quantity of labor embodied in it, it follows that all commodities, when taken in certain proportions, must be equal in value . . . [A]ll labor is, speaking physiologically, an expenditure of human labor-power, and in its character of identical abstract human labor, it creates and forms the value of commodities."

[18] See, for example, Marx's *Economico-Philosophical Manuscripts of 1844*: "Political economy proceeds from the fact of private property. It does not explain private property . . . When it determines the relationship of wages to profit . . . its final principle of explanation is the interest of the capitalist, i.e., it assumes what it is supposed to explain."

making shirts. But, says Marx, as toil, or undifferentiated labor, all labor is identical, and may be measured by the formula, Labor = (rate) x (time). As products of *undifferentiated* labor, all goods have a common measure, namely the amount of labor each embodies.

It would appear, then, that the self-evidence to Marx of the proposition that undifferentiated labor is the source of the value, and thus of the commensurability of goods, derives in part from his view that exchange is a transitory phenomenon. Marx's labor theory of value depends upon his dialectical materialism. That is, Marx must look to the quantity of labor as the source of value pure and simple, because he has nothing else to which to appeal, believing as he does that exchange has no natural or permanent basis in things.

This undifferentiated labor, however, is an *abstraction* from actual, concretely existing labor. Actual labor is always carried out for the sake of this or that purpose, and is thus always qualitatively determined. Actual labor is always undertaken for the purpose of satisfying some specific need or want. That is, only by abstracting from the *purposiveness* of actually existing labor is Marx able to assert that undifferentiated labor is the source of value pure and simple.

It is important to note this, because it indicates a difficulty with Marx's teaching, which he was apparently unable to overcome. On the one hand, Marx is a materialist. He teaches that human thought, or "consciousness," and therefore human society as a whole, is fundamentally a "reflection" of existing material conditions. Human rationality is derivative, not original or fundamental.

On the other hand, Marx himself is compelled to appeal to the human capacity for rational or intentional, and not merely economically determined behavior. For example, his entire program of revolutionary action presupposes the capacity for conceiving and originating action. On account of his materialism, however, Marx *must* abstract from the purposiveness of actually existing labor, and find the basis of exchange of qualitatively distinct goods in the sheer quantity of labor, a quantity which, although it may be considered in thought, has no independent existence in things. If, however, labor is an abstraction, then it begins to appear that human purposiveness is indispensable to the adequate or scientific account of labor. In that case, qualitatively distinct labor, and thus the category of exchange value, might turn out to be permanent categories of economic thought.

In our opinion, it is this unresolved tension in Marxism which is largely responsible for the inhumanity and repressive intolerance characteristic of communist societies. In such societies, human "consciousness" is divided into two kinds. The consciousness of the revolutionary is free and far-seeing, having been somehow liberated from the determinism of existing material conditions. The consciousness of the bourgeoisie is, on the other hand, literally "reactionary," that is, merely a reaction to existing material conditions, as well as to any attempt to change them. The revolutionary, having grasped the true direction of history, is thereby the rightful ruler of society, and may employ whatever means necessary to ensure the correct historical outcome. Thus, all so-called "natural" impulses or passions, being only the reflection of historical conditions, are suspect, and must be carefully controlled. It is partly for this reason that socialism, unlike capitalism, distrusts the capacity of "voluntary" exchange in the marketplace to set the exchange-values of capital and labor.

## IV

We saw above that, according to Lekachman, the U. S. Constitution and Bill of Rights make two promises which, because they contradict one another, cannot both be kept. The first "commitment" is to "political equality," by which, Lekachman asserts, without offering any evidence to support his assertion, the Constitution means "equality of political influence." The second commitment "is an open invitation to all comers to enrich themselves by their own efforts."

Why are these two promises, allegedly made by the Constitution, mutually incompatible? It is, says Lekachman, because

[p]olitical and economic markets overlap . . . and wealth translates into political influence, favorable legislation, and helpful decisions by bureaucrats. Rich people, not their poorer cousins, own newspapers, news magazines, and TV channels. The First Amendment protects a free press. To echo A. J. Liebling, only the wealthy own one. In the long run, political freedom cannot survive within the unfavoring [sic] context of plutocracy. Why are we willing to endanger *political freedom and equality* for the sake of capitalism?[19] [emphasis added]

Whereas Lekachman began by stating that the incompatibility "inherent" in the Constitution is caused by its promise of political equality (interpreted by Lekachman to mean equality of political influence), coupled with its alleged open invitation to "all comers to enrich themselves by their own efforts," he now re-states his position: it is capitalism which endangers both political freedom and equality. The danger Lekachman warns against is, not that our Constitution contra-

---

[19] Lekachman, "Capitalism or Democracy," 127.

dicts itself, but that capitalism cultivates "crass pursuit of profit," "individual gratification," and "avarice." That is, capitalism must be controlled, if not eliminated, if we wish to preserve political freedom and equality.

Now capitalism obviously cannot exist without free markets, that is, without freedom of a particular kind. Let us call it "economic freedom." Lekachman appears to believe, therefore, that there exists something which he calls "political freedom"; that political freedom can (and should) exist independently of "economic freedom"; that the latter inevitably prevails to the detriment to the former, and therefore must be controlled so as to prevent those who "enrich themselves by their own efforts" from acquiring inordinate political influence.[20] In any case, Lekachman seems to think that there is no use in merely having the right to a free press unless you are also wealthy enough to own a newspaper.

Lekachman's interpretation of our founding documents is not merely unsupported, but positively contradicted by what the Constitution actually says. Moreover, *the* authoritative interpreter of the Constitution, namely, *The Federalist*, states:

> The diversity in the faculties of men from which the rights of property originate, is not less an insuperable obstacle to a uniformity of interests [than is the connection between man's reason and his self-love]. *The protection of these faculties is the first object of Government. From the protection of different and unequal faculties of acquiring property, the possession of different degrees and kinds of property immediately results*: and from the influence of these on the sentiments and views of the respective proprietors, ensues a division of the society into different interests and parties.[21] [emphasis added]

It would be difficult to find a clearer rejection of the view that *political* freedom and equality cannot coexist with economic freedom: the "first object" of government is to protect the "faculties of men from which the rights of property originate." Not only that, but, because of the natural inequality of these faculties, the "possession of different degrees" of property immediately results. These assertions of Madison, who must be supposed to have understood the intent of the

---

20 One should recall here the results of Mikhail Gorbachev's efforts to "reform" communism in the Soviet Union. Gorbachev evidently agreed with Lekachman, that economic freedom may be divorced from political freedom.
21 *The Federalist*, ed. J. E. Cooke (Middletown: Wesleyan University Press, 1961), 58.

Constitution, can in no way be construed as advocating the view that political freedom requires the elimination of economic inequality.

Indeed, we recall that in *Federalist* #10 Publius argues that the republican solution to the problems of faction and the tyranny of the majority is to encourage factions to proliferate. This makes it unlikely that any one faction will gain sufficient power to become tyrannical. Publius goes on to say that

> [the] latent causes of faction are thus sown in the nature of man; and we see them every where brought into different degrees of activity, according to the different circumstances of civil society . . . [These causes] have in turn divided mankind into parties, inflamed them with mutual animosity, and rendered them much more disposed to vex and oppress each other, than to cooperate for their common good . . . [T]he most common and durable source of factions, has been the various and unequal distribution of property. Those who hold, and those who are without property, have *ever* formed distinct interests in society. [Emphasis added]

Thus, Publius would reject Marx's teaching that there is a dialectical movement in history, which leads eventually to the homogeneous society, one in which human beings are not alienated from one another by economic or other class interests: in free political societies there will always be division on account of economic interests. The encouragement of the proliferation of economic factions thus connects the teaching of *The Federalist* with Adam Smith's teaching concerning the system of natural liberty; and, Smith's system contains a mechanism by which to moderate the antagonism between conflicting economic interests, namely the creation, and diffusion throughout society of wealth.

Lekachman asserts that the "framers of our basic constitutional documents were serious people who must be credited with intending political entitlements to have consequences." Assuming that by "entitlements" Lekachman means what the framers meant by "rights," we find no basis in our founding documents for Lekachman's view that the framers meant to identify equality of rights with equality of the consequences of exercising one's rights, or with equality of result.

Lekachman states that the Constitution and Bill of Rights promise certain entitlements; but he does not tell us where these promises are made. He does refer to the Fourteenth Amendment's guarantee of equal protection under the law, but only to illustrate what he calls "an ambivalence in American attitudes," namely, the ambivalence between America's commitment to equality and its resistance to any attempt to rectify the "unequal distribution of wealth."[22] Lekachman does not consider the possibility that Americans view equality primarily as equality of opportunity, and believe the unequal distribution of wealth to be entirely consistent with that principle.

In particular, we find no statement in either the Declaration or the Constitution that may be construed as *promising* political equality; nor do we find any indication that equality, under our Constitution, means "equality of effect," or "approximate equality of political influence." Rather, we find that the Declaration speaks of *securing* rights which we already have by nature; and that among the rights secured by legitimate government is the right to liberty, and, by implication, to participate in all legitimate exercises of our political liberties. All human beings have been equally endowed by nature and nature's God with these rights.

Our Constitution does not grant or secure rights by explicitly enumerating a presumably exhaustive list of rights, which it then promises to guarantee to the people. Instead, its manner of securing rights is to state explicitly what the powers of the federal government are to be, and to limit those powers with respect to our rights. Our rights are not conferred upon us by the Constitution, but exist antecedently to any constitution. They are then secured by the explicit limitation of the powers of government. For example, Article I of the Bill of Rights does not positively guarantee or promise freedom of religion and speech to Americans. Rather, it places a restriction on Congress with respect to a preexisting right: "Congress shall make no law respecting an establishment of religion, or prohibiting the free exercise thereof."

Our Constitution's manner of securing rights by limiting the powers of government may be contrasted with the "Declaration of Human Rights and Freedoms," adopted by the Congress of People's Deputies of the Soviet Union in September, 1991, soon after the failure of the coup attempt. According to the *New York Times*, this declaration "is intended to act as an assurance on such matters until a new constitution comes into effect."[23]

The thirty-one articles of this declaration include the following: "Every person is ensured the right to the use of the native language, education in the native language and retention and development of ethnic culture." One may legitimately wonder how one knows that such a right exists, if in fact it does exist. According to the principles of liberal democracy, rights are things human beings have just by being

---

22 Lekachman, "Capitalism or Democracy," 130.
23 *New York Times*, 8 September 1991.

human, whereas one's native language and ethnic culture seem to be largely due to where and when one happens to have been born and brought up. It seems reasonable to conclude that, under the Soviet Union's Declaration of Rights, one has the right to use of one's native language because the Declaration says so.

Furthermore, under this Declaration, who will ensure this right, if not the government? Who will prosecute violations of one's putative right to the use of one's native language, or see to it that all receive adequate education in their native languages? Who will guarantee that one's ethnic culture is "retained"? The Soviet "Declaration," in granting and promising rights, thus obliges government to keep this promise, or to find an agent to act for it; but the very act of honoring such a promise makes inevitable the enlargement rather than restriction of governmental powers. Indeed, if the Declaration is the *source* of rights, it becomes difficult ultimately to distinguish rights from privileges. A privilege depends upon the will of the grantor, and not upon any claim, naturally justified or not, of the grantee. The Soviet Declaration thus ultimately justifies paternalistic government.

According to Lekachman, our Constitution promises us political equality, which he interprets to mean approximate equality of political influence; on the other hand, the Constitution promises equality of economic opportunity. The latter allegedly conflicts with the former because, inevitably, some will get more wealth than others, and thus will be able to command more than their fair share of political influence. We may put Lekachman's criticism in terms of liberty and equality. The contradiction inherent in the Constitution is that its promise of political equality is contradicted by its promise of economic liberty. Lekachman, along with other radical Leftist critics, evidently believes that justice requires that this contradiction be resolved in favor of political equality as he understands that term, and that the undesirable effects of economic liberty be replaced by economic equality, through the redistribution of wealth.

One wonders why this alleged contradiction ought not be resolved in favor of economic liberty. After all, our Declaration states that all human beings are naturally endowed with the rights of liberty and the pursuit of happiness. If I determine that my happiness depends upon my working hard in pursuit of material wealth, one might question my judgment or disagree with my goal; but, as long as I obey the law, what right has anyone else to meddle in my life, or tell me what to do? The answer to this question is that Lekachman believes that the fundamental form of all equality is equality of *power*, if not equality of influence.

Therefore, equality of economic liberty must be subordinated to political equality, because economic liberty produces unequal distribution of wealth, which in turn allows some people to wield more power than others. Apparently Lekachman accepts the Marxist dream, of a political society from which the baleful influence of the desire for wealth has been expunged.

V

Our disagreement with Lekachman, and those who share his views, is that he is able to argue for an inconsistency in the Constitution because he confuses securing rights—which the Constitution achieves primarily by simultaneously limiting both the powers of government relative to antecedently existing natural rights, as well as the exercise of the natural rights of those consenting to be governed—with promising or granting rights, which requires or mandates the expansion of those governmental powers necessary to keep its promises. In addition, he denies the Constitution's assumption that economic liberty is a part of political liberty.

It is true that, by means of the Constitution, our natural rights are transformed into civil rights, by our mutually agreeing to accept certain limits to the exercise of our rights, and by our consent to be governed by a common authority, whose rule is legitimate only to the extent that it is based upon the consent of the governed. One cannot, however, insist too frequently that the source of our rights is not the Constitution. We do not have rights because the Constitution promises or declares that we have rights. We have rights because we are human.

On account of the natural equality and liberty of all human beings, no one may be said to have consented to be ruled despotically; that is, the principle of consent implies that all legitimate government is limited government. Therefore, government's proper mode of securing our rights is through limiting its powers, as well as through enforcing our mutual agreement to limit the exercise of our rights. The view that rights *result* from constitutional promises implicitly contradicts the principle of the consent of the governed.

Moreover, Lekachman appears not to see that liberal democracy and capitalism rest on the twin principles of liberty *and* equality, not equality alone. It is the peculiar genius of our Founders to have hit upon a scheme for holding liberty and equality together, something rare in the history of political societies. In order, however, to understand this scheme, it is first necessary to inquire more deeply into what they meant by liberty and equality.

We thus return to the Declaration's opening appeal to the transcendent principles of nature and truth. Earlier we raised the question whether Americans today, liberal or conservative, still believe in the existence of the laws of nature and nature's God, self-evident truth, or the assertion that all human beings have been equally endowed by their Creator with certain unalienable rights. In any case, the Founders evidently believed that these principles and propositions are indeed necessary to the establishment of limited government, dedicated to the securing of rights, deriving its just powers from the consent of the government.

These terms, "laws of nature and nature's God," "self-evident truth," and "unalienable rights," are evidently intended to refer to things that really exist, which themselves are an indispensable part of the intellectual foundation of our society. If this foundation is ignored or rejected, it is difficult, if not impossible, to distinguish the notion of natural rights, those claims whose justification is the mere fact of our humanity, from any merely arbitrary desire or claim of privilege.

Moreover, the result of rejecting these principles is that rights must then be understood so as to make impossible any notion of public obligation or duty which may take precedence over factional interest. It is true, as we have stated earlier, that, under the scheme contemplated by the Declaration, naturally endowed rights have priority over duty; but certain public duties flow from and are grounded upon natural rights.

For example, the respect for the rule of law, as contrasted with the rule of men, follows from our mutually recognizing one another as being naturally equal in respect to ruling and being ruled. While it is true that our rights are subjective in origin, it is not true that they are merely arbitrary. They are based upon our common human nature.

Furthermore, the commonality of our rights, and the necessity for respecting our mutual consent to their limitation, may itself act as a uniting principle. That is, however else you and I may disagree, we have the same rights, and we agree upon the necessity to limit our rights in order to secure them. This is the American form of tolerance. We tolerate one another's differences because of our prior recognition of our common rights. To eliminate the natural, non-arbitrary basis for rights, however, is to eliminate both the obligations based upon them, as well as their commonality.[24]

---

[24] It is partly for this reason that the current infatuation, in education and elsewhere, with "multiculturalism" and "valuing differences" is misguided. Tolerating differences is not the same as "valuing" differences. Because each of us has the right to the pursuit of happiness however we may define

Even if it is true that few people now believe in the existence of self-evident truth, not to mention truth of any kind, or in the existence of nature and nature's God, it seems that "We," namely the ones who proclaimed the Declaration of Independence, did believe in the existence of these things. Specifically, "We" refers to "the Representatives of the United States of America, in General Congress assembled," who "in the name, and by the authority of the good people of these colonies, solemnly publish and declare" the independence of "these United Colonies." We justify the act of declaring ourselves independent, by publishing a list of the "injuries and usurpations," committed by "the present king of Great Britain . . . all having in direct object the establishment of an absolute tyranny over these states."

There then follows a long recitation of these injuries, all of which evidently contravene the unalienable rights we have merely as human beings. Nathan Tarcov makes this point quite well:

> The acts complained of in the Declaration imply the existence of other rights of which they are the violations. Some of the acts are 'abuses' of rightful power; others are 'usurpations' of power without right. The Declaration complains, for example, that George III vetoed laws 'the most wholesome and necessary for the public good' but does not treat the veto power as illegitimate, as it does parliamentary 'pretended legislation.' Other acts, such as keeping standing armies in time of peace and imposing taxes, are complained of not as being wrongful in themselves but as having been done 'without our consent.'[25]

"We" conclude this list by stating:

> In every stage of these oppressions we have petitioned for redress in the most humble terms: Our repeated petitions have been answered only by repeated injury. A prince, whose character is thus marked by every act which may define a tyrant is unfit to be the ruler of a free people . . . We must, therefore, acquiesce in the necessity, which denounces our separation, and hold [our British brethren], as we hold the rest of mankind, enemies in war, in peace friends.

---

happiness (within limits, of course), we ought to be willing to live and let live. If, however, you insist that I "value," or somehow "affirm" your way of life, then you are demanding that I go beyond tolerance—that is, leaving you alone to live as you please—and endorse your way of life.

25 Nathan Tarcov, "American Constitutionalism and Individual Rights," in *How Does the Constitution Secure Rights?* ed. Goldwin and Schambra (Washington: American Enterprise Institute, 1985), 103-104.

Accordingly, the argument of the Declaration proceeds as follows. It appeals first to the universal principles of nature and nature's God. There then follows a partial statement of the unalienable rights all human beings have as creatures of nature's God. The legitimate purpose and foundation of government are stated: governments are instituted for the purpose of securing rights, and derive their just powers from the consent of the governed. The wrongs inflicted upon the people of these colonies by King George III are described, evidently in order of their heinousness. The argument concludes that the King is thus "unfit to be the ruler of a free people."

The unfitness of King George for ruling a free people follows from his continued abrogation of the rights of the people, and his violation of the principle that government exists for the sake of securing rights, and rules legitimately only by the consent of the governed. We again note the connection between securing rights and the consent of the governed: government derives its just powers only from the consent of the governed, and thus is limited by that consent. Moreover, no reasonable person may be presumed to have given his consent to a government which did not pledge itself to securing his rights, precisely because no one enters civil society except for the sake of making his rights more secure than they are in the state of nature.

Up to this point, there is no indication that the Declaration has *promised* or granted us rights, or that the *effects* of our exercising our rights will be approximately equal. Instead, the Declaration proclaims that a government is justly empowered to rule only insofar as it both secures our rights, and rules by the consent of the governed. Each human being naturally has an equal claim on government to do these two things.

Governments are instituted to secure certain rights. This implies that, without properly instituted government, our rights are not secure; and in our discussion of Locke, we have seen why, in the state of nature, our rights are insecure. It also implies that, at least with respect to some rights, namely, the most fundamental rights, government cannot give or grant rights, nor can any constitution. Accordingly, as we noted above, it is not true that the Nineteenth Amendment gave women the right to vote.

This amendment, and others like it, in effect acknowledges that we Americans have not practiced what we preach. We have publicly proclaimed that our nation is based upon the principle that human beings are equally endowed with certain rights; but we have prohibited some people from legitimately exercising their rights implied by our proclamation. Specifically, if government rules legitimately only by consent of the governed, then the governed may not rightfully be prohibited from giving or withholding their consent by voting. As Nathan Tarcov puts it, certain rights "reflect the right to the rule of law implicit in the very granting of legislative, executive, and judicial powers in Articles I, II, and III [of the Constitution]. Americans have the constitutional right to be subject to no authority other than the legislated, executed, and judicially enforced law."[26]

Some of the Founders, including Madison himself, had reservations about adding a bill of rights to the Constitution. Madison's reservations were based, in part, on his view that a bill of rights would be an unnecessary redundancy, at best serving only to make explicit what was already implied by the Constitution itself. Accordingly, it was, in Madison's view, a mistake to say that the Bill of Rights contains *amendments* to the Constitution. Furthermore, he thought it prudent to meddle with the Constitution as little as possible.

On the other hand, by making explicit certain things already contained in the main body of the Constitution, the Bill of Rights helps us see the extent to which "We the People" are willing to go for the purpose of securing our rights by limiting them. For example, Article V of the Bill of Rights states that "No person shall . . . be deprived of life, liberty, or property, without due process of law; nor shall private property be taken for public use, without just compensation." This clause limits precisely those fundamental, unalienable natural rights named at the beginning of the Declaration of Independence: we may legitimately be deprived of life, liberty, or property, but only upon the observance of due process. Our rights even to life, liberty, and property are not absolute, or unqualified, at least not in civil society.

The manner of our being deprived of those rights must, of course, accord with the rule of law and our rights thereto. Due process of law and just compensation set limits to the power of government, by obliging it to observe certain procedures implied by the principles of the rule of law and consent of the governed. The specific content of "due process" is not stipulated, but this is as it should be. Specific legal procedures will vary with time, place, and circumstance, and no one can anticipate them all.[27] The point of Article V is that there shall be some

---

26 Ibid., 102.

27 There is another reason that the content of due process is not specified by the Constitution. Until approximately 1925, the Bill of Rights was understood as limiting the powers of the federal, not the state governments. It

lawful, promulgated, and nonarbitrary procedures, which must be observed, before one may be deprived of life, liberty, or property. It cannot be stated too emphatically, especially in a time when the meaning of "rights" is so widely misunderstood or distorted, that *no* right secured to us under the Constitution is unqualified or absolute, not even the right to keep and bear arms, or the alleged right to abortion.[28]

The negative character of the Constitution's language, as well as its manner of setting limits to powers and rights, therefore reflects the compromise from which civil society begins. The rights we have by nature are insecure without the protection of civil society. They are insecure for the simple reason that they are unrestrained. We the People therefore enter civil society by mutually consenting to constrain our natural rights, under the governance of a common authority, who rules by the consent of the governed.

This consent being obtained, civil government may rightfully be established. Civil rights are derived from, but are not co-extensive with, natural rights. It is the rule of law, manifested in part as the principle of due process, that simultaneously secures and limits our rights. As Tarcov puts it,

> Civil society exists to protect life, liberty, and property, but it does so precisely by wielding the power to deprive its members of life, liberty, and property. Those rights are more secure in civil society than in a state of nature, which is also to say they are more secure in a properly organized civil society than in a defective one, because they can be lost only in accordance with due process of law.[29]

There is, therefore, no absolutely unconditioned civil right. Indeed, "unconditioned civil right" is an oxymoron, precisely because civil rights result from the transforming and limiting function of the consent of the governed.

---

was therefore left to the state governments to determine those procedures that would constitute due process.

[28] The National Rifle Association and the National Organization of Women would initially appear to be the most unlikely of bedfellows. They are united, however, by the intransigence of their commitment to their respective causes. The NRA refuses to admit the legitimacy of any limitation upon the right to keep and bear arms; and the same is true of NOW with respect to right to have an abortion. In this, therefore, both groups display the characteristic common to all factions, namely, an unwillingness to compromise, coupled with an insistence that everyone else be willing to compromise in order to accommodate *them*.

[29] Tarcov, "American Constitutionalism," 102.

We may now begin to see more clearly what the Declaration and Constitution mean by freedom and equality. Indeed, it may be said that these two principles coalesce, in that, under the rule of the Constitution, each of us is equally free. Each of us has the same rights, equally protected under the law by our common consent to those limits upon the exercise of our natural rights necessary to secure them in civil society. Each citizen is equally free from certain governmental or other restraint upon his rights of political participation, and is equally free to exercise those rights as he sees fit. Finally, each of us is free to define and pursue his well-being, in accordance with his own best judgment, within the limits of restraint necessary to secure our freedom.

Articles IX and X of the Bill of Rights put the point this way:

> The enumeration in the Constitution, of certain rights, shall not be construed to deny or disparage others retained by the people. The powers not delegated to the United States by the Constitution, nor prohibited by it to the states, are reserved to the states respectively, or to the people.

That is, a right need not be explicitly named by the Constitution in order to be retained by the people. If the Constitution is silent about certain rights, it does not follow that the Constitution has thereby denied those rights to the people. It should be added, however, that we are not therefore free to claim anything we please as a "right," simply because the Constitution does not mention it. Rather, the Constitution's silence about a power creates the presumption that the power is retained by the states or the people. The burden of proof rests with the one who would deny that the power in question is retained by the states or the people.

The Constitution, therefore, contrary to Lekachman's assertion, does not promise "that any individual's vote, effect upon his neighbors, and influence upon his elected representatives is approximately as important as another's," if by this Lekachman means that the Constitution guarantees that our exercise of those rights to political participation will have equal results.

The Constitution *does* promise that our rights will be secured under limited government and the rule of law;[30] but it makes no promise

---

30 See Mansfield, *America's Constitutional Soul*, 185: "When rights are defined as wants, government is set the impossible task of guaranteeing those wants that happen to be defined as rights in our time, or in our decade. It cannot justify limiting rights or providing what is practicable in present circumstances since, in the absence of any distinction, every civil right is demanded with the full force of a natural right . . . And who does the demanding? When rights

whatsoever regarding the equal exercise of our rights. And how could it? The ideal of self-rule by means of elected representatives, requires a body of citizens, each of whom is able and willing to govern himself. If you do not undertake to exercise your rights under the Constitution, no one else can do it for you, without violating the very principles of self-rule and the consent of the governed upon which the Constitution is based.

The moral difference between making a promise and securing rights is that the obligation to keep a specific promise does not begin to exist until the promise is made; but one may not have been obliged to make the promise in the first place. Legitimately instituted government, on the other hand, is obliged from its inception to secure rights, because those rights exist antecedently to government. It is the necessary condition of the consent of the governed that imposes on government the obligation to secure rights; and, this obligation does not flow from a promise, or any other act of the government.

In sum: government is obliged to secure rights, but it is not obliged to guarantee equally effective exercise of those rights. Indeed, securing rights and guaranteeing the exercise of rights contradict one another. Government is obliged to guarantee the equal protection of the laws to *our* enjoyment and exercise of our rights. In general, freedom and equality, as constitutional principles, come together in the way rights are secured under the Constitution, by limitations placed upon the power of government. Each of us is equal in being equally free from abuse of governmental power and in being equally endowed with certain rights.

Tarcov makes this point as follows:

---

are wants, those who have the wants are no longer required to claim their rights, to fight for them, and to defend them once gained. Elite groups can make the necessary claims on behalf of those who want, who are regarded as too weak actually to enjoy the rights they have had until now in a merely formal sense. For in the constitutional understanding of rights, a right is a license or permission to be exercised on one's own; and some people by choice or circumstance will always excel others in the exercise of rights . . . But in the new *postconstitutional* understanding, any discrepancy between the formal possession of a right and its actual exercise cannot be tolerated: you do not have a right or a choice unless it is an equal right or choice . . . Guaranteeing rights now means guaranteeing their exercise. To do so, government does not by right have to seek your consent or the consent of your fellow citizens because you may feel too weak to consent and your fellow citizens may be overlooking your wants when they consent."

The form of our rights is that they are primarily rights to do, keep, or acquire things and corresponding rights not to have things done to us or taken from us. *This form contrasts, therefore, with alternative conceptions of rights to have things done or given to one.* It presumes that individuals already have some of the essentials (such as life and liberty) and therefore need only to be secured in enjoying them and ordinarily have the ability to acquire other essentials (such as property, respect, truth, salvation) and therefore need only to be secured in pursuing them. *Securing rights in this conception is a matter of providing security for enjoyment or pursuit, not of providing the desired objects of the rights themselves.*[31] [emphases added]

This view contradicts Lekachman's understanding of political equality under the Constitution:

The framers of our basic constitutional documents were serious people who must be credited with intending political *entitlements* to have consequences. Votes are shams *unless* they influence legislation. Free speech and press are meaningless *if they do not shape public opinion* . . . This is to say that the Constitution started life as more than a *capitalist* document. The Founding Fathers were unwilling to attach the weight of dollars to political rights (130). [emphasis added]

Lekachman also asserts:

Why are we willing to endanger political freedom and equality for the sake of capitalism? Even capitalism's most sophisticated apologists readily concede that their preferred system lacks the glamour, awe, and mystery that customarily hedge the courts of kings and pontiffs. As Alfred Marshall remarked in speaking of human motivation, crass pursuit of profit by sellers and of individual gratification by their customers is notoriously consistent with the strongest but not the highest of personal impulses-with avarice, not altruism . . . *[F]ree markets disperse income and wealth in patterns not entirely consistent with political democracy* . . . To its adherents, standard economics is a scoreboard on which people's unequal financial status appropriately reflects the wide range of their individual talents and energy. *By implication, inequality of income and wealth is actually quite equitable* (129, 131).

As we have seen in our discussion of Adam Smith, free markets are not intended to disperse or re-distribute income; rather, they are intended to create or increase wealth. The "diffusion of opulence" which, according to Smith, arises from free markets and the division of labor, is not intent upon the equal distribution of an existing amount of wealth, but upon spreading wealth by the creation of new wealth.

---

31 Tarcov, "American Constitutionalism," 118.

Critics of the Constitution and free market economies may prefer to ignore the fact that the Founders, including Thomas Jefferson, were firmly convinced that securing property rights is one of the principal ends of government. The Founders also knew that securing these rights leads inevitably to the possession of "different degrees and kinds of property."

Furthermore, the Founders generally believed that, human nature being what it is, appeals to altruism are likely to be ineffectual as means of achieving a just society. As Publius says in Federalist # 51:

> . . . [T]he great security against a gradual concentration of the several [governmental] powers in the same department, consists in giving to those who administer each department, the necessary constitutional means, and personal motives, to resist encroachments of the others . . . Ambition must be made to counteract ambition . . . It may be a reflection on human nature, that such devices should be necessary to controul the abuses of government. But what is government itself but the greatest of all reflections on human nature? If men were angels, no government would be necessary. If angels were to govern men, neither external nor internal controuls on government would be necessary. In framing a government which is to be administered by men over men, the great difficulty lies in this: You must first enable the government to controul the governed; and in the next place, oblige it to controul itself. A dependence on the people is no doubt the primary controul on the government; but experience has taught mankind the necessity of auxiliary precautions. *This policy of supplying by opposite and rival interests, the defect of better motives, might be traced through the whole system of human affairs, private as well as public.* [emphasis added]

The Founders may very well have agreed with Lekachman that altruism is nobler than avarice; but they also clearly believed that, however lamentable the "defect of better motives" might be, it is more prudent to construct a political system on the low but sure ground of self-interest, while channelling self-interest so that its benefits may be diffused throughout society.

## CHAPTER SIX

# *Conclusion*

We conclude by returning to the question of the relative moral merits of capitalism and communism. We have seen that one critique of our Constitution, which is fairly typical of the currently prevailing view, is able to accuse it of injustice only because that critique distorts our founding principles. According to this critique, the Constitution promises a kind of equality that includes equality of wealth, but encourages a kind of freedom that belies that promise.

In arguing as we have, however, perhaps we have proved too much. Perhaps we have confirmed a view to which Lekachman and others might assent, namely, that our founding principles *are* amoral and cynical, appearing as they do to encourage faction, strife, and economic disparity, in the name of security. As James Madison wrote, in a letter to Thomas Jefferson, "*Divide et impera*, the reprobated axiom of tyranny, is, under certain qualifications, the only policy by which a republic can be administered on just principles."[1]

Perhaps, after all, a political and economic system based upon the inculcation of selfless dedication to the common weal *is* morally superior to democratic capitalism. We appear, therefore, to have shown only that Lekachman understands "liberty" and "equality" in a manner that differs from the Constitution's understanding. We have, indeed, confirmed his assertion that the Constitution encourages economic disparity; but have we demonstrated that economic disparity is *not* unjust?

The question of the comparative moral worth of capitalism and socialism could not be addressed without the preceding effort to deepen our understanding of America's philosophic foundation. Still, it may appear to some that we have said relatively little about the positive moral ideals of democratic capitalism. Indeed, one may wonder whether democratic capitalism even has any positive moral principles, other than securing the right to own property.

---

1 Quoted in Marc Plattner, "American Democracy and the Acquisitive Spirit," in *How Capitalistic Is the Constitution?* (Washington: American Enterprise Institute, 1982), 6.

Moreover, we must wonder whether it is even possible to compare capitalism and socialism with respect to their moral worth. Is there any common standard to which both systems would agree, in the light of which such a comparison could be made? Without such a standard, is it even possible to show that one's preference for one system over the other is rationally or morally defensible?

The current view about moral judgments is that they are "values," or that they express one's "values." Values are said to be matters of personal preference. Values are either preferences, or they are the things preferred. In either case, values are believed to rest ultimately upon arbitrary acts of will, or upon one's "culture," which is itself a combination of happenstance and acts of will. That is, according to this view, there can be no such thing as *the* cultivation of *the* human mind. There is no objective or rational standard by which the various cultures may be ranked hierarchically. Thus, any attempt to argue for the superior truth or goodness of any particular set of values is misguided, not to mention narrow-minded or even tyrannical.[2] No rational justification can be given for asserting the superiority of any particular set of values to any other set.

The reader will have seen that we reject this view: in our opinion, moral judgments are rationally defensible. One cannot make sense of the passion with which the antagonists in the debate between socialism and capitalism mutually disagree, if there are no rational grounds for moral judgments. Neither side would agree that the question of the relative moral worth of capitalism and socialism is merely a matter of personal or arbitrary preference.

Indeed, if their respective preferences are merely preferences, the socialists and the capitalists have no genuine disagreement: they merely express different values. It is rather like saying you like horseradish and I don't. That is not a disagreement. It is a statement that you and I have different tastes. So, for example, if moral relativism is correct, the Cold War will turn out to have been merely a difference of taste, certainly nothing to get excited over. The rejection of socialism in favor of capitalism will then be nothing more than a change of taste on a very large scale, a world-wide change of fashion. Socialism is out. Capitalism is in.

It goes without saying that neither of the disputants will accept this analysis. From their point of view, the differences of principle which separate them are matters of life and death. If any proof of the serious-

---

[2] Although, if there are no objective values, why one should avoid being narrow-minded or tyrannical is difficult to understand.

ness of the disputants were necessary, it would suffice merely to recall the climactic paragraph of the Declaration of Independence: "And for the support of this declaration, with a firm reliance on the protection of Divine Providence, we mutually pledge to each other our lives, our fortunes, and our sacred honor." Or, consider Marx's stirring conclusion to *The Communist Manifesto*: "Let the ruling classes tremble at a Communist revolution. The proletarians have nothing to lose but their chains. They have a world to win. Workingmen of all countries, unite!"

Members of the radical Left, as serious critics of capitalism, will deny that their assertion of the moral superiority of socialism is merely the expression of a personal preference, for which no reasons can be given. The Left genuinely believes in the objective moral superiority of socialism. Indeed, the Marxist Left believes that historical, objective fact ultimately coincides with the demands of morality. That is the meaning of dialectical materialism. The overthrow of capitalism is *both* a historical certainty and a moral imperative. Otherwise it is impossible to make sense of the tone of high moral indignation that pervades Marx's writings. If history were the result merely of fate or chance, we would expect an intelligent man like Marx to have sounded more like the Stoic philosophers of old.

Likewise, the defenders of democratic capitalism will reject the assertion that private ownership of the means of production cannot be shown to be morally superior to ownership by the state. They will also insist that it is objectively unjust for the naturally gifted to be denied the opportunity to gain materially from the use of their talents, simply because others are not as gifted, or are otherwise prevented from succeeding to the same extent. Equality of rights and opportunity simply *is* the form of justice which best accords with democratic rule.

We ought also to recall the point made earlier, namely, that neither side in this debate is satisfied that the historical triumph of democratic capitalism over communism is equivalent to a demonstration of the moral superiority of the former to the latter. The melancholy inability of the West to celebrate its triumph, and the stubborn refusal of many socialists to accept the evidence of history as final, show that their quarrel is primarily one of principle. If we take seriously the seriousness of the very disputants themselves, we are compelled to search for a mutually agreeable moral standard, in the light of which we may assess their respective moral claims. Failing to discover such a standard, we must content ourselves with noting where capitalism and communism agree or differ, and judge accordingly. No other intelligent possibility exists, unless one is willing to grant that war is an intelligent possibility.

Perhaps we must be content to leave it at saying that the modern understanding of rights cannot be the common standard for judging between Marx's teaching and the principles of liberal democracy. The very sanctity of those rights, thought by writers like Locke to be the ground for guaranteeing the freedom and thus the humanity of men, is rejected by Marx. He views the assertion of those rights as the expression, if not the source, of man's dehumanization, his failure to become a whole human being. Marx rejects "individualism."

Modern natural right teaching, on the other hand, makes certain concessions, to paraphrase James Madison, not only to the better angels of our nature, but to the fallen ones as well. It is a form of individualism, to be sure, but one which, happily, shows how concern for the common good may emerge or be derived from individualism. The individualism of modern natural right is thus willing to settle for security, comfort, and sober decency, perhaps at the expense of man's nobler possibilities, to be sure; but, it is at least based upon a view of human nature and its political possibilities, which is both humane and patient.

Marx also appears to believe that the goal of society is to allow human beings to lead fully human lives; but, he rejects any appeal to a permanent human nature underlying all historical change, in favor of the view that man makes himself historically to be what he is. One must therefore wonder whether Marx is able to state coherently what he means by "fully human." Marx and Locke could agree that men in past ages lived under social institutions that presupposed and cultivated self-interest, to the detriment of their highest human possibilities. They disagree, however, regarding the status of self-interest, specifically with regard to its corrigibility, or malleability.

Perhaps the choice between liberal democracy and capitalism, and Marxism, comes to this: nature or history? That is, the choice between the two ways of life is a choice between believing either in the existence of a permanent human nature, or in the historical development of human society, culminating in the truly just society. To characterize this as a *choice*, however, is not to say that the decision in favor of one over the other is merely arbitrary or groundless. Implicit in our defense of the principles of democratic capitalism has been an agreement with their reserve concerning what is possible in political life.

To be sure, the ground of our reserve need not coincide exactly with the ground of Locke's or Smith's reserve. It is entirely possible that Locke, in an effort to show how to establish political stability and material well-being, aimed too low. Perhaps there are other human aspirations, for noble self-sacrifice, for wisdom, or for God, which Locke chose to ignore, or which he overlooked. Precisely if this is true, however, reasonable people ought to prefer a political system that, while it may encourage the pursuit of material wealth, is also dedicated to preserving individual liberty and tolerance, qualities which may themselves be the conditions required for the realization of our higher, albeit necessarily private, aspirations.

Perhaps there will always be those who, incapable of being satisfied with "empirically existing man," seek to establish heaven on earth. Given the overwhelming devastation wrought upon humanity by totalitarianism in the twentieth century, however, we are fully justified in concluding that man is better off either disbelieving in heaven altogether, or in being content to let heaven stay where it is.

## *Appendix to Chapter Two*

The history of the writing and publication of *The Federalist Papers,* which is the classic and authoritative defense of the Constitution based upon the principles proclaimed by the Declaration, is itself an example of concern for the common welfare overcoming individual differences of opinion. This history is an act of the kind of statesmanship displayed by the signers of the Declaration. *The Federalist,* presents itself as having been written by "Publius," the pseudonym chosen by its authors, John Jay, Alexander Hamilton, and James Madison.[1] (For practical purposes, Jay's contribution was sufficiently small that *The Federalist* may be regarded as the work of Hamilton and Madison.)

*The Federalist* consists of a series of essays, published during the period 1787-1788, immediately after the constitutional convention of 1787. Hamilton originally conceived the essays as a means of securing New York's ratification of the proposed Constitution. Thus, they appeared initially in the New York City press, addressed to "the People of the State of New York." However, even before the series was completely published in the press, the essays were collected in a book and published nationally, with the intention of winning support from the delegations sent by the states to their respective ratifying conventions.[2]

Although Madison and Hamilton privately disagreed over certain important issues pertaining to the system proposed by the Constitution, they put these disagreements aside for the sake of winning popular support for ratification. The decision to publish *The Federalist* as the work of one author thus reflected their support for the

---

[1] See Leo Strauss, "Liberal Education and Responsibility," in *Liberalism Ancient and Modern* (New York: Basic Books, 1968), 16: "[*The Federalist Papers*] reveal their connection by presenting themselves as the work of one Publius. This eminently sober work considers chiefly that diversity and inequality in the faculties of men which shows itself in the acquisition of property, but it is very far from being blind to the difference between business and government."

[2] See Martin Diamond, "The Federalist," in *History of Political Philosophy,* Third Edition, ed. Strauss and Cropsey (Chicago: University of Chicago Press, 1987), 659ff.

proposed Union, and willingness to suppress individual differences in behalf of the common good.

Moreover, the pseudonym chosen for the single author of the essays would have been familiar to educated readers of the day. "Publius" was Publius Valerius Publicola of ancient Rome, whose life was recounted by Plutarch. Plutarch says that Publius was "descended from Valerius, a man amongst the early citizens, reputed the principal reconciler of the differences betwixt the Romans and the Sabines, and one that was most instrumental in persuading their kings to assent to peace and union." According to Plutarch's account, Publius himself acquired so great a reputation with the Roman people as the friend of republican government, that he was widely known as "Poplicola, or people-lover."

In particular, Publius, looking to the example of the Greek legislator Solon for guidance in the formation of republican institutions, transferred to Rome certain of the latter's laws "empowering the people to elect their officers," thus restraining temptations to tyranny. Indeed, "the aversion to tyranny was stronger in [Publius than it was in Solon]; any one who attempted usurpation could, by Solon's law, only be punished upon conviction; but Poplicola made it death before a trial."[3] Thus, the choice of Publius as the pseudonym for the author of *The Federalist*, indicated the ancient lineage of the republican government the Founders sought to establish.

3 Plutarch, *The Lives of the Noble Grecians and Romans*, trans. Dryden (New York: The Modern Library).

# *Appendix to Chapter Three*

In his essay "What Is Enlightenment?" published in 1784, Kant writes:

> Enlightenment is man's release from his self-incurred tutelage. Tutelage is man's inability to make use of his understanding without direction from another. Self-incurred is this tutelage when its cause lies not in lack of reason but in lack of resolution and courage to use it without direction from another. Sapere aude! ["Dare to know!"] "Have courage to use your own reason!"—that is the motto of the enlightenment. Laziness and cowardice are the reasons why so great a portion of mankind, after nature has long since discharged them from external direction . . . nevertheless remains under lifelong tutelage, and why it is so easy for others to set themselves up as their guardians. It is so easy not to be of age. If I have a book which understands for me, a pastor who has a conscience for me, a physician who decides my diet, and so forth, I need not trouble myself. I need not think, if I can only pay—others will readily undertake the irksome work for me.[1] [emphasis added]

Who will release man from his self-incurred tutelage? Kant admits that "[f]or any single individual to work himself out of the life under tutelage which has become almost his nature is very difficult." Such a one, Kant continues, "has come to be fond of this state, and he is for the present really incapable of making use of his reason, for no one has ever let him try it out."

What is difficult for the individual human being, however, is less difficult for the public as a whole:

> . . . that the public should enlighten itself is more possible; indeed, if only freedom is granted, enlightenment is almost sure to follow. For there will always be some independent thinkers, even among the established guardians of the great masses, who, after throwing off the yoke of tutelage from their own shoulders, will disseminate the spirit of the rational appreciation of both their own worth and every man's vocation for thinking for himself . . . [However], the public can only slowly attain enlightenment. Perhaps a fall of personal despotism or of avaricious or tyrannical oppression may be accomplished by revolution, but never a true

---

[1] Immanuel Kant, "What Is Enlightenment?" in *On History*, ed. Lewis White Beck (New York: Bobbs-Merrill, 1957), 3.

reform in ways of thinking. Rather, new prejudices will serve as well as old ones to harness the great unthinking masses. For this enlightenment, however, nothing is required but freedom, and indeed the most harmless among all the things to which this term can properly be applied. It is the freedom to make public use of one's reason at every point . . . By the public use of one's reason I understand the use which a person makes of it as a scholar before the reading public.[2] [emphases added]

Kant evidently believes that, granted sufficient freedom, the independent thinkers among the people will be public-spirited. They will first liberate themselves from the yoke of tutelage, and then disseminate among their fellow citizens the spirit of "rational appreciation" for every man's "vocation for thinking for himself." The independent thinkers will inevitably dedicate themselves to inculcating among their fellow citizens the habit of thinking for oneself rather than submitting one's understanding to the teaching of books, even the oldest and most authoritative, or to the exhortations to virtue of pastors. That is, they will inculcate the habit and spirit of anti-authoritarianism.

Enlightenment, thus understood, may be contrasted with the teaching concerning the public use of reason, contained in Plato's little dialogue, *The Apology of Socrates*. In 399 B.C., Socrates was charged by Athens with crimes of impiety against the gods of the city, and of corrupting the young. The *Apology* (derived from the Greek *apologia*, meaning "defense") is Plato's dramatic presentation of Socrates' defense in court against his accusers. Socrates argues that his philosophic way of life, which is the life of reason *par excellence*, the life devoted to calling into question all opinions, even the most authoritative, is a life lived in obedience to the command of the gods. Thus, by living the philosophic life, Socrates refutes the charge of impiety. By living philosophically, Socrates demonstrates his great piety. Furthermore, by publicly questioning the prominent citizens of Athens, Socrates claims to be doing a great service to the city, particularly to the young, by exposing the ignorance of those public men who say they are wise about the most important human matters, when in fact they are not. Despite his efforts, Socrates is found guilty by a small majority, and is then condemned to death.

Apparently, then, Socrates' fellow citizens were not dissuaded from their view that his constant questioning of the city and its ways, its laws, and traditions, both sacred and poetic, is dangerous to that unity of opinion about the most important things, without which a political

---

2 Ibid., 4-5.

community cannot exist. The philosophic life undermines those opinions, without necessarily replacing them with anything else, unless it is the knowledge that one is ignorant about the most important things for human life. Perhaps there exist a few rare, wise human beings who can live a life which is somehow free of the authoritative opinions, a life based on "Socratic wisdom," or the knowledge that one knows nothing; but a political society cannot live such a life. Plato thus appears to teach a profound reserve about the ultimate harmony of the life devoted to reason and political life.[3]

---

[3] This does not mean that either Socrates or Plato taught that political life is simply irrational, or that standards of political justice are simply arbitrary or "culturally relative," or that they merely express the will of the stronger. Indeed, Socrates labored to distinguish himself and his way of life from the sophists, who were believed to teach precisely this view, namely, that all standards of justice are conventional, and aim, not at the general welfare, but at furthering the interests of the rulers. On the other hand, he appears to have agreed with the sophists that political life is necessarily concerned with the here and now, which changes from moment to moment. Political life thus inevitably depends upon opinion, not truth. Socrates showed his agreement with this part of the doctrine of the sophists to the extent that he taught, by word and deed, the necessity of rhetoric to political life. Socrates demonstrated, however that he, the one living the philosophic life, possessed an art of rhetoric superior to that of the sophists. But did Socrates the philosopher genuinely care about the political things, which are of such consuming importance to most normal human beings? There was at least one competent contemporary of Socrates, the comic playwright Aristophanes, who believed that Socrates secretly held political things in contempt, being more concerned with what we would now call natural science, while dissembling his genuine opinions about politics. It is, perhaps, difficult for us, the children of the Enlightenment, to take seriously the skepticism of the classical thinkers about the possibility of a purely rational public policy; but, our incredulity may in fact only be *prima facie* evidence of the success of the Enlightenment. Indeed, the current state in our colleges and universities of what are called the "humanities," may partially vindicate the classical view. In the nineteenth and twentieth centuries, the humanities, particularly political science, were transformed by being assimilated to the mathematical science of nature. The new mathematical physics was taken to be the paramount expression of reason; and the humanities, desiring to become more "scientific," copied and adapted the methods of mathematical physics, in wilful oblivion to the fact that the subject of the humanities, the human being, is not a number: the unity and wholeness of human life and experience cannot be reduced to numerical unity. It inevitably happened that the newly transformed humanities failed to find any confirmation in the "objective order," that is, in the world reduced

The classical understanding of the problematic character of the relation of philosophy to the interests of the political community is further indicated in Plato's *Republic*, in Socrates' famous allegory of the cave, which depicts the liberation from the constraints of public opinion. The one thus liberated, emerging from the "cave" of public opinion, is at first blinded by the brightness of the true world; but this benighted state is rapidly transformed into one of delight, as the liberated one becomes gradually better able to endure the sight of things as they really exist, undistorted by the authoritative public opinions. He desires to go higher, towards the sun, the source of the light of all intelligibility, which illuminates all the realities he sees, there to remain in contemplation of the realities, unconcerned with political matters; but, he is *compelled* by Socrates to return to the cave, that is, to the city, there to teach, or at least try to teach, his fellow citizens the truth about the world above the cave, albeit indirectly, by moderating their expectations of political life. Thus, for the lover of the pursuit of wisdom, public spiritedness is the result of compulsion, not of desire.[4] It is, as

---

to its merely quantitative dimension, for what matters most to us as human beings, things like justice and injustice, sin and grace, good and evil. Thus, these things were said to be "values," which are themselves merely the results of acts of "valuing," arbitrary, and ultimately mysterious acts of the will, or of we know not what. Thus the disciplines whose study was the human things, destroyed themselves in attempting to become purely scientific or rational, with what effect one may see for oneself with a brief glance at the humanities course offerings in almost any college catalogue. In particular, political science and economics, having transformed themselves into quasi-mathematical disciplines, failed to see the forest for the trees. How, for example, can any reasonable person take seriously a political science which, being bound to its quantitative methodology, hesitates to describe the former Soviet Union as an "evil empire"? Can it be doubted that the self-destruction of the humanities has profoundly harmed the public life of our nation? We have said that this result is only a partial vindication of the classical view concerning the relation of reason to politics, because the very meaning of the term "reason" was transformed by the success of the mathematical sciences of nature.

4 Plato, *Republic*, bk. VII. This brief statement necessarily fails to do justice to the complex, profound, and subtle teaching contained in Socrates' allegory of the Cave. For one thing, our account ignores the *ad hominem* character of the allegory. In telling his story, Socrates is primarily addressing Glaucon, a young man of high birth, an intelligent, ambitious man, motivated by a deep passion for what is noble and just. He is precisely the sort of man who, depending upon the circumstances, could become either a great statesman or a great tyrant. It is he and his brother, Adeimantus, who set the conversation

Glaucon himself points out, an act of injustice to the philosophers, "to make them live a worse life when a better life is possible for them."[5]

Still, according to Kant, enlightenment does not arise spontaneously among a people. Freedom is necessary but not sufficient for enlightenment. As Kant says, "there will always be some independent thinkers, even among the established guardians of the great masses, who, after throwing off the yoke of tutelage from their own shoulders, will disseminate the spirit of the rational appreciation of both their own worth and every man's vocation for thinking for himself . . . " There

---

of the *Republic* in motion, by compelling Socrates to answer their questions about justice, and its relation to human happiness. In the course of this conversation, Socrates invites Glaucon and Adeimantus to join him in founding a city, so that, by studying the city from its beginning, they might discern therein the true nature of justice. It is Glaucon who, in a passage just before Socrates tells his allegory of the Cave, displays his own immoderate desire for knowledge, in urging Socrates to tell him the truth, not only about the virtues of justice and moderation, but about the most important thing, the Good. Socrates replies to Glaucon's importunity by saying "let's leave aside for the time being what the Good itself is—for it looks to me as though it's out of the range of our present thrust to attain to the opinions I now hold about it. But I am willing to tell what looks like a child of the good and most similar to it, if you please, or if not, to let it go." Socrates then proceeds to employ certain *images* to teach Glaucon and Adeimantus. Thus, the premise implicit in the account which follows, including the account of the Cave, is that they are directed to young men who are not yet ready for a frank, unmediated philosophical discussion of the highest things, but are fit only to learn of them through images. The young men's passion for the noble and the just cannot be ignored, however, but must be moderated, so as to be of potential service to the city, without endangering it. Thus, when Socrates tells Glaucon that those who escape the cave will not be allowed to remain in the light, but will be compelled to go back down into the cave, he says that "our job *as founders* [of the best city] . . . is to compel the best natures . . . to see the good and to go up that ascent." However, adds Socrates, we founders will not permit them to remain there, for it would be unjust to the rest of the city not to compel these philosophers to care for the public good. That is, Socrates gets Glaucon to admit that he, as a co-founder of the best city, and a potential lover of wisdom, must consent to return to the city, for the benefit of the city he has helped establish. Although this thwarts Glaucon's desire for knowledge of the higher things, it also moderates his desire for political rule: he will serve his city, to be sure, but he will never forget that there exists a dimension of human life higher than the political, in comparison with which the goods of the political life appear paltry.

[5] Ibid., 519e.

must be one who, having first liberated himself from "tutelage," liberates his fellow human beings. Although the self-liberator may liberate others by imparting a positive teaching, it is at least, if not more important for him to "disseminate the spirit of the rational appreciation" of one's own worth, as well as "every man's vocation for thinking for himself." It is perhaps less critical that the teaching of the self-liberator be fully understood by those he liberates.

# *Appendix to Chapter Five*

No defense of the morality of the American system of democratic capitalism may ignore the fact of American slavery; but no intellectually honest critique of American slavery may ignore the attacks made by some of our greatest statesmen upon that institution, or the efforts, occasionally heroic, of this country to live up to its promise of liberty and justice for all.

It is entirely possible that slavery is the great tragic flaw of the United States. Perhaps no human effort can ever overcome the terrible devastation wrought by slavery upon what James Madison called "the unfortunate Africans" in America, who had no prospect "of being redeemed from the oppressions of their European brethren."[1] Under other circumstances, black people and white people have sometimes found ways to coexist peacefully; but, in the United States, it sometimes seems that the wounds of slavery will never heal. Many other racial and ethnic groups have been successfully absorbed into the American mainstream, and indeed, so have many blacks. But the social pathologies from which so many black communities suffer, and the resentment and hostility toward the United States displayed by so many black leaders, eclipse the otherwise solid achievements of middle and upper class black Americans.

There are some who believe this is largely because America is and always has been a racist country. Our founding documents are said to be racist in principle. Racial bigotry is said to inhere in our Constitution, in that document's infamous and shameful concessions to slavery: the United States has been racist from the moment of its conception. The defenders of the Constitution, including some of America's greatest black leaders, like the mature Frederick Douglass and Martin Luther King, based their defense in part on the belief that the Constitution is color-blind. According to our nation's severest critics, they were mistaken in that belief. Their mistake consisted in believing that the Constitution maintains the sanctity of *individual* rights, irrespective of considerations like race, or that justice requires that the rights of each individual human being be respected, not

---

[1] *The Federalist,* ed. J. E. Cook, no. 42 (Middletown: Wesleyan University Press, 1961).

because of his belonging to any group, but because of his humanity. The radical critique replaces this view with one which maintains that, because the Constitution's original bias was directed against certain groups of human beings, it must be rectified by policies that promote the interests of those same groups. The fundamental political entity is, therefore, not the individual, but the group.

After all, does not the Constitution itself justify a policy of restitution to certain groups of people, by saying, in effect, that black people are only three-fifths human? That is, doesn't the Constitution define one's humanity relative to the group to which one belongs? The constitutional commitment to equality, understood as equality of opportunity, is thus only a commitment to equal opportunity for those who are deemed fully human under the Constitution. It is only just, therefore, to subordinate the goal of equal opportunity to that of affirmative action, even if this subordination results in "reverse discrimination." Because the Constitution is thought to be racist in principle, it is necessary to take race into consideration in order to achieve a truly just society, even if certain otherwise innocent individuals must suffer as a result. In some cases, two wrongs *do* make a right. Nothing America has done or can do, short of tearing up its own foundations and starting over, will satisfy the radical critic. The civil rights movement of the 1960s, under the leadership of the Reverend Martin Luther King, Jr., shamed America into the effort to eliminate institutionalized racial bigotry, precisely by appealing to the principles of its Constitution, as well as to certain biblical principles. These principles combined to provide the moral foundation of the civil rights movement. The contemporary critique, however, goes beyond King and his principles, if it does not repudiate them altogether, condemning the Constitution as inherently racist.

To be sure, the arguments offered to support this view are often weak, and rely upon tendentious scholarship. One writer summarizes these arguments as follows:

> The argument that the Constitution depended on slavery . . . begins by concluding, from a negative, that because the Constitution did not abolish slavery, it therefore *preserved* slavery. Then it calculates, from the positive provisions touching on slavery, that the Constitution *encouraged* slavery. On the strength of that prima facie demonstration, the various acts and deeds of the individual founders are interpreted as if they were in the main consciously entertained with an eye to the putative result.

What follows from this is generally a fairly disingenuous debate about the extent of culpability of the various founders.[2]

One may grant the force of this criticism. On the other hand, it does indeed appear that the Declaration of Independence, which proclaims as self-evidently true that all human beings are equally endowed with certain unalienable rights, is contradicted by the Constitution, which capitulates to the interests of those who denied the natural equality of all human beings, namely, the slave-holders. It is thus difficult to resist the conclusion that, insofar as it compromises the principles of natural equality and liberty to accommodate the slave-holding interests, the system elaborated by the Constitution and defended by *The Federalist* is racist and hypocritical.

To this it might be replied that one should not judge the Founders too hastily. Jefferson, for example, had included in the original draft of the Declaration a paragraph condemning King George for having promoted the slave trade in the American colonies. In it, Jefferson said, in part: "He has waged cruel war against *human nature itself*, violating the most sacred rights of life and liberty . . . Determined to keep open a market where MEN should be bought and sold . . ." [capitals in the original; emphasis added]

This paragraph was deleted by the Congress of Representatives. Of Congress' action, Jefferson later wrote:

> The clause too, reprobating the enslaving the inhabitants of Africa, was struck out in complaisance to South Carolina and Georgia, who had never attempted to restrain the importation of slaves, and who on the contrary still wished to continue it. Our Northern brethren also I believe felt a little tender under these censures; for though their people have a very few slaves themselves, yet they had been pretty considerable carriers of them to others.[3]

On the other hand, the infamous Dred Scott decision of 1854 would seem to vindicate the charge that the Constitution capitulated to the interests of the slave states. In this case, the Supreme Court decided against the plaintiff, the slave Dred Scott, who had brought action against his owner, subsequent to the latter's removing Scott from the slave state of Missouri to the free state of Illinois. From there, Scott had

---

[2] W. B. Allen, "A New Birth of Freedom: Fulfillment or Derailment?" in *Slavery and Its Consequences: The Constitution, Equality, and Race* (American Institute Constitutional Studies series), 64-65.

[3] Quoted in *The People Shall Judge* (Chicago: University of Chicago Press, 1949), 1: 203.

been taken to what was then the Territory of Wisconsin, and thence back to Missouri. Scott claimed that he had become free, by his residence in Illinois, or in the Territory of Wisconsin, or both; and that, being free and a native of the United States, he was a citizen. A majority of the Supreme Court ruled against him on both claims.

In doing so, the Court also held the Missouri Compromise of 1820 unconstitutional. This compromise had been reached in order to admit Missouri as a slave state, and Maine as a free state, thus retaining the numerical equality of slave to free states. The Compromise stated that henceforth, slavery would be excluded from the Louisiana Purchase territory north of the line 36°30'. Accordingly, the Dred Scott decision not only set a precedent for denying black people their rights as set forth in the Declaration , but removed a principal obstacle to the spread of slavery in the United States.

In writing the majority opinion, Chief Justice Taney stated: "It is true, every person, and every class and description of persons, who were at the time of the adoption of the Constitution recognized as citizens in the several states, became also citizens of this new political body" when the Constitution was adopted. Despite this, Taney concluded:

> In the opinion of the Court *the legislation and histories of the times*, and the language used in the Declaration of Independence, show that neither the class of *persons* who had been imported as slaves nor their descendants, *whether they had become free or not*, were then acknowledged as a part of the people nor intended to be included in the general words used in that memorable instrument. [emphases added]

Taney then quotes the Declaration's assertions of the natural equality of mankind with respect to unalienable rights, to which he replies:

> The general words . . . quoted would seem to embrace the whole human family, and if they were used in a similar instrument at this day would be so understood. But it is too clear for dispute that the enslaved African race were not intended to be included and formed no part of the people who framed and adopted this declaration; for if the language, *as understood in that day*, would embrace them, the conduct of the distinguished men who framed the Declaration of Independence would have been utterly and flagrantly inconsistent with the principles they asserted; and instead of the sympathy of mankind, to which they so confidently appealed, they would have deserved and received universal rebuke and reprobation. [emphases added][4]

---

4 Ibid., 720-721.

In writing the majority opinion, Taney employed an argument which is now frequently used by some contemporary critics of the Declaration. There is a difference, certainly, between the use Taney makes of his argument, and that to which it is put by the contemporary critics; but there are also instructive similarities.

Taney argues, in effect, that the framers of the Declaration could not have intended the words "all men" to include the African slaves, because the framers were not hypocrites. That is, Taney infers the framers' "original intent" from his comparison of the language of the Declaration with the moral character and actions of its author and signers: the framers were incapable of acting in a manner "flagrantly inconsistent with the principles they asserted." The critics also conclude that the framers did not originally intend the words "all men" to include the slaves; but, their premise is that the framers *were* hypocrites, because some of them owned slaves. That is, both Taney and the radical critics *agree* that the framers did not really mean "all human beings" when they said "all men"; but they conclude this from premises which contradict each other.[5]

Taney and the radical critics appear to agree, however, in their assumption that the meanings of words are decisively determined by "the times," and not by reference to any timeless principles. This is why Taney could appeal to the way the language was understood "in that day," that is, during the time the Declaration was being written, as authoritative for his decision. Even though the propositions of the Declaration present themselves as universal, self-evident truths, applying to all human beings everywhere and always, Taney in effect says that they cannot be so understood. Why? Because "the legislation and the histories of the times" show conclusively that the Negro slaves were not originally "acknowledged as a part of the people nor intended to be included in the general words used in that memorable instrument."[6]

Moreover, "the public history of every European nation displays it in a manner too plain to be mistaken" that Negro slaves were never intended by the framers to be included in the class of "all men." The Negro was universally regarded as a piece of merchandise, to be bought and sold, to be

---

[5] It is interesting to note that many of those who now criticize the Constitution for being racist in principle, also deny the doctrine of "original intent."

[6] In this, Taney was not entirely correct, as Lincoln demonstrated, in his masterful critique of the Dred Scott decision, given as a speech at Springfield, Illinois, in 1857.

reduced to slavery for his own benefit . . . This opinion was *at that time fixed and universal* in the civilized portion of the white race. *It was regarded* as an axiom in morals as well as in politics, which *no one thought* of disputing, or *supposed* to be open to dispute; and men in every grade and position in society daily and habitually acted upon it in their private pursuits, as well as in matters of public concern, *without doubting* for a moment the correctness of this opinion. [emphasis added]

In short, Taney concludes that the framers, being determined by the prejudices of their times, could not seriously have meant that "All men are created equal" is universally and self-evidently true of all men . No proposition can be universally and self-evidently true unless the terms in it refer to things that remain the same from age to age and place to place; but, according to Taney, what matters is not whether a proposition is "fixed and universal," but whether it is "regarded" as fixed and universal at a particular time. Truth is relative to the opinions that prevail in any given historical epoch. It is this premise Taney shares with the contemporary critics. The contemporary critics and Taney agree that the framers could not have intended the words of the Declaration to apply universally to all human beings, because the customs or practice of the day failed to reflect such an intention.

There is, however, one competent contemporary of Justice Taney who did not share his views in this matter, namely, Abraham Lincoln. Lincoln's response to Taney's argument is equally pertinent as a rejoinder to the contemporary charge that our foundations are inherently racist. Speaking in Springfield, Illinois, on June 26, 1857, Lincoln said:

Chief Justice Taney, in his opinion in the Dred Scott case, admits that the language of the Declaration is broad enough to include the whole human family, but he [argues] that the authors of that instrument did not intend to include Negroes *by the fact that they did not at once actually place them on an equality with the whites.* Now this grave argument comes to just nothing at all, by the other fact that they did not at once, or ever afterward, actually place all white people on an equality with one another . . . [7] [emphasis added]

That is, Lincoln argues, one cannot have it both ways. If the authors of the Declaration did not "actually place all white people on an equality with one another," will it be inferred that they intended to exclude *them* from the "whole human family"?

Lincoln continues:

---

7 Quoted from Roy P. Basler, ed., *Abraham Lincoln: His Speeches and Writings* (New York: World Publishing Co., 1946), 352ff.

I think the authors of that notable instrument intended to include *all* men, but they did not intend to declare all men equal *in all respects*. They did not mean to say all were equal in color, size, intellect, moral developments, or social capacity. *They defined with tolerable distinctness in what respects they did consider all men created equal—equal with certain inalienable rights, "among which are life, liberty, and the pursuit of happiness."* This they said, and this they meant. They did not mean to assert the obvious untruth that all were then actually enjoying that equality, nor yet that they were about to confer it immediately upon them. In fact, they had no power to confer such a boon. *They meant simply to declare the right, so that enforcement of it might follow as fast as circumstances should permit.* They meant to set up a standard maxim for free society which should be familiar to all and revered by all; constantly looked to, constantly labored for, *and even though never perfectly attained*, constantly approximated, and thereby constantly spreading and deepening its influence and augmenting the happiness and value of life to all people of all colors everywhere. [emphasis added]

The Constitution thus acknowledges the *fact* of slavery, without recognizing the *right* of slavery.

Furthermore, Lincoln contradicts Taney's historical relativism. Equality of rights was declared as a *principle* by which we the people are to regulate our actions toward one another. Actions do not exhaustively determine the meaning of words; rather, words, and the standards they refer to, may be the authoritative guide to action. One may therefore reply to the contemporary critics, as Lincoln himself replied to Chief Justice Taney, that the Declaration does not describe practice; rather, the Declaration prescribes practice. The Declaration declares the right, "so that enforcement of it might follow." This declaration of right is not rendered nugatory simply by discrepancies of practice.

Even in the case of a man like Jefferson, who owned slaves, it does not follow that he was therefore a cynic or a hypocrite because he publicly asserted principles which his practice contradicted. We know that Jefferson was morally averse to slavery. He did not cease to be so because he owned slaves. If he did not free his slaves despite his aversion, it is not hard to imagine why. In the society of Jefferson's day, where it was widely believed, according to Chief Justice Taney, "that the Negro might justly and lawfully be reduced to slavery for his benefit," Jefferson's slaves were probably better off with him than they would be if they were "free," and thus liable to be "reduced to slavery" by a master who likely would have been considerably less benevolent than Jefferson.

Our point here is that something akin to Lincoln's understanding of the principles and natural theology of the Declaration is required by the very possibility of the radical critique itself. On what grounds will you condemn the Declaration and Constitution for being racist, unless it is true that all human beings *are* equal, in the politically relevant sense described by Lincoln, namely, equality of rights? The danger inherent in reducing the meanings of words to "the opinions of the day" is that, if you succeed, you make it impossible to appeal to any moral standard beyond contemporary opinion. To give moral legitimacy to their charge that the Declaration and Constitution are racist, the radicals must appeal to some transcendent principle of justice, similar to the principle of equality as stated in the Declaration. If there is no permanent standard in reference to which the just treatment of human beings may be distinguished from the unjust, then no criticism *or* praise of the Declaration, or any other political manifesto, has moral force. In that case, might makes right by default.

So, for various worthy reasons, it seems simpler and more reasonable just to admit that the Declaration of Independence means exactly what the critics think it *ought* to have meant: all human beings are equally endowed with certain rights, including life and liberty. That slavery is contrary to nature follows immediately, then, from the corollary that no human being by nature may rule over another, without the consent of the other: governments derive their *just* powers from the consent of the governed. In this respect, then, all just government is, ultimately, self-government. The conception of human nature underlying the Declaration is such that the only legitimate government is self-government. The Constitution elaborates upon this great principle.

This conclusion runs immediately, of course, into the undeniable fact that the Constitution makes certain concessions to slavery. The Constitution thus appears to qualify and limit the principle of the consent of the governed, in a particularly vicious and barbaric way. Lincoln's rebuttal notwithstanding, this fact appears to vindicate Chief Justice Taney's assertion that the framers *did* originally intend to exclude blacks from citizenship, and to protect and promote the institution of slavery.

Because our main purpose here is to set forth the conception of human nature underlying our national founding, we are unable to treat fully the complex issue of the Constitution's concessions to slavery. On the other hand, we cannot ignore the issue: indeed, it is our duty to face it squarely. Either the Constitution is pro-slavery or it is not. If the

Constitution is not pro-slavery, then we are obliged, in consideration of the intent stated in the Preamble, "to form a more perfect union, establish justice, insure domestic tranquility, and secure the blessings of liberty to ourselves and our posterity," to show that it is not. If the Constitution is pro-slavery, then we must conclude with the young Frederick Douglass that it is "a most foul and bloody conspiracy,"[8] a statement entirely unworthy of the moral aspirations of a free and decent people.

That the issue of the Constitution's treatment of slavery is complex is shown by the fact that Douglass himself later reversed his opinion of the Constitution, just quoted. In his "Address for the Promotion of Colored Enlistments," July 6, 1863, Douglass said:

> I hold that the Federal Government was never, in its *essence*, anything but an anti-slavery government. Abolish slavery tomorrow, and not a sentence or syllable of the Constitution need be altered. It was *purposely* so framed as to give no claim, no sanction to the claim, of property in man. If in its origin slavery had any relation to the government, it was only as scaffolding to the magnificent structure, *to be removed as soon as the building was completed.*[9] [emphasis added]

Douglass appears to use the term "essence" to mean something like Lincoln's "standard maxim for free society," something to guide or be approximated by practice. Similarly, Douglass' analogy of the "scaffolding to the magnificent structure, to be removed as soon as the building was completed," recalls Lincoln's assertion that the Declaration "declare[d] the right, so that enforcement of it might follow as fast as circumstances should permit." It is impossible simultaneously to believe that the Constitution is the fuller elaboration of the principles proclaimed by the Declaration, and that this elaboration is essentially decent, unless the "slavery clauses" of the Constitution are first understood in the light of their original intention.

We preface the following analysis with a general observation on the language of the Constitution. As Robert Goldwin reminds us, there is

---

[8] Quoted in Don E. Fehrenbacher, "Slavery, the Framers, and the Living Constitution," in *Slavery and Its Consequences: The Constitution, Equality, and Race* (Washington: American Enterprise Institute), 2.

[9] Quoted in Herbert J. Storing, "Slavery and the Moral Foundations of the Republic," in *Slavery and Its Consequences: The Constitution, Equality, and Race,* ed. Robert A. Goldwin and Art Kaufman (Washington: American Enterprise Institute for Public Policy Research, 1988), 51.

no direct reference to slavery or race in the main body of the Constitution:

> No words indicating race or color, black or white, occur in the text of the Constitution, and neither do the words "slave" or "slavery." Circumlocutions are used in the text to avoid the use of any form of the word "slave": for example, "person held to service or labor," and "such persons as any of the States now existing shall think proper to admit." In fact, the word "slavery" entered the Constitution for the first time after the Civil War, in the Thirteenth Amendment, which thereafter prohibited slavery anywhere in the United states. The words "race" and "color" were first used in the Fifteenth Amendment for the purpose of securing the right of all citizens to vote. The words "black" and "white" have never been part of the Constitution.[10]

Indeed, as Goldwin goes on to point out, a similar observation applies to terms designating gender. These omissions are not accidental, as we shall argue below. For those who believe that the discovery of a language which is neutral to race or gender had to await the advent of an enlightened age like our own, it may be especially instructive to reflect upon this remarkable achievement of the authors of the Constitution.

There are three clauses in the Constitution that deal with slavery. They are: 1) the "three-fifths" clause, Article I, section 2; 2) the "migration or importation" clause, Article I, section nine; 3) the "fugitive slave" clause, Article IV, section two. Our purpose is to show the manner in which these clauses were intended *temporarily* to accommodate slavery, but *eventually* to eliminate it. As Lincoln said, the framers treated slavery "as an evil not to be extended, but to be tolerated and protected only because of and so far as its actual presence among us makes that toleration and protection a necessity."[11]

The three-fifths clause states:

> Representatives and direct taxes shall be apportioned among the several states which may be included within this Union, according to their respective numbers, which shall be determined by adding to the whole number of free persons, including those bound to service for a term of years, and excluding Indians not taxed, three-fifths of all other persons.

---

10 Robert A. Goldwin, *Why Blacks, Women, and Jews Are Not Mentioned in the Constitution, and Other Unorthodox Views* (Washington: AEI Press, 1990), 10.

11 Storing, "Slavery and Moral Foundations," 55.

The standard interpretation of this clause is that it is racist because it implies, if it does not openly declare, that black people are only three-fifths human. Wendell Phillips, the abolitionist, called this clause "the chief pro-slavery clause in the Constitution."[12] In our time, Benjamin Hooks, former executive director of the National Association for the Advancement of Colored People, charged that "Article I, section two, clause three of the constitution itself starts off with a quota: three-fifths. That is how folks were counted in that original Constitution . . . [T]hey did not call us [black folk], they had a very good way of saying it—as three-fifths of a person."[13]

In fact, this clause resulted from a compromise reached during the Constitutional Convention, between the slave and free states, regarding the basis for taxation and for representation in the House of Representatives. The representatives of the slaveholding states to the constitutional convention categorically rejected union without slavery. On the other hand, it was clear that slavery absolutely contradicted the principles of the Declaration of Independence, upon which the Constitution was to be based. The difficulty faced by the framers regarding representation was this: given the existence of slavery in some states, how shall slaves be counted for the purposes of representation? The struggle was therefore joined, between the Southern delegates, who naturally wished to increase the political influence of slaveholding interests, and the Northern delegates, who wished to diminish it.

Had the slaves been counted as whole persons, the number of representatives from the slave states would have been substantially increased. For example, Virginia, by counting slaves as whole persons, would have had approximately 17 per cent of the seats in the House of Representatives. Excluding slaves would have reduced Virginia's share to about twelve per cent.[14] In regard to representation, then, it was clearly in the interest of the slave states to have slaves counted as whole persons; and, as James Madison recorded in his notes to the convention, the delegates from South Carolina "insisted that blacks be included in the rule of representation, equally with the whites." Therefore, even if the majority of whites in the slave states had agreed that black people are only three-fifths human, it was clearly in the political interest of the slave states to have blacks counted as whole persons.

The nonslave states opposed counting slaves as whole persons, for the obvious reason that it would give the South an inordinate number

---

12 Quoted in Fehrenbacher, "Living Constitution," 8.
13 Quoted in Goldwin, *Blacks, Women, and Jews,* 10.
14 Ibid., 7.

of votes in the House of Representatives. Furthermore, the principle of representation would be reduced to a sham. Slaves counted for the purpose of determining the basis of representation, would obviously not be represented in Congress in any meaningful way. Finally, if the South were allowed to count slaves as whole persons, it would obviously have an incentive to *increase* the number of slaves. The three-fifths clause thus substantially reduced the basis for representing slave-holding interests both in the House of Representatives (that is, in the more democratic branch of the Congress), and in the electoral college. As such, the clause was described by Frederick Douglass as "a downright disability laid upon the slaveholding states," eliminating as it did "two-fifths of their natural basis of representation."[15] Why then, apart from their desire for union, might the slave states agree to this compromise? In part because it reduced their basis of direct taxation by two-fifths.

Accordingly, the three-fifths clause was understood primarily, not as a reflection upon the humanity of black people, but as an agreement about numbering the population for the purpose of apportioning taxes and representation in Congress. Recalling that the Northern states did not want slaves counted at all, and that the Southern states wanted them to be counted as whole persons, if the three-fifths clause had indeed been a reflection upon the humanity of the slaves, we would then have to conclude that it was in fact the pro-slavery South that regarded blacks as fully human, and the anti-slavery North that regarded them as sub-human.

It should be pointed out that, as one writer notes, emancipation removed the "disability" referred to by Douglass: "[B]y the end of the nineteenth century, with blacks disenfranchised, white southerners had a greater advantage than ever in the apportionment of congressional and electoral votes."[16] That is, blacks were no longer slaves, and thus could be counted as "whole persons," thereby increasing the basis of representation for the southern states in Congress; but, because blacks were disenfranchised, the net effect was to augment the power of white southerners in the Congress and the Electoral College.[17]

The careful wording of the clause also indicates the intention of the framers that slavery not be mentioned in the Constitution, lest the appearance of sanction be given to it. Indeed, as we pointed out above, the words "slavery" and "slave" do not appear in the body of the

---

15 Quoted in Fehrenbacher, "Living Constitution," 9.
16 Ibid., 9.
17 This is the historical reason for the great importance placed by the civil rights movement upon registering black voters in the South.

Constitution as it was drafted and ratified; rather, the first explicit reference to slavery occurs in Article XIII of the Amendments, proposed in February and ratified in December, 1865.

The "migration or importation clause" reads as follows:

> The migration or importation of such persons as any of the states now existing shall think proper to admit shall not be prohibited by the Congress prior to the year one thousand eight hundred and eight, but a tax or duty may be imposed on such importations, not exceeding ten dollars for each person.

Again, we note the careful use of the word "person," and the concomitant absence of any direct reference to slavery.

The migration clause follows section eight, which explicitly sets forth certain powers of Congress, including the power to "regulate commerce with foreign nations, *and among the several states.*" [emphasis added] As such, section nine is clearly a statement of the *temporary* suspension of that power regarding the *international* slave trade. Indeed, in 1807, Congress passed an act prohibiting the importation of slaves. The natural inference was that, if Congress could reserve the right to regulate commercial traffic in the international slave trade, it could do likewise with the inter-state slave trade.

Moreover, the clause restricts this suspension to "any of the states *now existing.*" The clear implication is that no permanent and general right of property in slaves is recognized by the Constitution. Furthermore, Congress reserves to itself the power to regulate or even abolish the inter-state slave trade.

Although the slave states may have regarded the inclusion of this clause as a victory of sorts for their interests, a different view was expressed by James Wilson, of the Pennsylvania delegation:

> I will tell you what was done, and it gives me high pleasure, that so much was done . . . By this article after the year 1808, the congress will have the power to prohibit such importation, notwithstanding the disposition of any state to the contrary. I consider this as laying the foundation for the banishing of slavery out of this country; and though the period is more distant than I could wish, yet it will produce the same kind of gradual change which was pursued in Pennsylvania.[18]

Finally, the fugitive slave clause states:

---

[18] Pennsylvania state ratifying convention, December 3, 1787. Quoted in W. B. Allen, *Slavery and Its Consequences*, 68.

No person held to service or labor in one state, under the laws thereof, escaping into another, shall, in consequence of any law or regulation therein, be discharged from such service or labor, but shall be delivered up on claim of the party to whom such service or labor is due.

This clause, unlike the first two, does not appear in Article I, but Article IV. This difference is important. Article I treats of the enumerated powers of Congress, whereas Article IV concerns the several states. Section two itself deals with what is called "interstate comity," and may be understood as "a declaratory limitation on state authority."[19] It is instructive to contrast the language of the clause in its final form, with the two earlier versions considered by the Constitutional Convention.

The first read as follows:

If any person *bound to service or labor* in any of the United States shall escape into another State, he or she shall not be discharged from such service or labor, in consequence of any regulations subsisting in the State to which they escape, but shall be delivered up to the person *justly claiming* their service or labor. [emphasis added]

This version was then revised to read:

No person *legally held to service or labour* in one state, escaping into another, shall in consequence of regulation subsisting therein be discharged from such service or labour, but shall be delivered up on claim of the party to whom such service or labour *may be due*. [emphasis added]

Notice first that "bound to service or labor" was changed to "legally held to service or labour." The implication begins to emerge that "being held to service or labor" in the relevant sense, that is, slavery, is the creature of the positive laws of the states in which slavery exists. This implication is strengthened by the elimination from the second version of the reference to "the person justly claiming" the service or labor of the escapee. The final version drops "legally," to read "held to service or labor in one state, *under the laws thereof*," again making it clear, albeit with a certain degree of subtlety and circumspection, that the legal status of slavery is relative to the given state.[20]

So much must suffice for our treatment of this issue. We limit ourselves to the final observation that, if it is true that the framers of the Constitution of the United States *were* merely hypocrites, hiding their

---

19 Fehrenbacher, "Living Constitution," 11.
20 For a fuller treatment of this issue, see Storing, "Slavery and Moral Foundations," 53ff. I have largely followed his analysis here.

true intentions behind grand language and high principles, then it is hard to understand why so great a statesman as Lincoln should have so emphatically rejected this view.

Perhaps one might even say that Lincoln, in his debates with Stephen Douglas, and his campaign for the Senate, articulated a conception of our founding principles that decisively prepared the way for the Civil War. Indeed, it is difficult to understand his famous "House Divided" speech in any other way. Lincoln said that "slavery agitation" would not cease until

> a crisis shall have been reached and passed. "A house divided against itself cannot stand." I believe that this government cannot endure permanently half-slave and half-free. I do not expect the Union to be dissolved—I do not expect the house to fall—but I expect it will cease to be divided. It will become all one thing or all the other. Either the opponents of slavery will arrest the further spread of it and place it where the public mind shall rest in the belief that it is in the course of ultimate extinction or its advocates will push it forward, till it shall become alike lawful in all the states, old as well as new—North as well as South.

It is, to say the least, difficult to believe that a man of Lincoln's stature would have been willing to state the case so starkly, even to the point, perhaps, of helping to precipitate the very crisis to which he refers, had he believed the house to stand on a foundation of deception and hypocrisy.

# Index (Proper Names)